Alfred Williams Momerie

Preaching and hearing

And other sermons. Third Edition

Alfred Williams Momerie

Preaching and hearing
And other sermons. Third Edition

ISBN/EAN: 9783744744966

Printed in Europe, USA, Canada, Australia, Japan

Cover: Foto ©Lupo / pixelio.de

More available books at **www.hansebooks.com**

PREACHING AND HEARING

AND OTHER SERMONS

" Truth is the property of God : the Pursuit of Truth is what belongs to Man."
—*Von Müller.*

PREACHING AND HEARING

AND OTHER SERMONS

Delivered in the Chapel of the Foundling Hospital

BY

ALFRED WILLIAMS MOMERIE
M.A., D.SC., LL.D.

LATE FELLOW OF ST JOHN'S COLLEGE, CAMBRIDGE;
PROFESSOR OF LOGIC AND METAPHYSICS
IN KING'S COLLEGE, LONDON

THIRD EDITION, ENLARGED

WILLIAM BLACKWOOD AND SONS
EDINBURGH AND LONDON
MDCCCXC

CONTENTS.

PREACHING AND HEARING—

    I. THE GOSPEL, ... 1

    II. THE SCOPE OF PREACHING, . . . 15

    III. THE METHOD OF PREACHING, . . 27

    IV. HEARING, ... 40

COMMON DUTIES—

    I. THOUGHT, ... 55

    II. CULTURE OF THE BODY, . . . 70

    III. CULTURE OF THE MIND, . . . 83

    IV. CULTURE OF THE HEART, . . . 97

    V. CULTURE OF THE SPIRIT, . . . 111

    VI. HELPFULNESS, ... 127

COMMON SINS—

    I. SELFISHNESS, ... 140

    II. BAD TEMPER, ... 153

III. EVIL-SPEAKING,	166
IV. CANT: HYPOCRISY TOWARDS MEN,	180
V. CANT: HYPOCRITICAL CHURCH-GOING,	193
VI. CANT: HYPOCRISY TOWARDS GOD,	207
VII. BIGOTRY: ITS PREVALENCE,	219
VIII. BIGOTRY: ITS IRRELIGIOUSNESS,	233
IX. BIGOTRY: ITS MISCHIEVOUS EFFECTS,	246
OUR RIGHT TO IMMORTALITY—	
I. THE OBLIGATIONS OF THE DEITY,	260
II. THE HONOUR OF THE DEITY,	275
THE PRACTICAL NATURE OF CHRISTIANITY,	288
PAPER ON THE ANTAGONISM BETWEEN DOGMA AND PHILOSOPHY,	304

Preaching and Hearing.

I.

THE GOSPEL.

JUST before this chapel was closed I found, one Sunday morning, on the vestry table a copy of the 'Christian World Pulpit,' and in one of the sermons it contained the following sentences had been underlined. "We are often invited," said the preacher of this sermon, "to extend the scope of preaching, and if not actually to secularise the pulpit, to administer to that love of change and novelty which is so rife in this restless age. Sermons, it is sometimes said, ought to embrace a far wider range of topics, to be more varied and more entertaining. But, brethren, it is no part of our commission to tickle the ears of our fellow-sinners; we are not set apart and ordained as ministers of culture, to deliver amusing lectures on the questions of the hour. We are ordained to minister to perishing souls. From this place we speak to those who are met together, not for mental recreation, but as immortal beings exercised by the deepest of all human experience—to those who know what it is to be tempted, to stumble, and to fall because they are in darkness and want the light of life; and when he remembers this, the gravity of his task may well overawe the Christian teacher who is charged to minister to the souls of men. Here, we may well say, whatever our audience—here are the old universal needs, and must they not be met with the same universal helps? How dare I withhold these? How can I yield to the temptation to know any man's heart after the flesh, or offer anything in place of the one thing needful? And so we cannot forsake the old, old story: we preach, and we dare not but preach, the old, old truths."

As the paper containing this sermon was forwarded to me anonymously, I was unable at the time to thank the sender. But I take the present opportunity of doing so. I am much indebted to him for his suggestion. The passages which he was good enough to underline, and which I have just read to you, are a fair expression of views very commonly held. These views, at the instigation of my unknown friend, I will now ask you to investigate.

Before we can say anything in regard to the preaching of the Gospel, we must first of all ask and attempt to answer the question, What is the Gospel? This word Gospel we are apt to use through the mere force of custom, fancying that we understand perfectly what it means, though all the while the conception which we have formed of it may be extremely vague, or even positively erroneous.

I can best perhaps illustrate this by a foolish remark of my own which I made a good many years ago, and for which I received a quiet but telling rebuke that I have never since forgotten. I had been brought up, you must know, in that ultra-orthodox school which is generally called evangelical, but which really has no claim to such a title; and I had acquired the habit of looking upon all Broad Church-men with suspicion and distrust. Well, I was one summer morning strolling along the Tors at Ilfracombe, when I was overtaken by an old gentleman, with whom, after exchanging a few remarks about the scenery, I continued my walk. We exhausted various topics of conversation, and then began to speak of the late Charles Kingsley, upon whose noble character my companion discoursed with eloquence and enthusiasm. But at that time I was so very orthodox that I did not attach much value to character. My test question in regard to Kingsley and everybody else was—not "Is he good?" but—"Is he evangelical?" So I said—with shame I confess it to you—"Well, what you tell me about his character may be very true, but, after all, I don't believe he has much religion." I have often wondered since that the old gentleman did not lose his temper at such an exhibition of impertinent self-assurance on the part of a stupid boy. Many persons would have wished me an abrupt good morning on the spot, and it would have served me richly right. But with the unruffled serenity of superior wisdom, he merely replied, "What is religion?" This simple question reduced me to silence, and, better still, made me think. After a time I discovered that while I was thus talking glibly about the irreligiousness of others, my own ideas of religion, so far as I had any, were as bad as they could be.

Now a great deal of the same sort of nonsense is often talked about the preaching of the Gospel, —nonsense which is best answered by the question,

What is the Gospel? Many of those who have the word constantly on their lips would be quite incapable of giving any clear account of what they mean by it. And others, in the explanation they might offer, would show plainly enough that the Gospel about which they were clamouring was in all respects opposed to that of Christ.

Let us spend a few moments in trying to understand distinctly the essential nature of the Gospel that was preached by the founder of Christianity.

The word is a translation of the Greek εὐαγγέλιον, which signifies a good message. Now "spell" is the Anglo-Saxon term for story or narrative, and the word Gospel used to be regarded as a corruption of "good spell." It would thus mean the good story, and be etymologically equivalent to εὐαγγέλιον. But Professor Skeat thinks that this derivation is erroneous, and that the word is really equivalent to Godspell, and means God's story—that is, the life of Christ. Both definitions, however, amount to pretty much the same thing in the end. In either case the word Gospel stands for the story of Christ.

Now this story is called good, not only because it is the story of a good and perfect life, but also and chiefly because of its bearing upon the good or wellbeing of the human race. All believers, or professed believers, in the Gospel will agree that the evangelical narrative, interesting and beautiful though it be, was not intended merely to charm and delight us. It was meant to save us. St Paul describes the Gospel in the Epistle to the Romans as " the power of God unto salvation." In the First Epistle to the Corinthians he says, " Brethren, I declare unto you the Gospel by which ye are saved." St Matthew tells us it was because the Messiah's Gospel was the Gospel of salvation that His name was called Jesus. So that the question, What is the Gospel? involves another question, What is salvation? From what did Christ intend to save us?

From punishment, it has often been replied. Savages, and all races in a low moral condition, believe in bad-tempered deities, who are ever ready to inflict suffering upon them, but who may nevertheless be bribed or propitiated into letting them alone. Similarly it has not uncommonly been held, by persons calling themselves Christians, that the Almighty had determined to consign the whole human race to everlasting flames, but that Christ endured an amount of suffering which partially satisfied the requirements of the

Deity, and that in consequence certain individuals will be let off the tortures that would otherwise have been in store for them at death.

If there is any one present who holds this view, he will of course say that I have misrepresented him. And indeed with a certain small amount of plausibility he may urge—as has often been urged before—that the sufferings of Christ were required, not to appease the Divine wrath, but to satisfy the Divine justice. A moment's reflection, however, will suffice to show that justice is not, and cannot be, satisfied by suffering. Justice is satisfied only by repentance and reform, which this scheme of salvation altogether ignores. There is, however, no necessity to argue the matter upon abstract grounds. Who first invented this gospel, and by what authority it has been enforced, I do not know, and I do not care. It is sufficient for my present purpose to say it is not the Gospel of Christ.

The intention of Jesus was to save men from sin. " Thou shalt call His name Jesus," said the angel, " for He shall save His people from their sins." Not only in the Sermon on the Mount, but throughout the whole of His teaching, we find the Saviour constantly demanding from His disciples a certain kind of conduct, and asserting that without it all profession of discipleship would be vain. For example, " Not every one that saith unto me, Lord, Lord, shall enter into the kingdom of heaven, but he that doeth the will of my Father. Many will say to me in that day, Lord, Lord, have we not prophesied in Thy name, and in Thy name have cast out devils, and in Thy name done many wonderful works? And then will I profess unto them, I never knew you. Depart from me, ye that work iniquity." And in the Epistle to Titus, St Paul says, " Christ gave Himself for us, that He might redeem us from all iniquity, and purify unto Himself a peculiar people, zealous of good works."

Christ's Gospel, then, being a Gospel of salvation, and His salvation being a salvation from sin, there remains for us one further inquiry: What is sin? at least, what did Christ understand by it? Now we shall best arrive at Christ's conception of sin by seeing clearly what He meant by the kingdom of God. This phrase—as well as its equivalent, the kingdom of heaven—was, as you remember, constantly on the Saviour's lips. They were the expressions by which He designated the society of which He was the founder. And this new kingdom was to be distinguished from other kingdoms by a very remarkable characteristic. To its members the Saviour addressed, and still addresses, the words —" One is your Father, and all ye are *brethren*." In the kingdom of God there is but a single law —the law of brotherhood—obedience to which is the one all-comprehensive requirement of the Deity, disobedience to which is sin. And Christ asserted most unmistakably that those who had been excluded, by reason of sin, from the kingdom of God in this world, would be, for the same reason, excluded from the kingdom of God in the next.

That this was the Saviour's view of evil is proved conclusively by his description of the Last Judgment. "When the Son of man shall come in His glory, . . . before Him shall be gathered all nations: and He shall separate them one from another. . . . Then shall the King say unto them on His right hand, Come, ye blessed of my Father, inherit the kingdom prepared for you from the foundation of the world: for I was an hungered, and ye gave me meat: I was thirsty, and ye gave me drink: I was a stranger, and ye took me in: naked, and ye clothed me: I was sick, and ye visited me: I was in prison, and ye came unto me. Then shall the righteous answer Him, saying, Lord, when saw we Thee an hungered, and fed Thee? or thirsty, and gave Thee drink? When saw we Thee a stranger, and took thee in? or naked, and clothed Thee? Or when saw we Thee sick, or in prison, and came unto Thee? And the King shall answer and say unto them, Verily I say unto you, Inasmuch as ye have done it unto one of the least of these my brethren, ye have done it unto me. Then shall He say also unto them on the left hand, Depart from me, ye cursed, into everlasting fire, prepared for the devil and his angels: for I was an hungered, and ye gave me no meat: I was thirsty, and ye gave me no drink: I was a stranger, and ye took me not in: naked, and ye clothed me not: sick, and in prison, and ye visited me not. Then shall they also answer Him, saying, Lord, when saw we Thee an hungered, or athirst, or a stranger, or naked, or sick, or in prison, and did not minister unto Thee? Then shall He answer them, saying, Verily I say unto you, Inasmuch as ye did it not unto one of the least of these, ye did it not to me. And these shall go away into everlasting punishment, but the righteous into life eternal."

And the writer of the fourth Gospel, though he looks at Christ from a somewhat different point of view, is nevertheless in perfect agreement with St Matthew regarding the Saviour's teaching upon this fundamental doctrine. In the farewell address which St John records, Christ three times lays down the new commandment as a summary of all that He requires from men, and declares that their obedience to it would be a sufficient test of their genuine discipleship. (1.) "A new commandment I give unto you, That ye love one another." (2.) "This is my commandment, That ye love one another." (3.) "These things I command you, That ye love one another. By this shall all men know that ye are my disciples, if ye have love one to another."

At first sight it seems strange that Christ should thus reduce all sins to sin against one's neighbour —that is, to selfishness—and that He should say nothing of sins against God, of sins against Himself, of sins which men may commit against their own nature. But if you think for a little you may see, on the one hand, that selfishness implies and includes all forms of sin, and, on the other hand, that perfect *un*selfishness is really equivalent to perfect sinlessness. In the first place, I say selfishness implies and includes all other forms of sin. For when we sin against our neighbour, we at the same time injure our own moral nature; we displease the heavenly Father, who cares for him no less than for us; and we crucify the Son of God afresh, who, so far as we are concerned, seems to have lived and died in vain. And in the second place, I say that perfect unselfishness is equivalent to perfect sinlessness. He who would never sin against his neighbour must never sin against himself, nor against Christ, nor against God. For example, the very idea of human brotherhood is based upon that of divine fatherhood. Men are brethren because they are the children of a common Father. And just in proportion as they believe in Him, will they realise and fulfil their obligations to each other. Again, personal devotedness to Christ is the best means of fostering a universal devotedness to the welfare of the race. "If ye love me," he said, "ye will keep my words." And no other means will produce the same effect. A passionate enthusiasm for the welfare of humanity will be developed in us, just in proportion as we have learnt to admire and love Him who was the great example of self-sacrifice, who sought not to be ministered unto, but to minister, and who died, as He had lived, to redeem the world from evil. And lastly, with regard to sins against ourselves, we acquire an additional motive against committing them, when we become imbued with a love

The Gospel.

for others. In injuring ourselves we injure our brethren, both by our example and by our diminished power of usefulness; and just in proportion as we love our neighbour, shall we listen to the voice which bids us do ourselves no harm.

In one word, then, by the Gospel is meant Christ's method of saving men from sin; which consists in making them members of the kingdom of God, where they no longer act under the instigation of selfishness, but are invariably guided by the law of brotherhood. And this method of salvation was once and for ever, by Christ Himself, summarised and embodied in the simple but all-comprehensive maxim, "Love one another."

Now you may not like this Gospel. You may not think much of it as a method of salvation. But if you say it is not the Gospel of Christ, you virtually maintain that the writers of the New Testament have given us, either wittingly or unwittingly, an erroneous version of His teaching. If they did so wittingly, they were dishonest; if unwittingly, they were stupid. Unless, therefore, you are prepared to deny to the evangelists, I will not say inspiration, but even common intelligence and common honesty, you must admit that Christ did reduce sin to selfishness, and that He did attempt to save men by inspiring them with the spirit of love. At any rate, this is the Gospel which is contained in the New Testament, and which, therefore, ministers of the Christian Church have undertaken and are bound to preach.

How they should preach it, and how their congregations should listen to it, we must hereafter proceed to investigate.

Preaching and Hearing.

II.

THE SCOPE OF PREACHING.

THE passage I read last week [1] fairly represents a mental attitude towards the pulpit which is exceedingly common. There is a certain element of truth underlying the words, which keeps them from being recognised at once as nonsense. And indeed it might be possible, by a large amount of ingenuity, to extract an interpretation out of them, or to force an interpretation into them, which would be sensible and just. But the tenor of the passage, the impression it is meant to convey, is essentially mischievous, and is based upon the most unworthy, not to say ridiculous, notions of the nature and purpose of the Saviour's work.

[1] See pp. 1, 2.

It is quite true that the Gospel of Christ is the one thing needful for the salvation of men, and that therefore "we cannot forsake the old, old story, and dare not but preach the old, old truths." But if the Gospel is to save men, it will do so, not by being eternally reiterated, but by being universally applied. Let me give you a simple illustration. Think for a moment of the fundamental truths which are contained in the multiplication-table. It is impossible to overestimate their importance. They lie at the root of the mathematical and other sciences, and are implicated in the whole of our common existence down to its minutest details. But what would you think of a professor of practical engineering who should address his class as follows: " Gentlemen, all discoveries in mathematics and all inventions in art owe their existence in the last resort to a knowledge of the first principles of arithmetic. Unless you are acquainted with these principles, you will be incapable of performing successfully any engineering work—nay, your whole life will be an ignominious failure. I am so profoundly convinced of the overwhelming importance of these arithmetical laws, that I shall 'refuse to administer to that love of change and novelty which is so rife in this restless age,' and day after day, as you assemble in my class-room, I shall content myself with reciting to you the old, old truths of the multiplication-table." What would you say of such a man? Why, you would say that he was doing everything he could to turn arithmetic into ridicule. Similarly, the first principles of the Gospel of Christ may be monotonously repeated, apart from their bearing upon practical life, until they are made to appear utterly worthless—absolutely beneath the contempt of every reasonable man.

This much perhaps would be admitted, even by those who clamour most loudly for what they call the preaching of the simple Gospel. At all events, I never yet met with any one who even professed to desire, that the simple Gospel should be preached to him week after week in precisely the same form of words. For you will notice this curious fact—however much a man may inveigh against novelty in the pulpit, a certain amount of novelty he resolutely demands. Suppose, for example, that instead of preaching to you, it was now my misfortune to be preaching to a congregation entirely composed of persons who would listen to nothing, the gist of which they had not heard before—do you think they would be pleased with me if I had brought my last Sunday's sermon, and was at this moment preaching it to them again? There could be no mistake about its being a Gospel sermon. It was all Gospel, the whole Gospel, and nothing but the Gospel. And I may tell you, I took a great deal of pains with it. Several sentences cost me half an hour apiece. I shall never, as long as I live, be able to give a clearer exposition of the Gospel than I did in that discourse. Assuming now that the imaginary congregation agreed with my exposition—since it was based upon the New Testament rather than upon orthodox commentators, they probably would not have agreed with it—but assuming for the sake of argument that they had, do you think that they would have been overjoyed to hear it again to-day? And suppose that week after week, and month after month, I continued to deliver to them the same discourse, what would happen? Much as they profess to dislike novelty, much as they insist upon their yearning for the simple reiteration of the old truths, they would one and all desert me. Had I numbered among my hearers the celebrated old lady, who is reported to have told her minister that she enjoyed his sermons so much because she always knew exactly what he was going to say, even she, when she discovered that my words were as destitute of novelty as my thoughts,—even she would leave me, and for want of a congregation I should preach no more.

It cannot, therefore, be novelty as such which these good people dislike, but only a certain kind of novelty. They do not clearly explain what kind. So let us put the most charitable and the most reasonable interpretation upon their dislike which it is capable of receiving. And there is one interpretation which at first sight appears plausible enough. It may be said that those who are opposed to novelty merely desire, that the preacher of the Gospel should never touch upon subjects with which the Gospel has nothing to do. Now this is a perfectly legitimate demand, and it may seem to confine the sphere of the pulpit within exceedingly narrow limits. But upon reflection you will perceive that, in reality, it has no such tendency. For what, pray, are the subjects with which the Gospel has nothing to do? I know of none — absolutely none. The Gospel is coextensive with human life in all its fulness and variety.

It is very commonly held that salvation merely means escape from future punishment. But, as I pointed out last Sunday, this theory is in flagrant contradiction to the plain teaching of the New Testament writers. In the description of the Last Judgment as given by St Matthew, the Saviour says that hereafter men will be acquitted or condemned according as they have, or have not, in the present life been characterised by deeds of brotherly kindness. And St John relates that, in the farewell address to His disciples, Christ three times summed up all His commandments in the one simple precept—" Love one another." The Saviour's purpose, we saw, was to save men here and now from selfishness, which He regarded as equivalent to saving them from every possible form of sin. And the Saviour's method was to introduce men into the membership of the new society which He called the kingdom of God, where they would no longer act from selfish motives, but would be continually guided by the law of brotherhood.

That is the Gospel. And no doubt it has been so grossly misrepresented and so blasphemously parodied, as to render an occasional exposition of it, such as I delivered last Sunday, desirable, if not absolutely necessary. For in every congregation there are probably persons, professing and calling themselves Christians, who are nevertheless utterly ignorant of the first principles of

Christianity, and who do not in the least degree understand that, in order to enter into the kingdom of God, they must give up their selfishness and submit themselves to the law of brotherhood. For their sakes, therefore, we must now and again revert to elementary truths. But surely those who are in the *lowest* spiritual condition are not the only men whom the preacher must endeavour to help. Surely he may assume that some of his congregation are already genuine disciples of Christ. And to preach the Gospel to them is neither more nor less than this,—to show them how, as members of the kingdom of God—that is, in harmony with the spirit of love—they ought to think and feel and act.

For you don't suppose that it was by idle sentimentalism that the greatest of all reformers endeavoured to save the world. No! the spirit of love, with which He sought to inspire His disciples, was a spirit of practical beneficence never weary of doing good. The kingdom of God was often spoken of by Christ as the kingdom of heaven. And this is a very suggestive designation. Because it was a kingdom of righteousness, it was also to be a kingdom of happiness, No one can be a genuine disciple of Christ unless he has a real desire for the good of others, unless he actually does something to make the world happier.

Now this desire for the good of others, which is the beginning of the Christian life, it is the preacher's duty to foster and to guide. He must avail himself of all the means he can think of by which it may be stimulated; he must endeavour to weaken the force of all influences tending to diminish it; and he must continually direct it into wise and fitting channels of manifestation. For example, at any given time beliefs and modes of thought may be current, which tend to paralyse men's moral energies, and to make them indifferent to the welfare of others—almost indifferent to their own. All such beliefs and modes of thought it will be the preacher's duty to examine, and if possible to destroy. Again, there may be forms of conduct prevalent in society or in public life which the majority of men think unimportant, but which are nevertheless conducing to the injury of the world. All such conduct it will be the preacher's duty to expose and to denounce. Or once more: the science and art, the literature and the recreations of the day, all have a bearing, for good or for bad, upon the temporal and spiritual welfare of mankind.

It will be the preacher's duty therefore, on the one hand, to warn men against everything in these pursuits which is evil; and on the other hand, to use everything that is best in them for the furtherance of the interests of the kingdom of God.

Such matters you may call, if you like, "questions of the hour"; but on what grounds they are to be regarded as beneath the notice of the pulpit I cannot possibly conceive. Slavery was once a question of the hour, and so was polygamy: pessimism, materialism, and atheism are at present questions of the hour. And do you mean to tell me, because a subject happens to be keenly discussed in his own age, that *therefore* a preacher must have nothing to say to it? Why, it is with this class of subjects that he is preeminently called upon to deal. It is his business to preach, not in vague generalities applicable throughout all ages, but definitely and distinctly to the particular age in which he lives. It is in questions of the hour that his hearers are chiefly interested; it is by questions of the hour that they are supremely influenced; and it is therefore precisely these questions of the hour that the preacher is bound above all others to discuss.

To say they must be avoided in the pulpit, is virtually to assert that the Gospel is a system of barren abstractions, which have no practical bearing upon the exigencies of human life.

But people are so terribly frightened lest the pulpit should be "secularised"! Now it strikes me they would be less afraid of the secularising of the pulpit, if they were more anxious for the spiritualising of the secular life. Why, the whole of our existence is secular, with the exception of the few moments we may spend in religious exercises; and even those moments, few though they be, are wasted—nay, worse than wasted— unless they have some effect upon the secular moments that follow. It can be only at the suggestion of the devil that men endeavour to keep the secular and the spiritual apart; for it is the very purpose of religion to bring the secular and the spiritual together. The essential business of the preacher is to apply the principles of the Gospel to all the interests and pursuits of the secular life.

"The Christian teacher, then, may well be overawed by the gravity of his task."[1] But if he take a worthy view of the Gospel he is called

[1] See p. 2.

upon to preach, he will not be afraid of widening too much the sphere of its application. His dread will be lest he should unduly narrow it. There is no danger of his speaking on subjects with which the Gospel is *not* concerned; but there is very great danger of his omitting to speak on subjects with which it *is* concerned. If the preacher's business were simply to reiterate old truths, he would have an easy, though inglorious, task. But to apply these truths, as he is bound to do, to the ever-varying circumstances of human life,—that is a work of surpassing interest, but, at the same time, of tremendous difficulty and responsibility. Who shall estimate the knowledge and the skill which preachers require, and the labours which they are called upon to undergo, if preaching is to be anything better than a farce— if it is to exercise a real and profound influence over a single human life? There is no position which makes such demands on a man as the position of a spiritual teacher. All the beliefs and practices which are current in the world he must investigate, discovering how far those beliefs are true or false—how far those practices are conducive or prejudicial to the welfare of the race. And he must acquire the power of persuading men, so that by listening to him they will be prepared for any self-sacrifice—even on behalf of generations yet unborn. Truly the vocation of a preacher, if a man but exercise it faithfully, is at once the hardest and the grandest in the world!

Preaching and Hearing.

III.

THE METHOD OF PREACHING.

I POINTED out to you last Sunday that this view of preaching,[1] though a very common one, was radically false. The old, old truths, no doubt, are as needful now as they ever were; but their usefulness consists, not in being repeated as abstract propositions, but in being practically applied to the ever-changing circumstances of human life. If this be to secularise the pulpit, then the pulpit must be secularised; for only in this way is it possible to spiritualise the secular life. It is with questions of the hour that the preacher is pre-eminently called upon to deal, because these are the questions which, for good or for bad, exercise the greatest influence over

[1] See pp. 1, 2.

his hearers. In a word, the Gospel is — and therefore the preaching of the Gospel should be —coextensive with human life in all its fulness and variety.

So much for the scope of preaching. To-day I wish to speak about its method.

Now, whatever be the right method, it is clear that the common method is wrong. For, little as the pulpit has accomplished in the world hitherto, its power is every day becoming less. "It is said by some, 'Has not Christianity in all ages been preached by plain men, who contented themselves with repeating the old, old truths?' It has, and what have eighteen centuries to show for it? To-day three-fourths of the globe is heathen, or but semi-civilised. After eighteen hundred years of preaching, how far has Christianity gone in the amelioration of the condition of the race? . . . The torpors, the vast retrocessions, the long lethargic periods, and the wide degeneration of Christianity into a kind of formalistic and conventional usage, show very plainly that the past history of Christian preaching is not to be our model."

Besides, as I have already said, not only has preaching done little, but it is continually doing less. The majority of respectable women go to church on Sunday morning, but the number of men to be found there is always becoming smaller. They virtually say, with Crabbe's convert,—

> "That from your meetings I refrain, 'tis true:
> I meet with nothing pleasant, nothing new;
> But the same proofs that not one text explain,
> And the same lights where all things dark remain."

And of those who do go to church, both men and women, a very large proportion, so far at any rate as the sermon is concerned, would have been more honest had they stayed away. There was a time when the preacher was cultured and his hearers were not, and when they therefore naturally looked up to him for guidance and help. But, with the spread of general education, the average culture of the laity has become equal, and even superior, to the average culture of the clergy; and so the old feeling of respect on the part of the audience is gradually changing into a feeling of contempt. What proportion, do you imagine, of those who now listen to sermons, ever dream that they will *learn* anything in church, or that they will hear anything there at all likely to influence them in their common, daily conduct? In high churches, I admit, where the clergymen lay down rules as to fasting communion, or the keeping of Lent, there is a certain amount of influence exerted by the pulpit over the pew. These instructions do actually influence the conduct of a considerable number of the hearers. But, with this exception, the preaching of the Gospel, as it is called, has, generally speaking, about as much effect upon a congregation as if it happened in one building while they were out of hearing in another.

And I may go further still. The majority of church-goers are becoming, not merely indifferent to preaching, but positively antagonistic to it. In places of worship where it is not a breach of etiquette to leave before the sermon, large numbers avail themselves joyfully of the opportunity; and most of those who remain, to judge by their faces, wish that they had done the same. From the force of custom, or some other equally absurd reason, ladies and gentlemen may sit out the sermon Sunday after Sunday; but as a rule they expect to be bored, and they are. And so the poor preacher is beginning to be regarded, not only as a useless person, but as a positive nuisance. Men think of him as the obnoxious individual, who week after week inflicts upon them fifteen or twenty minutes' suffering more or less acute. In fact sermons, preachers, and pulpits are becoming by-words,—synonyms for all that is tiresome and stupid. As dull as a sermon, as dry as a preacher, as wooden as a pulpit, are expressions that not unfrequently occur in common conversation. And I once was startled by hearing a public speaker, when he fancied he was becoming tedious, endeavour to conciliate his audience by saying, "Don't be afraid, I'm not going to preach;" by which I suppose he meant that, however dull his address might seem, it would be liveliness itself compared to the dulness of a sermon.

Now I feel that I must enter a protest on behalf of myself and my brethren. We are not exclusively to blame. If we have preached badly, as undoubtedly we have, it is partly the fault of our hearers. For they have presented to us the horns of a very awkward dilemma. When we were not interesting, they called us dry; but when we were interesting, they called us irreverent, declared that we were secularising the pulpit, and described our sermons by the opprobrious epithet of "lectures." In order to avoid the second horn of the dilemma, we have thrown ourselves upon the first. It may seem strange, but it is true, that, much as society grumbles at the dulness of sermons, it really would not like them to be anything else. For if they were not dull, they might be practical; and it would be so extremely disagreeable to listen to a man who made one feel that there was anything wrong either with one's opinions or with one's conduct. Society does not want to be disturbed. It desires only the confirmation of its prejudices. In order to protect itself from interference, and to preserve the pulpit in a state of uselessness, it has laid down a number of rules to which the preacher is expected to conform.

These unfortunate restrictions have been very well described by Professor Mahaffy in his book on the 'Decay of Preaching.' "The preacher is required," he says, "on fixed and very frequent occasions, however indisposed or empty he may feel as regards teaching, to ascend a narrow pulpit, where he has no power of movement or action. Indeed all action, but that of speaking very loud or thumping the cushion before him, is prohibited; and even these symptoms of energy have come to be considered excessive and ill-bred. He is obliged to find a text of Scripture from which to draw his lessons, even though there be none exactly appropriate, and though he be forced to employ many quibbles and subtleties to graft on his discourse. He is not to speak too loud or too low; he must not be too long or too short: if the former, he offends the worldly and idle, who only come to church from habit, and desire to escape as soon as may be convenient; if the latter, he annoys the serious and respectable people, who think that such brevity reflects upon the importance of his subject. If he employs anecdotes and descends to particulars, in order to give colour to his sermons, he is thought familiar. In fact every sort of departure from a fixed norm—a fixed way of speaking, a fixed way of thinking—is resented by some section of his congregation. Above all, to be amusing is a great crime. The shadow of Puritanism still hangs over our churches, and if a generation ago all ornament in churches was thought to savour of worldliness or of false doctrine, so all levity, as it is called, is considered improper on account of the solemnity of the subject. And yet men pleading for life and death, for great issues of poverty and wealth, for great party struggles which involve the weal and woe of millions, do not disdain to distract and divert their audience by an appeal to that peculiarly human faculty— the faculty of laughter. There is no orator in the world, speaking on the subject nearest his heart and most vital to those he addresses, who avoids this great help to persuasion—except the preacher."

"Such are the bonds of uniformity with which modern society trammels the preacher, and from which only a strong and exceptional nature can free itself. The average preacher, who feels no special force or originality, never even thinks of struggling against them; and so, if we walk into any strange place of worship, we may anticipate, in nine cases out of ten, exactly the sort of thing we shall hear. It will be respectable and commonplace, delivered with a voice and tone implying official seriousness. It will generally be all true when not too narrow, and it will be excellent advice for people to follow. But we also know that, in nine cases out of ten, the members of the congregation take no interest in it whatsoever. Modern society has done its best to make preaching into a perfunctory duty, and it has succeeded."

Society, then, is very mainly responsible for our dulness. But I am afraid I must admit that we have yielded to the demands of society partly from a love of what is called dignity. We have looked upon ourselves and our position as so exalted that we have been loath, even when society might have permitted, to descend to the discussion of the common affairs of common life. "Many men sacrifice the best part of themselves for what is called the dignity of the pulpit. They are afraid to speak of common things. They are afraid to introduce home matters. Things of which men think and speak, and in which every day a part of their lives consists, are thought to be beneath the notice of the pulpit. But there are few things that have power to make men good or bad, happy or unhappy, that it is not the duty of the pulpit to handle. Men hear plenty from the pulpit about everything except the stubborn facts of their everyday existence, and the real relation of these immediate things to the vast themes of the future. There is much about the divine life, but very little about human life. There is much about the future victory, but very little about the present battle. There is a great deal about divine government, but there is very little about the human governments under which men are living, and the duties which arise under those governments for every Christian man. There is a great deal about immortality and about the immortal soul, but very little about these mortal bodies that go so far to influence the destiny of the immortal souls."

There is one thing more that I must just mention, which may seem at first trivial, but which is really of great significance. The ordinary preacher is not content with confining his remarks to conventional platitudes, but he delivers those remarks in an artificial and unnatural tone of voice. He speaks not as a man but as a priest, with a pious and sanctimonious accent, which he assumes or discards along with his ecclesiastical vestments. No one can tell how fatal has been this blunder from a religious point of view. It has tended more than anything else to keep up the popular delusion that religion is for Sundays and churches, and not for common everyday life.

And the worst of it is, that this kind of preaching, which society approves, and which the preacher may adopt partly to please society and partly to please himself—this kind of preaching is often regarded as most conducive to the welfare of the Church itself. "The man who avoids unpleasant doctrines, who avoids all bold statements of his own opinions, who keeps within the narrowest bounds set him by the theological public, and takes no lead in the march of thought, will never be a good, far less a great, teacher. But he is what is called a safe man. Safe such men may appear at the moment; in the long-run they contribute to the ruin of the Church they represent."

But, at any rate, one thing is certain. If the Church is to live, not merely as an establishment but in any form at all, preaching must be either abolished or improved. English Churchmen love their Church, with its liturgy, its architecture, its old associations; they love everything about it but its preaching—and *that*, as a rule, they hate. I fear me this is—

> "The little rift within the lute
> That by-and-by will make the music mute."

How often have I heard people say they received more harm from the sermon than good from the prayers! And every such sermon has a tendency to weary and disgust men with the Church to which the preacher belongs. It is sometimes said that the day for preaching is over. If so, let us have no more of it. I do not believe, however, that its day is over. One of the greatest orators of this or any age has said, "True preaching is yet to come." I think so too.

But if we are ever to have this higher preaching, there are three rules which must be observed.

(1.) Preachers must have something to say,—in other words, they must possess a certain amount of knowledge and ability, and have time allowed them for the preparation of their sermons. It is one of the crying evils of the day, that an overworked parish priest is often required to preach two or even three sermons a-week. The consequence is, that by his inevitable weakness *in* the pulpit, he is constantly counteracting much of the good which he would otherwise have accomplished *out* of it.

(2.) Preachers must understand the scope of their work. They must know that preaching the Gospel means, not repeating old truths in their abstract sameness, but developing those truths, and applying them to the ever-changing conditions and requirements of human life. If we could but remember this, and act upon it, our sermons would have one charm at any rate—the charm of infinite variety.

(3.) Preachers must be in earnest. They must be moved by one supreme desire—the desire to influence for good the minds and hearts and lives of those who hear them. If this be really their aim, they will shake off the trammels of conventionalism, and avail themselves of all the expedients by which they know that men may be persuaded and convinced. The more fully they realise the transcendent importance of their work, the more firmly will they resolve that sermons shall be distinguished from other discourses, not by greater dulness, but by greater power. If men only knew how to preach them, sermons would be at once the most valuable and the most interesting of all works of art.

Preaching and Hearing.

IV.

HEARING.

"Take heed what ye hear."—MARK iv. 24.

WE have been engaged the last three Sundays in considering the duties of the pulpit. I should like this morning to offer a few remarks in regard to the duties of the pew.

The first duty of the hearer is, to make himself acquainted with the purpose of preaching. Those who are endowed with reason ought to act reasonably; and, therefore, every one who is in the habit of hearing sermons, ought to understand why he does so, ought to have some definite expectation of being the better for them, ought to know exactly the results which sermons may be expected to accomplish. Now the Gospel, as we have seen, is concerned with conduct. And since the conduct of men is determined by their beliefs and their emotions, the preacher's business will be to help them to such beliefs, and foster in them such emotions, as will tend to bring their conduct into harmony with the law of Christ. In other words, preaching has a twofold object—instruction and exhortation. This should be clear to every member of a Christian congregation.

Secondly, it will be the hearer's duty to make a judicious selection of the preacher, or preachers, whom he will attend. If a man be under an obligation to live in accordance with the Gospel of Christ, he must be also under an obligation to seek the best help he can obtain towards the accomplishment of that result. I admit that in some cases any real help is difficult or impossible to find. There are hundreds of parishes where there is but a single clergyman, and he has to preach so often as to be virtually compelled to talk nonsense. For such a system I have no suggestion to offer, except that it should be changed. But I am speaking now to those who live in London; and here, at any rate, there is no excuse for the man who persistently listens to sermons by which he is unmoved. He must be very singularly constituted unless the metropolis contains one or two preachers at least, from whom he might receive some help. It is to me a marvellous and inexplicable thing, that people will go Sunday after Sunday to hear the same clergyman, and invariably grumble at his sermon. They knew quite well before they went that they would find fault when they came away. Then why, in the name of common-sense, were they there? They are not compelled to hear sermons the only effect of which is to spoil their temper. Nay, I will go further; they *ought not* to hear them.

Now the kind of preaching that a man needs will depend very much upon his education, disposition, and other such circumstances. Last Sunday I pointed out certain general qualities by which all preaching must be characterised, if it is ever to do good to anybody. But you must remember that though, in these general respects, all successful preachers are alike, they will still be distinguished from one another by much diversity of style. And this diversity will correspond —more or less—to the requirements of different kinds of hearers. For instance, there is the question of taste. Persons of culture are not likely to be benefited by a preacher who drops his *h*'s and speaks ungrammatically, although he may be extremely earnest and clever,—capable of doing much good to those who would not notice his little peculiarities of diction. And, conversely, a preacher may be too cultured to deal very successfully with the lowest classes. They prefer to listen to a speaker who is more manifestly one of themselves, and who gives them rougher and more striking illustrations than would be tolerated in Belgravia.

And there is another and more important difference between hearers—namely, a difference in mental constitution. "All men do not take in moral teaching by the same sides of the mind." Some men can only be influenced through the reason. All they require from the preacher is,—instruction. If you prove to them, by reasoning, the legitimacy of certain beliefs, they will accept them, and ever afterwards act in accordance with them. If you show them the reasonableness of certain conduct, you have done all that is necessary. It needs little or no exhortation to make them act in harmony with the dictates of reason. Others, on the contrary, in whom the intellect is weaker and the emotions stronger, require very little argument. They will believe, or imagine they believe, almost anything that you tell them. But these abstract beliefs do not much influence their conduct. *That* is chiefly governed by emotions. And so what they require is mainly exhortation.

Now you may say it is our duty to address ourselves in the course of our ministry, and even in the course of every sermon, to both these classes. I admit it. But you must not expect too much from preachers; and if you do expect it, you won't get it. The natural bent of a preacher, just like that of a hearer, is either intellectual or emotional. He cannot change his nature, nor would it be desirable for him to do so if he could. He will accomplish the best work for God when he is truest to the nature God has given him. If persons to whom he is not adapted will persist in hearing him, it is not his fault, but theirs, if they get no good. It is most undesirable for those whose bent is mainly intellectual, to listen regularly to a preacher who is nearly always emotional; and it is equally injurious for those who are supremely emotional, to hear nothing but sermons which are for the most part intellectual. The natural bent of preacher and hearer should correspond.

And, in addition to these broad differences, there are many others, which I need not now enumerate, less marked perhaps, but still of importance in determining the kind of hearers for whom alone any particular clergyman is adapted. There is no preacher in the world adapted to everybody. A sermon may be useless to one man, and yet—or I may say, and therefore—specially adapted to another whose requirements are totally different. It is with sermons as with books. You may have outgrown an author, and he may now be beneath you. But on the contrary, it is possible that you may not like him because he is above you, and moves in an atmosphere in which you cannot comfortably breathe. The fact, then, that you do not care for the preacher whom you are accustomed to hear, is no argument whatever against *him*, but it is a very strong argument against *you*. If you had done your duty, you would have found some one else from whom there was at least a chance of your receiving good. In the selection of your preachers, as in every other important act of life, you need common-sense and moral earnestness.

There is a third requisite for the proper hearing of the Gospel—namely, a spirit of humility. The congregation should be possessed by a desire for spiritual help, and they should also feel that there is some likelihood of their getting it. This spirit of humility is remarkable for its absence in a very large number of church-goers. There are many persons much more anxious to teach the clergyman than desirous that he should teach them. Disregard for the opinions of the minister, though common enough in the English Church, is, if possible, more flagrant among Dissenters. I dare say you remember how well this is described in Mrs Oliphant's 'Salem Chapel.' There is another less known but equally interesting book, called 'Frederick Rivers,' written under the *nom de plume* of Mrs Williamson. It is really the autobiography of William Kirkus, who was at one time an Independent minister, but afterwards joined the Establishment. He describes in a very amusing manner how his deacons were always sitting in judgment on him and finding fault with him. And in particular he relates how on a certain occasion one of them, named Bung, came into the vestry and said, " I have heard it rumoured, Mr Kirkus, that you read the works of Frederick Maurice." "Certainly," said the minister, "rumour is correct. I do. Why shouldn't I?" The deacon replied, "Because Maurice is an infidel." "Indeed," said Mr Kirkus, "is he? who told you so?" "Well," replied Mr Bung, rather driven into a corner by this cross-examination, "Mrs Bung told me." So because Mrs Bung told Mr Bung that Maurice was an infidel, therefore the minister must not read him! In the Church of England there is more outward show of respect for clergymen, but behind their backs criticisms are often made that are little less absurd.

Those, however,—both Churchmen and Dissenters,—who have taken pains to find out the preacher or preachers adapted to their requirements, will generally be characterised by a spirit of humility. And when I say that hearers should possess this spirit, you will please understand that I do not mean to claim for clergymen anything miraculous or supernatural. I should be the last man in the world to assume priestly superiority over the humblest member of my congregation. All I mean is this: If a clergyman has devoted the greater part of his life to the study of subjects connected with his vocation, there is certainly a presumption that he will know more about them than his hearers, who have devoted their lives to other pursuits. However great his ignorance, and however liable he may be to error, his ignorance and his liability to error must be less than theirs, in regard to subjects which he has studied more. At any rate, if they think not, why do they sit and listen to him? What would you say of a patient who never took the doctor's medicine, but only criticised his prescriptions? You would say, Why on earth does the man have a doctor? Now there are many church-goers who, as they think, know all about everything. They could teach the clergyman a great deal, but he can teach them nothing. Then why do they have a clergyman? It does not cost them much. But still, little as it is, it is a waste of money—not to speak of the waste of time. No doubt the preacher may make mistakes, and therefore his opinions should not be blindly accepted. But if you do not think them worthy of consideration, it can be nothing but the rankest hypocrisy which causes you to sit and hear them.

I think it cannot be doubted that there are in every church a great number of these hypocritical hearers, men and women, who come, not intending to listen, and never dreaming of being helped. The only thing they like about a sermon is the end; and the preacher's sole business, according to them, is to get through with it. If, during paroxysms of coughing or any other interruption, he pauses till he can again be heard, they are astonished. Why should he want to be heard? Why should he waste those precious seconds, in which he might have been bringing his sermon to a close? This kind of hearer, moreover, wants the sermon to proceed, not only fast, but smoothly, so that he is not obliged to listen. He has a great dislike to being what he calls "startled." And the preacher who has the power of compelling him to listen and forcing him to think, will be regarded by him with the greatest repugnance. Mr Perrin, in his comparison of Christianity and Buddhism, has the following suggestive passage: "The laxity of thought in religion, which is so prominent a feature in the Christian world, has its counterpart in the greatest religion of the East. The Buddhist monks of Siam do not, as a rule, endeavour to make their sermons interesting, or even intelligible. They are satisfied with monotonously chanting or intoning a number of verses in the dead language Pali, to which they add an almost incomprehensible commentary in Siamese. Nor do their hearers care. Crouching on the ground in a reverential posture, they acquire merit (as they think) by appearing to listen; and they do not believe that that merit would be one whit greater if they understood the language of the preacher. It certainly would not require much imagination to establish a resemblance between such devotion and that which distinguishes many Christian congregations."

Preaching and Hearing.

To sum up this part of my subject: From every member of a Christian congregation is required—(1) a clear understanding of the meaning and use of sermons; (2) an honest endeavour to discover the preacher, or preachers, best fitted to minister to his own personal requirements; and (3) a spirit of genuine humility—that is to say, a consciousness of deficiency and a sincere desire for help.

Before closing, I should like to say a word or two about the influence which hearers may exert over those who preach to them. I pointed out to you last Sunday how much society had done to the prejudice of preaching, by laying down all sorts of foolish rules and conventionalities, the tendency of which is to render sermons insipid and monotonous. But now let me ask you to notice the power which the individual hearer possesses over the individual preacher. In the first place, as he sits there in the pew, he contributes something to the success or failure of the sermon. Every discourse is as much the production of the audience as it is of the man who delivers it. I have preached the same sermon on consecutive Sundays to different audiences, and in the one case, where the congregation was sympathetic and interested, I felt that I was preaching well, or at any rate that I was doing my best; in the other case, where the congregation was antagonistic or (worse still) indifferent, I felt I was preaching so badly it would have been better for me to have stayed at home. Only those of you who are accustomed to public speaking will be aware, how depressing it is to address an audience that takes no interest in what you say. Every one, therefore, whose presence would be likely to damp the enthusiasm of the preacher, will best do his duty by absenting himself.

Secondly, I have a remark to make in regard to criticism. There are two kinds of criticism, one of which is useless and injurious, while the other is of the utmost value. The first kind I may call captious criticism. It is what is vulgarly designated as "picking holes"—that is, finding faults, or rather making them, where they do not actually exist. You will hear people, for example, condemning a sermon because the preacher wore a coloured stole or a black gown; because he said—or did not say—the invocation at the beginning of it; because he turned—or did not turn—to the east at the end of it; or abusing it on account of a hundred and fifty other irrelevant trivialities. After the Archbishop preached last year at the festival service of the Temple Church, I made some inquiries as to the subject of his sermon. But I could discover very little about it. All I learnt for certain was this: the benchers had been furious because he began without a text! There is no other public speaker in the world who is subjected to the same peurile and—the word is not classical, but there is no classical word to express anything so contemptible — *pottering* criticism that is every Sunday lavished on the preacher. When it comes to his ears it may annoy, or sadden, or merely amuse him. In any case, however, it is morally injurious, like every other kind of pettiness, to the man who is guilty of it.

But there is a kind of criticism which is of great use. The two varieties of criticism are distinguished very well by the Rev. Phillips Brooks in his 'Lectures on Preaching': "One difficulty of the preacher's office is its subjection to flippant gossip, along with its exemption from severe and healthy criticism. There are people enough always to find out a minister's little faults and let him hear of them; but it is wonderful how he can go on year after year without being once brought up to the judgment-seat of sound intelligence, and hearing what is the real worth of the words that he is saying and the work that he is doing." Personally, I must say I have been very fortunate in receiving a good deal of useful criticism; and to those who have given it I owe a debt of gratitude which I shall never be able to repay. Just let me point out to you one or two instances of the sort of criticism which might with great advantage be offered to a preacher. He may have little tricks of manner, little oddities of style, which are offensive and distracting, and which really tend to make his best sermons ineffective. If so, by all means tell him of them. Again, you may think that the arguments which he has advanced on a given subject are weak and insufficient. Then it will be a kindness to inform him of the fact, —more especially if you are able to suggest anything by which his position could be strengthened. Or, again, he may have helped you; you may be at this moment wiser, better, happier—a different kind of being altogether to that which, but for him, you would have been. If so, do not hesitate to thank him. It will be his best reward and his strongest stimulus.

Now I trust that the few simple suggestions I have offered will enable you to see the kind of preaching and the kind of hearing which the Gospel deserves and requires. When we have such preaching and such hearing as that which I have endeavoured to describe,—then, and not till then, will the Church be really prosperous; then, and not till then, will the world at large begin to feel that the Gospel is the power of God unto salvation; then, and not till then, will men perceive the infinite beauty of the old, old story that is ever new, and the infinite significance of the old, old truths that are ever capable of fresh expansion and development; then, and not till then, will the Saviour's prophecy be fulfilled,— "I, if I be lifted up, will draw all men unto me."

Common Duties.

I.

THOUGHT.

"As a man thinketh in his heart, so is he."—Prov. xxiii. 7.

I MUST ask you, at the outset, to distinguish between two kinds of thought—viz., between the sensuous and the non-sensuous, between that which is exclusively concerned with matters taken cognisance of by the senses, and that which involves other and higher elements. The first kind of thought belongs to all sentient beings. Paradoxical as it may seem, it may be truly said of a man who would by universal consent be called thoughtless, that in spite of his thoughtlessness he is always thinking. Ideas of some sort are constantly passing through his head. He thinks, so far as he cannot help thinking. Thought of this kind can be escaped only by the unconsciousness of sleep or of death. In this sense it may also be said of animals that they are incessant thinkers. They can, and do, think about their own sensations. When a dog sees a stick, for example, he thinks of the circumstances under which he might be made to feel it. The two ideas are associated in his mind, just as flogging and robbery are associated in the mind of a garrotter. And every animal, no doubt, just like a human being, has an incessant succession of ideas passing through his mind; he has, just as we have, recollections of good times gone by and visions of good times to come.

Now these sensuous thoughts, which are common to men and brutes, are for the most part involuntary. They spring up of themselves; they enter the mind with no more effort than is required for the passage of the air through the lungs. And even when there is a measure of voluntariness about them, you will observe that these sensuous thoughts are still instinctive— that is, they are prompted and controlled by feeling. Burns, you remember, speaks about "the best laid schemes of mice and men." And this is no poetic fancy; it is scientifically and psychologically true. Mice, as well as men, have their well-laid schemes; and for the maturing of these schemes a certain amount of voluntary thought and effort is necessary. But the schemes of mice, so far as we can make out, are always concerned with sensuous objects, and the thinking of mice is always controlled by the desire to obtain some pleasure or avoid some pain. The old scholastics defined man as a rational animal. This definition, however, did too much honour to the human race, considered as a whole, and too much dishonour to the race of brutes. All animals are rational up to a certain point, and many men give no evidence of being rational beyond it. In regard to sensuous matters, animals can reason as well as we can, perhaps better. But to these sensuous matters their thinking is restricted. A cat thinks, before she attempts to jump over a high wall— deliberately thinks as to whether she can manage it, or what amount of effort it will require. But she is influenced simply by her desire to get to the other side. She does not debate with herself the question as to her right of going there; she does not ask herself whether it might be an act of trespass. And just as animals control themselves by sensuous motives, so by the same kind of motives, and by those alone, we can succeed in controlling them. A dog, for example, may be kept out of the cupboard, by the thought of what will happen if he is found in it; but he is not to be influenced in his conduct by any abstract conception of duty, by any non-sensuous respect for the rights of property. And the mental range of some human beings is precisely the same. "Wisdom for a man's self," says Bacon, "is in many branches thereof a depraved thing. It is the wisdom of rats, that will be sure to leave a house somewhat before it fall. It is the wisdom of the fox, who thrusts out the badger that digged and made room for him. It is the wisdom of the crocodiles, that shed tears when they would devour." And this is the sole wisdom to which some men can lay claim. The thoughts they think are just those which happen to come to them; or if they voluntarily deliberate, their deliberation is, always and exclusively, concerned with the ways and means by which they may secure for themselves something agreeable, or ward off something disagreeable. The end of such a man's existence, the sole purpose for which he lives, is precisely identical with that of the lowest kind of animal. The man lives for pleasure, and so does the brute. The objects which please may be different in the two cases. One may like thistles, the other may prefer bread and meat;

one may feel happy over a trough, the other may require an æsthetic dining-table; the dress of the one may be provided by nature, that of the other by art; one may go on all-fours, and the other may walk erect. But the thoughts of both are concerned exclusively with objects that will minister to their own sensuous enjoyment.

Whether he use it or not, however, there is in man what there does not seem to be in animals, a capacity for another and higher kind of thought. The thinking of animals seems, as I have said, to be necessarily confined within the circle of their sensuous experience; it seems to be always excited and regulated by feelings of pleasure or pain. But man has a faculty for non-sensuous, abstract thought. He can think without the stimulus of pleasure or pain. He can think about objects of which the senses can take no cognisance. He can form conceptions of right and wrong, of duty, of God. He can voluntarily criticise the thoughts that involuntarily arise in his mind, and say whether they should be cherished or dismissed. He can create for himself a moral and spiritual ideal, in the light of which he will often condemn his past conduct, although it was pleasant—or approve it, notwithstanding its having been painful. And he can resolve that his future conduct shall be less determined by the consideration of sensuous consequences; for he sees that "because right is right, to choose the right were wisdom, in the scorn of consequence."

It is the possession of this higher faculty of thought that alone entitles us to be called men; or rather, I should say, it is the *use* of the faculty that entitles us to the designation. To possess it and not to use it, is the most utter conceivable degradation. As one thinketh in his heart, *so is he*. As one thinketh not in his heart, *so is he not*. Not to think as a man when one has the power, is in reality to be of even less value than a beast.

Now this higher faculty of thought — our glorious human prerogative—is the basis of morality. Without it morality would be impossible. It is just because they do not possess it, that animals are incapable of doing wrong. It is just because we do possess it, that we are capable of doing right. To use this faculty is the most fundamental duty, because it is the essential prerequisite to the performance of all other duties. In order to do right, it is absolutely necessary that we think about what we are doing. I cannot agree with Wordsworth when he says in his apostrophe to duty—

> " There are who ask not if thy eye
> Be on them,—who in love and truth,
> Where no misgiving is, rely
> Upon the genial sense of youth :
> Glad hearts ! without reproach or blot,
> Who do thy work and know it not."

Now duty, I conceive, is never done unconsciously. We cannot do it without knowing that we are doing it.

That thought is necessary to the performance of duty, may be shown in several ways.

First, it is implied in the very meaning of the word duty, which signifies something due. Now, whether we regard it as due to ourselves, to our fellows, or to God, it is in the nature of a debt or obligation that it can only be recognised by thought. In a vague sort of way we might be said to feel a debt; but, for anything like an exact knowledge, thought is of course indispensable.

Secondly, there is manifestly no virtue in mere yielding, in thoughtlessly yielding to natural inclinations. The instinctive carrying out of impulse, unsanctioned by thought, is self-gratification. We cannot help liking a person of a sympathetic and kindly disposition; and we are apt to forget that if the disposition was given him to start with, he deserves no credit for it, nor for the actions to which it prompts. I shall have occasion to point out to you another day, how such a temperament may be cultivated and strengthened. So far as it has been thus voluntarily improved, it does possess a moral value; but only so far. The man who received ten talents was not rewarded for having so many, nor was the man who received one punished for having so few. They were rewarded or punished respectively, because they had increased, or failed to increase, their original gifts. Some men find it easy to do what to others is a task of almost superhuman difficulty. Some have instincts strongly prompting them in one direction, while the instincts of others as strongly impel them to an opposite course. And so the self-same act, in the one case may involve heroic self-denial, while in another it is scarcely distinguishable from self-indulgence. Well does Mr Greg say, "One man is generous and open-handed, another niggardly and mean; but the generosity of the one, and the niggardliness of the other, may be a mere yielding to native temperament. In the eye of Heaven, a long life of beneficence in the one may have cost less exertion, and may indicate less virtue, than a few rare, hidden acts of kindness, wrung by duty out of the reluctant and unsympathetic nature of the other." In order that an act should be right, it is not necessary, of course, that it should be performed in opposition to impulse— it is not necessary that great effort should be expended in performing it; but whether prompted or resisted by impulse, it is necessary that it should receive the sanction of thought. To take a simple illustration: The hatching of her chickens by a hen, and the bringing up of her offspring by a human mother, so far as they are the result of instinct, stand precisely on the same level. A mother's training only rises into the sphere of duty, when instinct becomes the servant of thought; when she has realised the possibilities, for good or for evil, that lie bound up in the child's nascent nature, and when she has clearly apprehended an ideal—a physical, intellectual, moral and spiritual ideal—to which she is striving that her child should be conformed. A conception such as that will serve to moralise the simplest maternal acts. Everything we do acquires a moral value, as soon as we recognise its connection with the fulfilment of a moral purpose.

Thirdly, thought is essential to morality, because the best of impulses may sometimes lead us astray. There is no kind of action which is always right or always wrong. Circumstances, as the proverb has it, alter cases. The rightness or wrongness of an action depends on the circumstances under which it is performed, so that what, at one time, is highly praiseworthy, may be, at another, highly culpable. Liberality, *e.g.*, is a man's duty, *if he can afford it*. But to lavish money on strangers, while leaving one's own children in poverty, is a crime. Similarly, it is right to make one's self agreeable to one's neighbours, to endeavour as far as possible to amuse and please and instruct them. But here, again, one's duty is first to those of one's own household. The man who is a pleasant companion to everybody but his wife, who spends all his energies in pleasing strangers, so that at home he is too exhausted to do anything but yawn, commits a grievous wrong. Impulses, good enough in themselves, must sometimes be checked in one direction, in order that they may have their legitimate force in another. Since, then, the rightness or wrongness of actions depends on the circumstances under which they are committed, not to think about these circumstances is to prove ourselves indifferent as to whether we act well or ill. And such indifference is sin.

Fourthly, thought is necessary to moral conduct, because in most men, if not in all, there are more impulses, and stronger impulses, prompting to evil than to good. You may call it original sin, or you may call it by its modern name of heredity; but, call it what you please, it is certain that there is something amiss with our moral constitution. The impulses to self-indulgence, either in the form of sloth or of pleasure, are the strongest impulses in our nature. If they are to be successfully resisted, it must be by something stronger than themselves; and there is nothing stronger than impulse except reason or thought. You remember the old Socratic paradox, that no one ever knowingly does wrong. Whoever has a full knowledge of what he is about, will do right. You are sometimes inclined to say with the old Roman poet,—I see and approve the better course, and yet I choose the worse. But to this Socrates would reply—and

I think Socrates is right—your knowledge is incomplete. You have not looked long enough at the better course to see its beauty; you have not thought sufficiently of the worse to discover its vileness. If you thought a little more about the wrong you proposed to commit, you would see so much mischief involved in it, that you would shrink in horror from its perpetration.

These few remarks may suffice to show the general connection between thought and morality. The particular connection of thought with particular duties we may notice hereafter from time to time.

Before I close, may I say something to those of you who are very young? My subject you find, perhaps, far from attractive. At your age thought is apt to be irksome. You are possibly inclined to avoid, rather than to cultivate it. It is all very well, you say to yourselves, for book-worms and professors and other uninteresting people of that sort, but for you it is too slow; it would diminish the vivacity, and mar the enjoyment, of your fresh young life.

Now all history, all experience, go to prove that in the long-run enjoyment is not diminished, lives are not marred, by thought, but by the want of thought. No one was ever known to mourn for having thought too much. And there is no period in human life when impulse is more dangerous, and thought more necessary, than in early youth. "I have no patience," says Ruskin, "with people who talk about the thoughtlessness of youth indulgently. I had infinitely rather hear of thoughtless old age, and the indulgence due to that. When a man has done his work, and nothing can be materially altered in his fate, let him forget his toil; but what excuse can you find for wilfulness of thought, at the very time when every crisis of future fortune hangs on your decisions? A youth thoughtless, when all his happiness for ever depends on the chances or the passions of an hour! A youth thoughtless, when the career of all his days depends on the opportunity of a moment! A youth thoughtless, when his every act is a foundation-stone of future conduct, and every imagination a fountain of life or of death! Be thoughtless in any after-years rather than now." Ruskin is right. You would be safer in mid-ocean on a rudderless ship, you would be safer travelling full speed in a train which had lost its driver, than in a world like this, at an age like yours, under the dominion of impulse, unchecked, uncontrolled by thought. Not only will your character in the future be good or bad, admirable or despicable, in proportion to your thoughtfulness or thoughtlessness now, but your physical condition, your intellectual worth, your social status, your success in life or your failure, your happiness or your misery, will all be determined in the self-same way. Fate often hangs upon seeming trifles. At any moment something may occur which will irrevocably seal your destiny, as far, at any rate, as this world is concerned. At any moment an impulse may arise in you, which, but for thought, will hurry you on to your destruction. At any moment, but for thought, you may say or do something which will irretrievably blight your life. You remember George Macdonald's words, sung carelessly enough oftentimes in our drawing-rooms, though they embody one of the profoundest and saddest truths,—

> " Alas! how easily things go wrong!
> A sigh too much, or a kiss too long:—
> Then comes a mist and a blinding rain,
> And life is *never the same* again."

Will you not listen to me, then, when I urge

upon you, which I do with all the earnestness of which I am capable, the importance of thought? Use your great prerogative. Cultivate the faculty of thought. Get into the habit of thinking. Think about everything, but especially about your own conduct. Think before you speak. Think before you act. Think, for God's sake, I beseech you—think!

Common Duties.

II.

CULTURE OF THE BODY.

"Be perfect."—2 COR. xiii. 11.

CULTURE, just like thought, is a comprehensive and far-reaching obligation: it has a bearing upon the performance of all other duties. By culture I mean self-development; the education of all our latent powers; the bringing to maturity of the various parts of our nature; the carrying out the injunction of the text and becoming perfect.

All these words—culture, development, education, maturity, perfection—are suggestive, if we look at them etymologically. We shall often find that in the commonest terms of our everyday speech, our ancestors have bequeathed to us great and important thoughts. So here. The

Culture of the Body.

word "culture" means tilling or farming, and reminds us that the soil of our nature, just like the soil of the land, will depend entirely for its ultimate value upon the care we take of it. The word "maturity" means ripeness, and suggests, therefore, when used as a synonym for culture, that it is but the seeds of our faculties, so to speak, which are given us to start with—that if those faculties are ever to blossom or to fructify, there is much which we must do to them. "Education," again, means a drawing out; "development," an unfolding or unwrapping. Just as there lies concealed in every block of marble a beautiful statue, which may be drawn out or unfolded by the sculptor's art, so the most glorious manhood, or the most exquisite womanhood, lies latent in every human life, and may be developed by voluntary effort. We often hear of men being the architects of their fortunes: but they are more than this; they are the sculptors of themselves. And lastly, all the ideas suggested by the terms culture, maturity, education, development, are included and summed up in the word "perfect," which means finished or completed. "Be perfect," says the apostle—that is, finish or complete yourselves.

Now, let us inquire how we are to succeed in

this task of self-completion. We have already seen the importance of thought. Yet thought alone is not sufficient. For culture it is essential, not only that we think ourselves, but that we avail ourselves of the thoughts of others. The perfection of humanity is only to be attained by co-operation. In the task of self-completion, it is impossible for us to dispense with the assistance of others. We might think for ever, shut up in our isolated individuality, and yet remain thoroughly imperfect and uncultured. But the fulfilment of the duty of thought will lead, almost inevitably, to the fulfilment of the duty of culture. As soon as we begin to think about our own knowledge, we discover its insufficiency. When we think over our own ideas of things, we find out that they are vague, or obscure, or erroneous. And thus we are driven to ask—What do others think? Have they more accurate knowledge and clearer views than we?

Now culture—the developing or perfecting of one's nature—may be best considered under four heads, viz., the culture of the body, of the mind, of the heart, of the spirit. These are the four constituent elements of our humanity; and for the perfecting of that humanity, it is necessary that they be completely and harmoniously developed. "As the harmony and solidity of a building," says Bishop Otter, "can only be secured by a strict attention to every part of the structure, which can then, and then only, be considered complete, when nothing can be withdrawn or altered without a striking injury to the whole; so also in education, if any part whatever be either omitted or displaced, there will always be some fault or obliquity remaining, which injures the whole effect."

First, then, we have to consider the culture or education of the body. It is our duty, as far as lies in our power, to preserve our health and increase our strength. But religious enthusiasts have not generally thought so. The poor body has been hardly dealt with by them. They have starved it, plagued it, bullied it. They have practically committed suicide; for, as the result of all their penances, they have died years and years before their time.

The ascetics have assumed that the best way of strengthening the higher nature is to weaken the lower; that injuries inflicted on the body are so many benefits conferred on the mind; that spiritual vitality is increased exactly in proportion as physical vitality is diminished. Now it is easy to show that this assumption is false. The body is the instrument through which the mind and heart and spirit receive their impressions and perform their duties. A blunt knife will not cut, and an impaired body will not work. Everything that injures the health of the body, must inevitably injure the life of the spirit. If it be objected that the greatest thinkers — the men who have had the widest influence on their generation — have usually been, like the late Charles Darwin, men of a delicate constitution,— to this I reply that their delicacy generally consists, not so much in weakness as in the possession of a very susceptible nervous system. This extreme sensitiveness, which seems to be an almost invariable accompaniment of originality, of course renders the nervous system liable to be easily thrown out of balance; but at the same time it often carries with it its own compensation. For men of this description are compelled to take more care of themselves, to be more watchful in avoiding every kind of excess, than men who are naturally stronger and therefore more reckless. But at any rate, it may be considered self-evident that, other things being equal, a strong man in good health will do more work than a weak man in bad health. Hence arises the extreme importance of bodily culture.

The Greeks and Romans were very wise in paying so much attention to the physical education of the young. In most of the countries of modern Europe the gymnastic part of education is altogether neglected. In England it is left to look after itself. If a boy has no taste for outdoor games, he is quietly allowed to discard them; and a girl is supposed to have had a very superior training, when she has been through a few exercises in calisthenics. There are not many of you—may I say it?—there are not many of you, I expect, who pay sufficient attention to the physical training of your children. If your boy is deficient in mathematics, if your girl is backward with her music, you are seriously perturbed; but you should be even more concerned if they show an indifference to football or to tennis. The mathematics and the music can be learned in the future; but physical stamina, if not gained in youth, will never be acquired at all. The work which your children will succeed in accomplishing for themselves, for their fellows, for God, will depend to some extent, no doubt, on their mathematics and their music, but it will depend far more upon their health. Neither mental, nor moral, nor spiritual culture can be based upon a foundation of bodily decay. It is of no avail for the spirit to be willing when the flesh is weak.

The body, then, being the instrument by which alone the mind and heart and spirit can discharge their proper offices, the weakening of the body is the prevention of good. But that is not all—that is not the worst. The weakening of the body is the direct fostering of evil. In proportion as it becomes unfitted for the performance of good deeds, in exactly the same proportion is it impelled to the performance of bad. There is no worse temptation than ill health. I admit that among the weak and suffering we sometimes find the sweetest and noblest characters. But in such cases, the weakness and the suffering are never the result of any personal folly or neglect. Those who are afflicted through no fault of their own, seem sometimes to be in possession of a "special grace preventing them," saving them from the natural effects of their affliction, and turning even the curse into a blessing. But in cases where it is possible to trace suffering to the sin or folly of the sufferer, you will never find it productive of anything but evil. The weariness, the lassitude, the pain that follow dissipation, almost inevitably drive men into further excesses. And the bad health which is not due to sin, which at first sight may seem to be a pure misfortune, how often do we find it making a man morose and disagreeable! It was Carlyle's indigestion that caused him to pollute the pages of his diary with so much virulent abuse, the publication of which has sadly darkened his character and terribly weakened his influence. In all probability a little more culture, a little more acquaintance with the laws of health, might have saved him. The story goes that he once consulted a doctor, and the doctor advised him to give up smoking. He did so for a short time; but as the indigestion continued, he took to smoking again, called the doctor an ass, and sought no further advice. The only anodyne he ever used thereafter was vituperation. How much better a man, but for his indigestion, might not Carlyle have been!

And even the bad health which is due to a mistaken religious zeal, is no less disastrous in its consequences. When I was a curate in the north of England, one of my best friends was an old ritualistic vicar—so ritualistic that we always called him "Father." It was his practice during Lent to live almost entirely on bread and water, and also to give up smoking, which, from long habit, had become to him one of the necessities of life. Now the result of this abstinence was, that towards Easter his temper—always a weak point with him—became perfectly ferocious; if one had not known the cause, one would have been almost inclined to call it fiendish. Dear old man! he fancied that by his stern abstinence he was subduing the flesh to the spirit, but in reality he was subduing the spirit to the flesh. It is possible to keep too strictly to the letter of the collect for last Sunday. We there pray for grace to use abstinence; but you will observe, the abstinence is not an end in itself,—it has a definite purpose; it is "*such* abstinence as will help to subdue the flesh to the spirit." Now this subjugation is often, no doubt, to be effected by eating less; but sometimes by eating more. For all persons in perfect health, occasional abstinence from food is a good thing, and tends directly to the preservation of health. Without such abstinence they will in the long-run eat too much. All such persons will be benefited by taking a fish dinner once a-week, by going without their dinner altogether now and again, and by invariably acting upon Luigi Cornaro's rule: "Always rise from table feeling you could take a little more." But there are others whose appetite is feeble, who often find it disagreeable to eat at all, whose bodies, so far from being over-nourished, are in a state of semi-starvation; and such persons, if they wish to make an extra effort for the subjugation of the flesh, must try and devise means for taking *more* nourishment than usual.

Now for the culture of the body it is necessary, as I have already intimated, not merely that we think, but that we avail ourselves of the thoughts and discoveries and knowledge of others. Health and life depend upon laws as certain, and many of them as clearly formulated, as the laws which govern the planetary motions. With these laws of health and life it is our bounden duty to make ourselves, so far as possible, acquainted. We are just beginning to wake up—thanks to the labours of Professor Huxley and others—to the importance of bodily culture. It has been one of the greatest defects of civilised education, that, till quite recently at any rate, neither boys nor girls were taught anything of the most elementary hygienic laws. The ignorance among the lower classes in these matters is almost inconceivable. I remember hearing the late Dr Lankester say, that dozens of infants died annually from suffocation, simply because their mothers imagined they could live without air. Anxious to keep their babies warm, they tucked them up so effectually with the bedclothes, that the poor little creatures never woke again. And ignorance in regard to the laws of health is not confined to the lower classes. "If any one doubt," says Herbert Spencer, "the importance of an acquaintance with the principles of physiology, as a means to complete living, let him look around, and see how many men and women he can find, in middle or later life, who are perfectly well." Now a knowledge of physiology would not keep us always well. Some of our ailments may be due to recondite causes, which science is not yet advanced enough to discover. But by far the larger proportion of human diseases are curable, and, still better, preventable, when men will but systematically act upon that physiological knowledge which has been already obtained. And if we do not avail ourselves of this knowledge, we are, in the present day, without excuse. Small, readable, portable books are within the reach of every one; and they are written by the greatest experts, in the most simple language, so that he who runs may read; as, for example, Lewes's 'Physiology of Common Life,' the papers on the chemistry of food, which Mattieu Williams contributed to

'Knowledge,' or that invaluable little set of primers called the 'Health Series.'

Most appropriately is the last-named series published by the Society for Promoting *Christian Knowledge*. No one was ever more careful for the bodies of men than He whose life-work it was to save their souls. How often He exerted Himself to alleviate pain, to remove disease, to ward off death! How often He took the trouble to provide His followers with a meal! Almost the last words on earth which He is reported to have said were these—" Children, have ye any meat?" The ascetics have assumed that the body is essentially despicable, and that their chief business was to dishonour it and punish it and bring it to an end. Now, whatever may have been the origin of this doctrine, it certainly was not the doctrine of Christ. One of the most remarkable features of the New Testament is the manner in which it glorifies—I had almost said deifies—the body. "Know ye not," says St Paul, "that your body is the temple of the Holy Ghost, and that your members are the members of Christ?" The body is represented as being essentially deathless and eternal. The natural body, we are told, is *the seed* of the spiritual body. It is to be buried, but only as a grain of wheat is buried. It will die, but only in order that it may come to the maturity of its life. From the natural body, which the ascetics would teach us to despise, there is to come, as an outgrowth, the spiritual body—the body with which we are to see the face of our Father, the body in which our likeness to the Deity will become apparent, the body by which it will be made evident that we are the sons of God. Since, then, this spiritual body is to be an outcome or development from the natural body, to despise the one is virtually to despise the other. Contempt for the body— I care not who professes it—is a sin little short of blasphemy. What God has honoured, it is not for man to despise!

Common Duties.

III.

CULTURE OF THE MIND.

"Be perfect."—2 COR. xiii. 11.

WE are engaged in discussing the duty of culture, which consists in the complete and harmonious development of all sides of our nature, in educating or perfecting—so far as possible — body, mind, heart, spirit. Culture has been well defined as follows : " It is the pursuit of our total perfection, by means of getting to know, on all the matters that most concern us, the best which has been thought and said in the world; and through this knowledge, turning the stream of fresh and free thought upon our stock notions and habits, which we now follow staunchly but mechanically; vainly imagining that there is a virtue in following them staunchly, which makes up for following thus mechanically."

That is a suggestive definition. The uncultured man is the man of stock notions, the man whose ideas have come to him — he can't tell how. He finds them in his head, and that is all he can say about them. Whether other people have the same ideas or different ones, he does not know, and he does not care. Similarly, he is a man of stock habits. He does what he does, not because thought has shown him that it is wise or right to do it, not because those on whose judgment he can rely have advised him to do it; no, he does it simply because he is accustomed to do it. Somehow or other he has acquired the habit of acting in certain ways; and, for this reason, he will go on acting in these ways to the end of the chapter. He reminds one of the first law of motion, which is, that a piece of matter, when once set going, will continue to move for ever in the same direction, unless interfered with by other objects; it will never stop itself; it will never change its course. That, I say, is an emblem of the uncultured man. When he has once fairly started in life with certain ideas and habits, he goes on, for ever, under their absolute control. He possesses all the inertness of *matter*. His stock notions and habits, which are the motive-powers of his life, have been formed for him by purely external causes, and they carry him where they will. His actions are determined from the outside, just like those of a billiard-ball. Such a man is, in the emphatic language of the Bible, "*dead.*"

We have discussed already physical culture —the thoughtful, systematic, scientific development of the body. Its importance depended, we saw, upon the fact that the body is the instrument through which the mind and heart and spirit work. The body should be strengthened and disciplined as nearly as possible up to the point of perfect health; since at this point it is best fitted for employment in the service of the higher faculties. And when the body has been thus disciplined and prepared, the exercise of the higher faculties is directly conducive to health. There is nothing incompatible, for example, between physical and mental development. Some persons seem to imagine that using the mind, except in the most mild and moderate fashion, tends necessarily to weaken the body and to shorten life. No such thing. Brain-work is as healthy, even more healthy, than muscle-work. Statistics prove the peculiar longevity of brain-workers. The longest livers are those who make an abundant use both of brain and muscle —men, for example, like Tyndall or Gladstone, who are capable of great physical exertion, and who also go through severe and protracted mental labour. And so far from the use of the mind being prejudicial to health, it is further proved by statistics that brain-work, even without muscle-work, is more conducive to longevity than muscle-work without brain-work. The average life of a bookish recluse is longer than that of an agricultural labourer. There is nothing, then, chimerical or impossible in the attempt to develop different sides of our nature. Bodily health is the best preparation for mental work; and mental work, rationally pursued, is the surest preservative of health.

But *how* to bring the body into just that condition, in which it is best fitted to be the servant of the mind, is not a simple problem; it is one which will certainly never be solved by accident or by guess-work. If the body is to be an efficient instrument in the development of the mind, it is necessary that we give it a certain amount of training, exercise, and discipline. A certain amount; but this amount will differ in different cases. The stronger the body is to begin with, the more training it can endure; and the more training it can endure, the stronger it can be eventually made. All this shows how important it is that, in early years, a youth should form for himself, with the guidance and assistance of others, a scheme of life. He should try and discover, both in regard to physical and mental pursuits, what he can do, what he might do after a time with practice, and what he never would be able to do at all. It is given only to a very few to row in the "Varsity" eight or to play in the "Varsity" eleven, and at the same time take a high degree. It is given only to a few to be first in anything. Sometimes a man may succeed in placing himself first, when nature intended that he should be second, or third, or thirtieth. If he does so, the effect to himself is always disastrous. Such a man dies prematurely, in mind if not in body. It is proverbial, that a large number of senior wranglers are never heard of after they have taken their degree. They work themselves out in their teens. If they had been content with a lower place in the tripos, they would have taken a higher place in the world. Hence the necessity for a scheme of life. We need not only to develop, but to some extent to husband, the resources with which nature has endowed us. A certain amount of rivalry no doubt affords a very useful stimulus; but what I would impress upon every youth's mind is this,—his chief duty in the world is not to surpass his competitors, but to perfect himself.

Now mental culture involves, first, the acquisition of facts; and, secondly and specially, the development of the faculties. These, the faculties, are to be educated—educated from the latent into the developed state. The mere acquisition of facts is not education. We pick up a considerable number of facts involuntarily, and education always involves effort. A man would not be considered educated for knowing that fire burns, that food nourishes, that pain is unpleasant, or a thousand similar facts, which he could not help knowing if he tried. And a very large proportion of what is actually dignified with the name of education, does not deserve to be so called. Much of what we learned at school, learned perhaps with a very disagreeable amount of effort, was yet acquired in such a way, that its tendency was to weaken rather than to strengthen the mind. For example, in the interesting acticle on his school-days, which the Dean of Westminster contributed to a recent number of the 'Nineteenth Century,' he tells us how much time in his childhood was wasted in purely memoriter work; how he was obliged to learn by rote lists of the kings of England, of the metals, of the planets, and so forth, and was not obliged, was never expected, to attach any meaning to the names. "I really think," he says, "that we might almost, without rebuke, have substituted one list for the other." Things learned in this way, with the sole motive perhaps of escaping the birch, do not improve the faculties. The intelligence cannot be unintelligently developed. And the same remarks apply to very much of the work which is exacted in colleges and universities. There is a considerable amount of information which has to be acquired previous to the exercise of any profession. There are certain sciences, or parts of sciences, of which every one must have a smattering, before he is allowed to start in life. Before we can practise as doctors, as lawyers, as clergymen, we must know something about medicine, or law, or theology; at least we must pass examinations in these subjects. Such sciences, or parts of sciences, the Germans call *Brodwissenschaften*—that is, bread sciences, the sciences by which a man is enabled to earn his living. In England this kind of training is generally called professional, as distinguished from liberal, education. But in the strict sense of the word, there is nothing necessarily *educative* in the mere professional training. A man's having passed examinations, is no proof whatever of his being ready for duty in the world. Why, I have known a medallist in surgery expelled from a hospital for some gross act of incompetence. If a man's only qualification for the practice of a profession is the fact that he has passed examinations, God help those who intrust themselves to his care! As a rule, the peculiarly technical or professional parts of a science are the least interesting, the least suggestive, and, pecuniary considerations apart, the least valuable. Hence any one who possesses but the minimum of information, which has enabled him to scrape through his professional examinations, can only by courtesy—dishonest courtesy—be called educated; and no one, in the greatest excess of politeness would ever dream of calling him cultured.

It is curiously, sadly suggestive, however, that in common speech the word useful would generally be applied to professional, and not to liberal, education. The term "useful" has come to mean that which pays. The most useful education is the one that can be the most readily converted into cash. An education that merely enlarges a man's mind and develops his faculties, in whatever terms it might be eulogised by those who approved of it, would hardly ever, even by them, be called useful. As if, forsooth, it was of no use for us to educate ourselves, unless we were going to be paid for it! But so long as it is customary to estimate a man's worth in pounds sterling, self-culture will never be properly appreciated. Why, those very pounds, if a man has sacrificed his higher nature in gaining them, are so many evidences of his worthlessness! The only real worth a man can possess lies in himself. It is determined, not by what he has, but by what he is. The end of life is, not to get, but *to be*.

Mental culture, then, consists essentially in the enlarging of the mind, and in the strengthening and stimulating of all the mind's powers. Culture involves, no doubt, the learning of new facts, but it is not enough that they be learnt. They must be understood; they must be seen in their relation to other facts. Beauty, mystery, wonderfulness, must be discovered in them. And for this we are not left to ourselves. We can have, for the asking, the assistance of the ablest of our fellows. We live in a golden age, when the vast resources of science and literature and art are within easy reach. You remember Whewell's definition of an educated man,—the man who knows something of everything and everything of something. That is a high standard; but the first part of it, at any rate, is becoming every day more feasible, thanks to the multiplication of short, simple books upon difficult and abstruse subjects. If we, living so fortunately at the end of this nineteenth century, do not cultivate our minds, we have no excuse. There is nothing to prevent us; there is everything to help us.

But, unhappily, numbers of persons, bearing the outward semblance of men and women—persons, too, of means and of leisure, live on day after day, week after week, year after year, without ever receiving into their minds a new thought. They will be as ignorant at sixty as they were at sixteen. And when it is required of them, before the throne of God, to declare what use they have made of their intellectual opportunities, they will have to remain absolutely speechless. So far as mental development is concerned, they might as well have been born in the wilds of Africa, they might as well have been born tadpoles. Would that some looking-glass for the mind had been invented, in which these mental pigmies could see their embryonic souls! They might then be induced to throw off their lethargy for very shame. Rational animals, we are sometimes called. Animals we may be, but rational we certainly are not, if we care to know nothing of the mysterious workings of nature; especially now, when so many of her phenomena have been explained and so many of her laws have been discovered. Animals we may be, but rational we certainly are not, if we care to know nothing of the still more mysterious workings of the world's great master-minds; especially now, when the best of their thoughts are to be obtained without any laborious research, without any undue mental strain, when, in fact, we can only avoid making some acquaintance with them by persistently refusing to read.

The way in which new ideas lead to mental development—actually enlarge the mind itself—I have only time to illustrate by one example. It is probably familiar to you all. What an intellectual revolution was worked in us, when we exchanged the old view of the universe for the new! As children, we believed that the earth was but six thousand years old, that it was the largest and most important of created objects, and that the stars and planets had been brought into existence merely for the purpose of adorning the terrestrial firmament. Now we know that our globe was millions of years in the making, and that it is but a tiny speck in infinity, one of the very least of the myriads upon myriads of worlds with which never-ending space is studded. In receiving a new idea like that, we seem to pass at a bound from mental babyhood to youth; or, to use the simile of Wendell Holmes, the mind is *stretched* by it, so that it never shrinks back again to its original proportions. Ever thereafter we have humbler views of ourselves, loftier views of God, correcter views of everything.

But true culture is, as I have said, the development of all sides of our nature. It remains to speak of the education of the heart and spirit; and this I hope to do in the two succeeding sermons.

"That will make four sermons upon culture," I hear some one say; "and what has culture to do with religion? The pulpit is not the place from which such subjects should be discussed. A clergyman has no right to interfere with the minds of his hearers; his business lies entirely with their souls. You keep on telling us to perfect ourselves, and you ought to be telling us to glorify God." Now, my friend, I have been all along exhorting you to glorify God. Every word I have said was intended to stimulate you to that most sacred duty. At first sight it may seem as if perfecting yourself was something quite different, something quite the contrary of glorifying God. But a little consideration will show that the two ends of life are identical. Just think. The only conceivable way in which the Creator can be glorified, is by the perfection of the beings whom He has created. There is but one thing we can do for God, and that is to finish or complete ourselves. Religious exercises, such as prayers, hymns, or the Communion, are only valuable so far as they express our desire to become perfect. Those who are anxious to circumscribe the sphere of religion, who keep such a jealous guard that nothing secular shall ever be introduced into it, prove conclusively thereby that they are, in their heart of hearts, essentially irreligious. Religion is not to be restricted to certain ceremonies gone through, and certain words repeated, at regular, stated intervals. Religion is not to be restricted even to exalted spiritual emotions, which, from the circumstances of our human existence, we can only at times experience. Religion, properly so called, must comprehend our whole nature, must be coextensive with our whole life. There are men who waste or prostitute every faculty they possess, and who yet imagine themselves very religious: they fancy they do God much honour, because on a Sunday they sing Him a few hymns and say Him a few prayers. Honour! "The sacrifice of the wicked is an abomination to the Lord." To profess to care for Him, when all the time we are abusing, or failing to use, the gifts with which He has endowed us, is the grossest conceivable blasphemy. The man who comes into the house of God, and takes the words of saints and prophets into his polluted lips, when his whole nature is in ruins, and he is quite content to have it so—that man insults the Almighty to His face!

Common Duties.

IV.

CULTURE OF THE HEART.

" Be perfect."—2 Cor. xiii. 11.

CULTURE consists, as we have seen, in the complete and harmonious development of all sides of our nature, in the educating or educing the latent powers of, body, mind, heart, and spirit. We have already noticed something of the importance which attaches to physical and mental education. Our business to-day will be with the culture or education of the heart.

The term education is generally restricted in common usage to intellectual development. But if we are to be perfect, we stand as much in need of moral as of intellectual education. We are no more born with cultivated hearts than with fully developed minds.

By the education of the heart I mean the development of sympathy. This word sympathy signifies etymologically, as you know, suffering or experiencing with—that is, with others. I say suffering, or *experiencing*, with; for the Greek word παθεῖν means not only to suffer pain, but to have any kind of passive experience, joyful no less than sorrowful. Sympathy is therefore experiencing with others, having more or less similar—if not the same—feelings that they have, rejoicing when they rejoice and weeping when they weep.

It has been much disputed how far sympathy is natural to man. Indeed its possibility has, not unfrequently, been denied. It has been maintained, in other words, that we have no heart to cultivate. We are sometimes told that, so far from sympathy being part of our nature, there is rather an anti-sympathetic tendency in us— a tendency to experience, not similar, but quite opposite, feelings to those which others are experiencing, to rejoice when they weep and to weep when they rejoice. Boys, for example, are proverbially cruel; they seem to find the greatest pleasure in inflicting the greatest pain. And Rochefoucauld has asserted universally of us all, that we are, by our very constitution, inclined to rejoice in the sorrow, rather than in the joy, of our neighbours. "In the adversity of our best friends," he says, "we always find something that is not wholly displeasing to us."

Now as to the argument drawn from the cruelty of boys, I think it may be shown that the pleasure which they seem to take in suffering is more apparent than real. We cannot take pleasure in that of which we are ignorant; and, as a rule, boys scarcely know the meaning of the word "pain." When they know what pain is, the contemplation of it generally becomes disagreeable to them. Delicate boys are seldom, if ever, cruel. And further, cruel boys delight in the sight of pain, not because it is pain, but because it testifies to the successful issue of their own labours. When they pull off the legs of flies, for example, what amuses them is, not so much that the poor insects have been incommoded, as that they themselves have been skilful enough to incommode them. In other words, what they really take pleasure in is, not the pain of another, but the power of themselves. And as to Rochefoucauld's maxim, it implies that the calamities of our friends, though not wholly, are yet partially, displeasing to us. As calamities, it seems to me, they are displeasing; but in so far as they serve to illustrate our own superior skill in having avoided them, to that extent they may be actually pleasing.

Some persons, it must be admitted, appear to be absolutely indifferent both to the pleasure and to the pain of their neighbours. They are not in the least affected as a rule by either. They are like Hetty in 'Adam Bede,' whom Mrs Poyser compares to a peacock, that would spread his tail if all the folks in the parish were dying. Such want of heart may, I think, be traced ultimately to a want of mind, to defective powers of observation or imagination. If they realised what their neighbours were suffering, they might feel it very much; but they do not realise it. The peacock in question would not know that his fellow-parishioners were dying; or if he did, he would be incapable of conceiving all that the fact involved. Similarly with people like Hetty, the entire energy of their poor little minds is expended on what they themselves are doing or suffering; and they have not sufficient mental power left to imagine, or even observe, the experiences of their neighbours. Suffering of a kind that involuntarily stimulates their imagination, awakens even in them a certain low kind of sympathy. The peacock, for example, would probably feel perturbed, if he saw a brother peacock being strangled. This would awaken in him a certain minimum of sympathy — that minimum, at any rate, which Hobbes dignified with the name of pity; there would arise in his breast the painful feeling that "the same calamity might happen to himself."

That we have been endowed by nature with the germs of a heart seems indicated by the fact, that the youngest infants are generally pleased by laughter and merriment, and discomposed by tears or other signs of woe. And that this instinct of sympathy becomes in later life almost inevitably developed, seems clear from the fact that the Stoics took such pains to urge upon their disciples the necessity for crushing it. "Thou mayst put on," says Epictetus, "a look of sorrow, but take care that thy sorrow be not real." I think, upon the whole, we must agree with Hume and Bishop Butler, that to take pleasure in pain is an altogether unnatural and acquired vice. "Would any man who is walking along," asks Hume, "tread as willingly on another's gouty toes, whom he has no quarrel with, as on the hard flint and pavement? Let us suppose him ever so selfish, let private interest have engrossed ever so much of his attention, yet, in instances where that is not concerned, he unavoidably feels some propensity to the good of mankind," he unavoidably is pleased with their pleasure and pained by their pain. If so, every human being possesses, to start with, the germs of a heart.

But only the germs. For undoubtedly, at first, our sympathy is more or less selfish, and so far, in the strictest sense of the word, unsympathetic. We are pained, not so much because others feel pain, as because we have to see them feeling it. It is a depressing sight, and we wish it removed for our own sakes rather than for theirs. Now this lower kind of sympathy, which we possess from our birth, is developed to some extent, without any effort on our part, by the circumstances of life. We saw, in the previous sermon, that there was a minimum of mental development, which we could not avoid. And the same is true in the moral sphere. He who has experienced suffering is likely to shrink from the very thought of it, by the mere process of mental association. The sight of another's grief brings up remembrances or suggestions of the suffering which he has himself experienced, and these remembrances and suggestions are in themselves painful. Again, the most self-centred of men cannot help finding out that his own interests are more or less bound up with those of others. It is in this way, as George Eliot says, that political molecules—the most selfish and self-isolating members of the body politic—get educated, by the nature of things, into a faint feeling of fraternity. They come to desire the condition of affairs which would be advantageous for others, because it is often just this condition of affairs that is likely to be most advantageous to themselves. But it is evident that this interest in their neighbour is not really disinterested. When their own happiness clashed with his, they might, for anything that such sympathy could do to prevent them, cause him an immense amount of pain, in order to secure for themselves the smallest amount of pleasure. And yet, beyond this stage of selfish sympathy, many men never pass.

We saw in the last sermon that it depended on ourselves whether the mental faculties with which nature had endowed us should, or should not, be developed into what could properly be called a mind. The intellectual faculties become sensualised, so to speak, if they are always sensuously employed. If we devote them exclusively to the promotion of our physical comfort, we do not deserve to be called rational. Similarly, without our own determined efforts our original faculty of sympathy will never be developed into anything properly called a heart. What distinguishes the human race from the race of animals is, not that men *are* rational and moral, but that they *may be*. We have power to develop, if we please, an intellectual and moral existence, of which animals never manifest more than the germs. But morally, as intellectually, there are men who always remain at the lowest stage of being. As children, the only love they ever had for their parents was what is vulgarly called " cupboard-love." As grown-up men, they regard wife, family, servants, mankind, as so many personal appendages, so many ornaments or ministers to themselves. Their faculty of sympathy will be no more developed on the day of their death than it was on the day of their birth.

The circumstances of our earthly life do much, if we will only let them, towards developing our nascent instinct of sympathy into a genuine human heart. Most of us, I suppose, made some little progress in the home of our childhood. There we learned, in the true sense of the word, to love. The instinctive affection of infancy changed into the intelligent affection of youth. There for the first time we took a disinterested interest in human happiness and misery. The experience of those with whom we lived pleased or pained us, irrespective of its direct effect upon ourselves. We learned to rejoice in the joy of others, not merely because it was a pleasant thing for us to look upon, but because it was a pleasant thing for them to feel. We began to grieve over the sorrows of others, not merely because we ourselves were depressed by them, but because we realised what they meant for those who were actually experiencing them. We began to sympathise—to feel with others, not in the sense of having self-regarding feelings of our own awakened by their experiences, but in the sense that our feelings became self-disregarding. We were not occupied entirely with the pleasure or pain instinctively caused to ourselves by the sight of their joy or grief, but we actually felt what they were feeling; and in this unselfish experience, our own personal feelings were almost, if not entirely, forgotten. It was thus in our home that we gained the first glimpse of what we were capable of eventually becoming. We discovered that we were more than self-contained individuals; that we might live a larger, fuller life than such as pertained to us as isolated units; that when we aimed directly at the happiness of others, our own happiness was indirectly enormously increased; and that we only began truly to live when we took up into our own the lives of others.

And the sweet, blessed influences of home were intended to help us to a yet fuller and higher development. He who has once learned the incompleteness of an isolated existence, is prepared to go on identifying his own life with an ever-widening sphere of life beyond himself. Love of kindred will thus expand into love of country. We learn to identify ourselves with the members of the community to which we belong. Their joys become our joys, and their sorrows our sorrows. We absorb their life, so to speak, into our own. We may even feel what they are suffering, more really and keenly than any experience which could pertain to us as mere individuals. There have been men who have so sympathised with their fellows, that for them pain and pleasure became words which had almost ceased to have any personal significance. "Self-indulgence at the expense of others would be a greater self-denial, a thing fraught with keener anguish, than any private suffering; it would be an injury done to a dearer self, for the sake of a self less dear. There have been men who actually felt in their country's humiliation and loss a far sharper pang than in any personal suffering; and the offering up of life itself has had a strange sweetness in it, if the sacrifice could avert or retrieve her ruin."

And as the love of kindred may expand into the love of country, so the love of country may expand into the love of race. We may take up the vast life of humanity, and make it part of our own. "It is an indication," says Professor Caird, "of the highest moral progress, when nationality ceases to be the limit of sympathy, when the oppression of the remotest nation begins to appeal to us with a sense of personal injury, or when the story of a great act of injustice, done to a single human soul, breaks down for a moment the barrier of national exclusiveness, and evokes from all lands a cry as of pain and indignation for a universal wrong. In such incidents there is a witness to the slow advance of mankind towards that ideal of goodness, which Christians have ever recognised in One who loved all men with a love more intense than the love of kindred and country, and who offered up life itself a sacrifice for 'the redemption of the world from evil.'"

And let me ask you to notice that this culture of the heart, this education of sympathy, this merging of our own life into the life of our fellows, is in reality nothing more than self-development. It is an illustration of the words of Christ, "He that loseth his life for my sake, shall find it." The isolated individual, as Caird points out, is not, properly speaking, a man, but only a fragment of humanity, as really dead as an amputated limb, which, in being cut off from the organism, is virtually cut off from itself. "Considered from a merely individualistic point of view, the duties which we owe to family, state and race, the taking upon ourselves the heavy weight of their many burdens—all this is a limit to our freedom. But considered from a higher point of view, it is just here that there is provided an escape, from the narrowness and poverty of the individual life, and the possibility of a life, which is other and larger than our own, and yet is, at the same time, most truly ours. For to be ourselves we must be more than ourselves. What we call love, is, in truth, the finding of our own life in the life of another, the losing of our individual selves to gain a larger self." As the scope of our sympathy widens till it embraces the complex life of the family, the nation, the race, at each successive step we are only expanding the range of our own moral life, escaping further and further from the finitude of the individual self, and approximating more and more to a life which is unlimited and universal. And until we enter upon this inheritance of the universal life, we shall never be truly perfect. A man cannot realise himself within himself, cannot come to perfection by himself, but only in and through communion with others. Well has Mr Phillips Brooks said, there are some parts of the individual's life which are always in his brethren's keeping, and which he can only receive from them. A deeper selfhood, a richer personality, comes to a man from communion with others and sacrifice for others, than he could possibly have gained by any amount of solitary contemplation or self-aggrandisement. It is only as our individual, narrow, exclusive, isolated self is developed into a larger, inclusive, sympathetic self, that we come to our highest life. "To go forth out of self, to have all the hidden wealth of feeling of which I am capable called forth towards others, and to receive back again this wealth redoubled, in reciprocated affection and increased power of loving—this is to live wisely and well; not to do this is to eliminate from life all that makes it most truly human, all that makes it most really valuable." *He who loveth his life shall lose it.* If any one's affections are always centred on himself, he will never have any self worth caring for; he will eternally be a mean and contemptible creature, undeserving of the name of man. *He who loseth his life shall find it.* He who has taken up, into his originally isolated being, the lives of his fellows, has thereby perfected his own moral life. The old, meagre, paltry life is gone. The life which he now lives is broad and deep, noble and heroic, Christ-like and divine.

Common Duties.

V.

CULTURE OF THE SPIRIT.

"Be perfect."—2 Cor. xiii. 11.

IT is impossible to-day,[1] and it will be impossible for some time to come, to mention the word culture without being reminded of that noble example of it, whose sudden and premature death we are all deploring. A Prince by birth, he was deprived of much of the stimulus to work which men of lower rank enjoy; he was surrounded by many inducements to idleness which men of lower rank escape; and, in the physical weakness, from which he was never altogether free, he might have found—had he wished it—a good excuse for taking life easily. Yet, from his childhood upwards, he manifested

[1] The Sunday after the Duke of Albany's death.

the most untiring assiduity in the task of self-culture. And his judgment was not inferior to his zeal. At Oxford he resisted the tendency—common to all universities—of a narrow and one-sided education, his own studies being of the widest and most varied kind. And, better still, he was not contented to be a highly educated man; it was his great ambition to be useful. He took the deepest interest in the wellbeing of his fellow-countrymen. His talents and acquirements were consecrated freely to their service. He was always ready to encourage every good work by his presence, and by his wise, stimulating counsel. And morally, as intellectually, his sympathies were of the widest. Prince though he was, and scholar, he was interested in the pleasures and recreations of the poorest and most uncultured. In one of his latest speeches he asked, "How could a man feel himself so separate from his fellow-creatures, as to think that the pleasures which were worth his own attention, were quite superfluous trivialities in the case of poor men and women?" The direct and indirect influence of such a man is incalculable, and his loss to the world irretrievable. But there is one thing he may yet do for us, one thing which I am sure he would yet wish to do for us—he may stimulate us to imitate, so far as we can in our humbler sphere, his most illustrious example. And may his royal mother—of whom, though she is the best of Queens, her subjects love rather to think as the most womanly of women—may his royal mother find some consolation, even in the sadness of his death, by remembering the beauty and the value of his life.—

The heart, we have seen, is the faculty which unites us to our fellow-men, which enables us to live in the lives of others, and to make them part of our own. This expansion of our isolated existence is morality. There is nothing more unwarrantable than the prevalent restriction in the sense which is attached to the term "moral." In common parlance it generally means, abstinence from one or two glaring vices. To be moral, nowadays, it is not necessary even to be honest. A swindler who has caused widespread ruin by his chicanery, is sometimes described as a moral man, because, forsooth, he has been a tolerably good husband, or, at any rate, not bad enough to be divorced. But *genuine* morality is the identification of one's own life with the lives of others. The truly moral man finds much of his own happiness in the happiness not only of his family, but of his neighbours and acquaintances and fellow-citizens; he feels their sufferings almost as keenly as—sometimes, as we saw, even more keenly than—those which fall directly upon himself. And as he approaches to moral perfection, his loving sympathy goes on expanding, till at last it comprehends the whole human race.

Now manifestly he who is living this wide-reaching life is a higher type of man—a more finished and completed man—than he who is living a mere isolated existence. But though the moral man is more finished and completed than the immoral, morality alone will never make any one quite perfect. For this reason: even though his life should have been expanded till it embraced within itself the whole of his fellow-men, they are, one and all of them, like himself — imperfect. "The individual at any period of human history may identify himself by absolute self-devotion with the life of the family and state, with the organic life of the world, but that life itself is ever far short of perfection. Beyond the corporate life of mankind there is a wider life, of which all nature and history, all finite existences present and future, are the manifestations. Beyond the highest point to which the moral life can ever attain, there is always a far-off goal which recedes as we advance." The moral life, therefore, though indefinitely progressive, can never, from the nature of the case, be absolutely perfect or complete. It approaches ever nearer and nearer to perfection, but cannot actually reach it. Perfection, if it is to be obtained at all, must be achieved through union with that Infinite life from which all finite lives have come. In other words, if we are to be perfected, religion must be added to morality. We can only be perfected in God.

Religion is conscious, voluntary union with God, as morality is conscious, voluntary union with the race. And just as we have a special faculty—namely, the heart—by which the latter union is effected, so we have a special faculty for the former—namely, the spirit.

It has often been maintained, we saw, that we have no heart; that we are, and must always remain, selfish to the core; and that every appearance of kindliness is only an elaborate, and therefore disguised, form of selfishness. Similarly, it has been maintained that we have no spirit, no faculty for discerning God; that religion is nothing but the fanaticism of an undisciplined intellect; that what religionists call their spiritual vision is only the working of a diseased imagination; that God Himself is a nonentity, or, at any rate, a Being who has given us no proofs of His existence, and that His name is but the last survival of a feeble and worn-out creed. This is the kind of talk to which we are constantly subjected nowadays. We cannot open a magazine, we can hardly take up a newspaper, without statements of this kind staring us in the face.

The most curious thing about it all is the airs which these atheistic and agnostic writers give themselves; their self-satisfied assurance that they are the people with whom wisdom will die, or that if any wisdom survives them, it can only be such as has received the benefit of their sanction and authority. The ill-disguised contempt on the part of these gentlemen for those who make any profession of religion, appears extremely remarkable, when one remembers that God has been recognised and worshipped by men of infinitely higher genius, of infinitely greater eminence, than any atheist or agnostic living or dead. Comparisons are proverbially odious, and I do not wish to be offensively personal: but every one knows, all the world acknowledges, that now and then a man arises who towers a head and shoulders above all his fellows, who stands out conspicuously superior, not only to the illustrious men of his own age, but even to those of previous and succeeding generations. Two such men were Goethe and Hegel, and both of them were ardent theists. I trust I shall not be considered rude if I venture to say, that Mr Frederic Harrison must not expect to be ranked as a thinker with Hegel, nor should Mr Bradlaugh blame us if we do not regard him as a second Goethe. Of course the mere fact that Hegel or Goethe had a certain belief, does not prove that belief to be true; but it does effectually stop the mouths of those who would persuade us that none but a fool could hold it.

If you do not read German fluently (and no one ever yet read Hegel's German fluently) you will find the arguments by which that prince of thinkers proved the existence of God, proved it so that it could never again be for an instant doubted, by any one who had taken the pains to master the demonstration,—you will find all this simplified, popularised, and expressed in the most perfect and eloquent English, in Professor Caird's book entitled 'The Philosophy of Religion'—a work which, I take it, is the most important contribution to theology[1] that has appeared in the present generation. If you read and master this book of Professor Caird's, you will understand

[1] I use this word here in its best sense.

something of the *rationale* of the doctrine of doctrines, the doctrine in regard to which Hegel is at one with St Paul, the doctrine, namely, of an Infinite Person, in whom we live and move and have our being, and in whose realised presence we may find fulness of joy. Perhaps I may give you some slight indication of the drift of the argument by quoting a single sentence: "That we are capable of a perpetual progress in knowledge and goodness, and yet that every actual attainment leaves us with an ideal that is still unsatisfied; that we are conscious that our knowledge is limited, while yet we can set in thought no absolute limit to our knowledge; that we are conscious of our moral defects, and nevertheless can feel that there is no point of moral advancement beyond which we may not aspire;—in this boundless possibility of advancement, combined with a latent standard of excellence which throws contempt on our highest actual attainments, we may see that there is in our nature a potential infinitude." In other words, a careful analysis of our own finite life shows that it is inextricably bound up with an infinite life. God — though perhaps we know it not—has been latent, so to speak, within us from the first. He lives implicitly, if not explicitly, in the life of every one of us. He stands at the door, according to Christ's beautiful metaphor,—He stands at the door of our spirit and knocks, waiting to be recognised and loved.

It is in the constant and joyful recognition of our union with God that true religion consists. But there is no word which has been so unpardonably misused as the word "religion." It is frequently supposed to consist in a certain process or transaction which, if we are to escape the flames of hell, must be gone through sometime before we die. But as any time will do, this transaction is generally postponed indefinitely. Till the thunderbolt falls, says the Russian proverb, the peasant never crosses himself. And you remember, in Shakespeare's "Henry V.," Mrs Quickly's account of the death of Falstaff. "He cried out," she says, "God, God, God, three or four times; and I, to comfort him, bid him he should not think of God. I hoped there was no need to trouble himself yet with any such thoughts." Others look upon religion as a *series* of processes or transactions, which must be gone through systematically at stated times. There are people who fancy themselves religious because they go regularly to church. They remind one of Tennyson's Yorkshire farmer. When that worthy lay upon his deathbed, he could not understand the parson's anxiety about his spiritual condition. For, as he quaintly puts it—

" I hallus coom'd to's choorch afoor moy Sally wur deäd,
An' 'eerd 'um a bummin' awaäy loike a buzzard-clock ower my 'eäd,
An' I niver knaw'd whot a meän'd, but I thowt a 'ad summut to saäy,
An' I thowt a said whot a owt to 'a said, an' I coom'd awaäy."

Now there are many persons, possessing a certain amount of intellectual education and culture, who, so far as religion is concerned, stand upon no higher level than this Yorkshire clodhopper. They may, perhaps, not take the sermon so quietly, they may chafe under it and disagree with it, and think that the parson has said what he ought *not* to have said—but that is all the difference. Like the farmer, they fancy there is a saving merit in mere attendance at a place of worship, and that they will by-and-by be well paid for the systematic manner in which they discharge this irksome duty. What nonsense! "You might as well call the daw a religious bird, because he is often heard cawing from the church steeple," as call a human being religious because he is often found sitting in a church pew. There is no more religion in sitting in a pew than there is in sitting on a steeple. The abuse of the term religion, when it is applied to the routine work of external observance, is only surpassed by the abuse of the term God, when it is applied to a Being supposed to be propitiated by such hollow, stupid mockery.

Religion consists in the constant and joyful recognition of our union with God. We *are* united to Him, whether we recognise it or not, by the very fact of our existence. But when we realise in our own consciousness the actuality of the Infinite life, out of which we have come and by which we are encompassed, we realise at the same time the comparative paltriness of all finite things, and we give ourselves up to be possessed and suffused by the Infinite life of God.

The culture of the spirit—of that faculty by which we see God, by which we live a religious life — is essential to our own self-completion. We only become perfect when we begin to live an infinite and divine life. One of the correspondents, with whom I have here made an epistolary acquaintance, has suggested to me that Christianity might be called the apotheosis of personality—an expression of which I gladly avail myself. No religion ever required so much self-sacrifice as the religion of Christ; and yet the self-sacrifice demanded is a most reasonable service. For we sacrifice only a lower self to gain a higher; we lose a life which is finite and imperfect and not worth keeping, to gain a life which is in a sense infinite and divine. The sacrifice demanded of us leads to our own apotheosis. "Religion is the surrender of the finite will to the infinite, the abnegation of all desire, inclination, volition that pertain to me as this private individual self, the giving up of every aim or endeavour that points only to my exclusive pleasure or interest, the absolute identification of my will with the will of God. And it is just in this renunciation of self that I truly gain myself, and realise the highest possibilities of my nature." Everything that can accrue to me as a mere isolated individual, nay, even that deepening and widening of my life which comes from sympathy with kindred and community and race, leaves me incomplete and imperfect. It is possible for me to gain the whole world, and still to lose my soul—my true and proper self. My life—my true life—is "hid with Christ in God."

I am only "complete in Him." To be perfect I must be filled with the fulness of God; I must be able to say,—God liveth in me. Nothing short of this is legitimately called Religion. "In the act which constitutes the beginning of the religious life—call it faith, or trust, or self-surrender, or by whatever name you will—there is involved the identification of the finite with the infinite life. It is the elevation of the spirit into a region where hope passes into certitude, struggle into conquest, interminable effort and endeavour into peace and rest. As the life of the organism is one and indivisible, because ·the whole life —and not a part or portion of it merely—is present in every member, so it is not a finite, but an infinite life, which the spirit lives. It is a divine spirit which animates and inspires it. In all its actions, it is a divine will that moves it. Every pulse-beat of its life is the expression and realisation of the life of God."

And if you ask me by what means the spirit —the faculty by which we see God and realise our union with Him—is to be developed in us, I reply, mainly by use. For the culture of the spirit, as for culture in general, we cannot dispense with the assistance of others. We must all of us avail ourselves of the assistance of those whom we find able to impart it. But we must rely chiefly upon our own voluntary efforts. Just as a bodily organ is strengthened by every attempt we make to use it, so is it with the faculty of spiritual vision. We shall see God in proportion as we look for Him. And let us shake ourselves free from the fancy, if we have ever been possessed by it, that He is only to be found at certain times and places, and through the instrumentality of certain ceremonies. If we have had no communion with God *out of* church, we are not at all likely to meet with Him *in* church. Its services are useful and helpful only to those who, having already seen Him, desire a clearer and fuller vision. God is not tied down either to Mount Gerizim or to Jerusalem; nay, we may possibly fail to find Him even in those sacred spots. But the quickened spiritual vision sees God everywhere and in all things, recognises the simplest object in nature as one of the dwelling-places of the Most High. This is beautifully expressed in a poem of Lowell's, with which I must conclude:—

> " Worn and footsore was the Prophet
> When he gained the holy hill;
> 'God has left the earth,' he murmured;
> '*Here* His presence lingers still.

'God of all the olden prophets,
   Wilt Thou speak with man no more?
Have I not as truly served Thee
   As Thy chosen ones of yore?

'Hear me, guider of my fathers,
   Lo! a humble heart is mine;
By Thy mercy, I beseech Thee,
   Grant Thy servant but a sign!'

Bowing then his head he listened
   For an answer to his prayer:
No loud burst of thunder followed,
   Not a murmur of the air.

But the tuft of moss before him
   Opened while he waited yet,
And, from out the rock's hard bosom,
   Sprang a tender violet.

God, I thank Thee,' said the Prophet,
   'Hard of heart and blind was I,
Looking to the holy mountain
   For the gift of prophecy.

'Still Thou speakest with Thy children
   Truly as in eld sublime;
Humbleness, and love, and patience,
   Still give empire over time!

'Had I trusted in my nature
   And had faith in lowly things,
Thou Thyself wouldst then have sought me
   And set free my spirit's wings.

'But I looked for signs and wonders
   That o'er men should give me sway:
Thirsting to be more than mortal,
   I was even less than clay.

'Ere I entered on my journey,
  As I girt my loins to start,
Ran to me my little daughter
  The beloved of my heart:

'In her hand she held a flower,
  Like to this as like may be,
Which,—*beside my very threshold,*—
  She had plucked and brought to me.'"

Common Duties.

VI.

HELPFULNESS.

"The law of Christ. . . . Bear ye one another's burdens."
—GALATIANS vi. 2.

WHEN we discussed the culture of the heart, we recognised the obligation we were under of teaching and training ourselves to feel with our fellow-men, to rejoice with them when they rejoice, and to mourn with them when they mourn. We saw sympathy might be developed to such a point, that we should rejoice and mourn with others, not only because the sight of joy is instinctively pleasing and the sight of sorrow instinctively saddening *to ourselves*, but because we had entered into their experiences, and actually felt what they were feeling. Their joys, we saw, might become literally our joys, their sorrows our sorrows. Their lives might be so completely incorporated into our own, that our narrow private interest would sink into insignificance, when compared with the broader demands of the common weal. John Stuart Mill, in his tract on Utilitarianism, has finely said, that "when we have received a proper moral education, the feeling of unity with our fellow-men will be as deeply rooted in our consciousness as the horror of particular crimes; the good of others will be to us a thing naturally and necessarily to be attended to, like any of the physical conditions of existence; we shall be unable to conceive the possibility of getting personal happiness by conduct opposed to the general good; and we shall never think of, nor desire, any beneficial condition for ourselves in which others are not included." The ideal end of moral education is to cultivate the heart up to this point; to develop the nascent feeling of sympathy, which is latent within us from the first, into this far-reaching, all-embracing emotion, which unites us more or less closely to every member of the human race.

But sympathy, like every other feeling implanted in us by nature, is intended to prompt us to action. It is of no use to feel with others, unless we are thereby stimulated to do something for them.

Helpfulness.

> " For if our virtue go not forth of us,
> 'Tis all the same as though we had it not."

Life, in the true sense of the word, is not feeling but work. Napoleon's test, " What has he done ? " is perfectly applicable in the moral sphere. The good man, no less than the great man, is the man who has done something. Out on the sympathy of those persons who shed floods of tears over the imaginary woes described in a novel or a play, and never do anything to lessen the actual woes around them of which those descriptions are but copies ! Out on the sympathy which always tries to thrust the burden of relief upon some one else's shoulders ! I think it was Sydney Smith who jocularly remarked that the world was full of sympathy, because if A was in trouble B would always ask C to help him. But it is manifest the world is not benefited by these attempts at vicarious helpfulness. If C is as lethargic as B, he will pass the matter on to D, and D will transfer it to E, and so on. In the meantime poor A's trouble remains unalleviated. For all the good effected by the sympathy of Messrs B, C, D, and E, they might just as well have been blocks of marble. Sympathy, then, is of no use unless it leads to action.

And further, it is of no use unless it leads to

the right kind of action. It is possible to act on the instigation of impulse, and at the same time to do more harm than good. "Some rub the sore when they would heal the wound;" and so the sufferer would have been better off if they had *not* sympathised with him. We are all sometimes made to smart, by the foolish treatment of friends who mean to be kind; and we are compelled to hope that, in future, if they cannot get wiser heads, they will at least obtain harder hearts. Many good-natured persons do quite as much mischief as they could possibly have done by being ill-natured. You know the kind of people—the people who are generally described as "meaning well"—a polite and pleasant way of saying that they usually do the opposite. There are few persons in the world who more often act ill, than those who are always declared to mean well. It is not enough, then, to have sympathy; it is not enough to act on the instigation of sympathy. If we would be really helpful, we must be sure that we are acting rightly. And to do this, we must see the bearing of our action upon the circumstances of the case. Helpfulness may be defined as the judicious carrying out of sympathy.

Here we have another and a striking illustration of the importance of thought. We shall never be helpful until we learn to think. If our sympathy is to be of any use, it must be thoughtfully, and not thoughtlessly, acted on. Just as it is not enough to desire our own good, but if we are to achieve it, we must carefully consider the best means to be employed; so it is not enough to desire the good of others, if that good is to be promoted by us we must give the subject at least as much reflection as prudence would require us to give to the promotion of our own. To be really, wisely helpful, we must make the interests of others part of our own scheme of life.

Let me give you two illustrations of the necessity there is for thought, if sympathy is to be converted into helpfulness. Let us take the case of speech. It is impossible to overestimate the amount of good, as it is impossible to overestimate the amount of harm, which we are capable of doing, by the use or abuse of the tongue. Sometimes, when we think of the misery wrought by speech, we begin to wonder whether, on the whole, human happiness would not be greater if all men and women were dumb. And yet, a word spoken in season, how good it is! Many a man has been saved from moral ruin, many a man has been prevented from throwing up the game of life in despair, by a few well-chosen words of remonstrance or encouragement. But the mere feeling of sympathy alone will not suggest the seasonable word; that can only be arrived at by thought.

There is nothing about which we ought to be so careful as our speech; and yet there is nothing in regard to which most of us are so careless. We say whatever first occurs to us, without waiting to consider the result. And there are many of us, to whom it is generally the wrong thing that occurs first. It is a hackneyed quotation—but hackneyed because it is so true:—

> " Full many a shaft at random sent,
> Finds mark the archer little meant ;
> And many a word at random spoken,
> May soothe, or wound, a heart that's broken."

There is a large number of well-meaning persons, who always manage — quite contrary to their intention — to wound instead of soothe. They say what is harmful through sheer stupidity. And this stupidity is sin; for it is merely a form of laziness — laziness shrinking from the fatigue of thought. When they find they have caused pain, they try to excuse themselves by saying they "didn't think." A pitiful excuse! Why didn't they think? What is the use of being a man if you don't think? If their remorse for the mischief they have done is very poignant, they will declare that they feel "inclined to bite their tongues out." But what is the good of that? It might certainly keep them out of mischief in the future, but it would not cure the pain they have already caused. A little thought, before the harm was done, would have been much more useful than the cutting out of their tongues afterwards. Such people would appear to be driven into speech by an inordinate dread of silence. They seem to imagine that a terrible disgrace would have befallen them, could they ever be accused of having for an instant held their tongues. They will say anything rather than say nothing. But this dread of silence is extremely silly. It was a maxim of the Duke of Wellington's, "When you don't know what to do, do nothing." And the corresponding maxim is just as self-evidently valid,—when you don't know what to say, when you are not sure of the right and wise thing to say, say nothing. Not only in politics, but in conversation, there is much need oftentimes of a "masterly inactivity." Silence may occasionally be more helpful, nay even more eloquent, than speech.

I do not agree with the following sentence in

'Mr Isaacs': "How little sympathy there must be for any one, even our dearest, when it is so hard to look forward to speaking half-a-dozen words to comfort some poor wretch of a friend, who has lost everything in the world that was dear to him. We would rather give him all we possess outright, than attempt to console him for his loss." Now in such a case, it seems to me, we are often silent, not because we have so little sympathy, but because we have so much. We feel so acutely what our friend is feeling, that it seems to us, as if anything we could utter by way of mitigation, would only be a mockery and an insult. And sometimes we are right. There are occasions upon which nothing ought to be said: a silent pressure of the hand is all the consolation we should presume to offer. When poor Job's friends first arrived, "they sat down with him upon the ground seven days and seven nights, and none spake a word unto him; for they saw that his grief was very great." That was the only comfort he ever received from them. As soon as they began to speak, they did nothing but irritate and chafe him.

Still, if we would take the trouble to think, we might generally, even in the most desperate cases, after the first paroxysms of the sufferer's anguish were over—we might generally find something to say that would be really helpful to him. The present Postmaster-General[1] affords a remarkable illustration, of the enormous amount of good that may result from a few judicious words of sympathy. He lost his sight when about four or five and twenty by a shooting accident; and he was utterly crushed by the weight of the disaster. When we meet him now, he seems so cheerful and contented, that we can hardly believe he could ever have felt it so acutely; and yet he did. He was in the most absolute despair; he was convinced that the rest of his life must be without value or use. But at this crisis a friend suggested to him that there was much to be done, in the world and for the world, which did not require sight; nay, that there were some things, such as abstract thinking, which the want of sight would facilitate rather than hinder. The result was, that Mr Fawcett shook off his despair, gathered up his energies afresh for the battle of life, and how nobly and successfully he has fought it you all know.

So much for the helpfulness of speech. If

[1] Mr Fawcett's sad and unexpected death occurred while these pages were passing through the press (Nov. 1884).

we want a second example of the necessity of thought, for the conversion of sympathy into helpfulness, we may find it in the case of what is called charity. You all know that the word translated "charity" in the New Testament should have been rendered "love," and is so rendered in the Revised Version. A very great improvement; for the word charity in modern English has come to mean giving money, and most frequently giving money to beggars — a thing which any one, who has the least rational love for his fellow-creatures, will rarely, if ever, do. Miss Muloch, in her 'Sermons out of Church,' has some very good remarks on what she terms the crime of benevolence. "Many a man called benevolent," she says, "is simply wasteful, and the cause of waste in others. The really deserving neither beg nor borrow; they suffer silently; while the loud-complaining, ever-greedy applicants for aid always get the best of what charity is going. I often think that much of the benevolence in the world is poured out like pig-wash; the pig who makes the most noise, or who succeeds in getting his two feet in the trough, while the others get but one, is the animal who swallows most and fattens fastest." You see you must distinguish between benevolence and beneficence. Benevolence is wishing well, beneficence is doing well. Now it is no good wishing men well and doing them ill. Everybody who has ever looked into the matter knows that, in nine hundred and ninety-nine cases out of a thousand at least, beggars are impostors. They might, if they chose, work for their living; but they do not choose. To give money to them, therefore, is not to help but to harm them. There is no greater injury you can inflict on a man, than to do for him what he might and ought to have done for himself. You may fancy you are conferring a benefit, but you are not; on the contrary, you degrade and demoralise him. And the pity of it is, that the money wasted in pampering impostors, might have relieved so many cases of *bonâ fide* necessity. But as the deserving cases are unobtrusive, it would have taken a little trouble to discover them. It is easier to give one's money to the undeserving rascals at hand. For the helpful distribution of charity, thought and trouble are indispensable; and therefore, I suppose, we must always expect to find a large amount of harmful distribution.

There is one other point very apt to be overlooked, to which, before I close, I should like to direct your attention. I refer to the helpfulness of example. By what we say and do, we are not only directly affecting the *comfort* of others, but we are indirectly changing their *characters*. We may not only contribute to their happiness, but we may make them morally better. By acting rightly ourselves, we may help others, may make it easier for others, to bear their burden of duty. There is no surer way of helping a man to cope with his difficulties and to conquer his temptations, than by showing him that we have obtained the mastery over ours. There is no surer way of stimulating a man to give up bad habits, than by exemplifying, in our own lives, the beauty and the charm of good ones. And the stimulus of our example will not end with death. Mark Antony was wrong when he said, " The evil that men do lives after them. The good is oft interred with their bones." The good may be less noticeable perhaps, but it lives, no less than the evil. The scientific doctrine of heredity teaches us, that our dispositions and tendencies—be they good or bad —are inevitably transmitted to our descendants. If we always remembered this, how careful we should be of our actions, of our words, of our thoughts. We may lighten the burden of duty for generations yet unborn. By living wisely and well, we shall confer incalculable blessings upon many who will never know us, who may never even hear of us. We may give them a better moral start in life than, but for our efforts, they could possibly have had. But alas for those who come after us, if we live unwisely and ill! Through no fault of their own, but entirely because of our misdeeds, it may be next to impossible for them to be anything but bad. We may make their burden of duty a burden too heavy to be borne.

> "They *enslave* their children's children, who make compromise with sin."

Common Sins.

I.

SELFISHNESS.

"Let every man please his neighbour for his good to edification."
—ROMANS xv. 2.

I WISH to speak to you to-day about selfishness, the commonest of all common sins.

Let me ask you at the outset carefully to distinguish between self-love and selfishness. Self-love, says one of Shakespeare's characters, is not so vile a sin as self-neglecting. He might have put it much more strongly. Self-love is not a sin at all. The interest we take in our own well-being, as Bishop Butler long ago pointed out, is one of the most important elements in our moral constitution. It enables us to keep in check the various appetites and passions and desires, which would otherwise bring about our ruin.

Selfishness. 141

Without it we could never attain to the stature of perfect men.

Ardent enthusiasts have sometimes spoken as if it were a sin to do anything on one's own account,—as if the whole of one's thoughts and efforts and energies should be devoted to the welfare of our fellow-men. For example, Faber says in one of his hymns—

> "O Lord, that I could waste my life for others,
>   With no ends of my own;
> That I could pour myself into my brothers,
>   And live for them alone."

But a moment's reflection will show that such self-effacement is rendered impossible by the very conditions of our existence. Suppose, for instance, that we devoted ourselves exclusively to the satisfaction of other people's hunger and refused to satisfy our own, death would very soon put an end to our labours. If we are to supply our neighbour's wants, it is first of all necessary that we satisfy our own. Lecky relates a curious legend of an aged hermit paying a visit to a brother recluse, who was celebrated for extraordinary holiness, but who unfortunately at the time possessed only a single loaf, just big enough to constitute a meal for one. The two saints spent four-and-twenty hours each trying in vain to persuade the other to eat it. The visitor maintained that it belonged to his host on account of his superior sanctity; the host replied that it was the right of his guest on account of his superior age. At last, when they grew too faint to carry on the discussion, the expedient suggested itself of dividing the loaf between them, and afterwards going together in search of more. You see the self-effacement of these holy men was very nearly being the death of both of them. And if, by some sudden miracle, the principle of self-neglect were to be universally substituted for the principle of self-love, the human race would be extinguished in a week. We are not only at liberty, we are bound to seek our own good; it is advantageous to others that we should do so. Even the rivalry and competition in which we try to surpass our neighbours is (within due limits) wholesome and healthy for them as for us, affording as it does the necessary stimulus for those efforts which are essential to their self-development. Such rivalry is part of the divinely appointed discipline of life.

Selfishness, then, is not the love of self, but the exclusive or excessive love of self. It does not consist in regarding our own welfare, but in

Selfishness. 143

disregarding that of others; it is manifested not when we take ourselves into consideration, but when we leave others out.

Now there is in the world an extreme form of selfishness, which actually derives pleasure from the pain of others. So exquisite is the enjoyment which is sometimes afforded by the sight of suffering, that there have been men who imagined it to be the highest conceivable joy both for this world and for the next. The torments of the lost have been regarded as important elements in the happiness of heaven, and as contributing largely to the serene satisfaction of the Deity. Of this state of heart which delights in agony we find an illustration in the domestic tyrant. You will remember, I daresay, a striking passage on this subject in Oliver Wendell Holmes' 'Autocrat': "What torment," he says, "may be caused you by one of your own flesh and blood, or of a certain grade of intimacy. No stranger can get a great many notes of torture out of a human soul. It takes one that knows it well—parent, child, brother, sister, intimate. Some of them have a scale of your whole nervous system, and can play all the gamut of your sensibility in semitones, touching the naked nerve-pulps as a pianist strikes the keys of his instrument. I am satisfied that there are as great masters of this nerve-playing as Vieuxtemps or Thalberg in their lines of performance. Married life is the school in which the most accomplished artists in this department are found. A delicate woman is the best instrument—she has such a magnificent compass of sensibility. From the deep inward moan which follows pressure on the great nerves of right, to the sharp cry as the filaments of taste are struck with a crashing sweep, is a range which no other instrument possesses. A few exercises on it daily at home fit a man wonderfully for his habitual labours, and refresh him immensely as he returns from them." All the fiends in hell could not cause more suffering than is sometimes inflicted by a man, for his own amusement, upon the unhappy woman whom he has promised to love and to cherish.

More commonly, however, selfishness shows itself by simple indifference. Many persons are made neither happier nor unhappier by their neighbours' joys and sorrows. They are as unsympathetic as if their hearts were made of cast-iron. They remind one of Wordsworth's sexton, who would—

> "Wrap an old acquaintance up in clay,
> As unconcerned as when he plants a tree,"

Selfishness. 145

Such persons have no objection to their neighbours finding life pleasant, but they have equally little objection to their finding it unpleasant. As for trying to make anybody happier or better, unless their own private interests were to be served thereby—why, they would as soon think of standing on their heads.

This kind of person, you may say, is rare. Well, I hope so. But I want to point out to you that men are often much more selfish than we should at first be inclined to suspect. Selfishness, you must know, sometimes decks itself in the outward semblance of unselfishness. Very frequently men are in reality thinking of themselves, when to all appearance they are thinking of others:—

> "They use their love of others for a gilding,
> To make themselves look fair."

Generosity Rochefoucauld has defined as the vanity of giving. Though I believe this to be a libel on human nature if laid down as a definition capable of universal application, yet there can be no doubt that it is often but too accurate. A man, for example, will subscribe to a hospital because he likes to see his name in print; he will give away large sums of money in order that it

K

may be known he is well off; he will confer considerable benefits on the community with the view of obtaining a peerage. In a word, there is a good deal of apparent generosity, to which people are only prompted by the desire of receiving a great deal more again. In social life you will find many illustrations of the essential selfishness of much apparent unselfishness. Politeness, for example — which implies respect for others—is often nothing but respect for one's self. Our manners may be agreeable, not because we take any interest in others, but because it would be bad form to show our indifference. We think it due to ourselves to act up to a certain standard of deportment. Or, once more, just think of the immense number of hospitalities which are offered, not with a view of increasing happiness, but for the purpose of diminishing it,—the only aim of the host or hostess being to vex their neighbours by the unapproachable splendour of their own entertainments. Many of the customs and practices of modern civilisation, which would be highly Christian if prompted by a spirit of genuine kindliness, are at the same time quite compatible with a spirit of the most anti-Christian selfishness.

I must also draw your attention to a yet more subtle form of this common vice. If we are genuinely benevolent, we shall try and please our neighbour, as our text advises, "for his good to edification,"—in other words, we shall prefer his permanent good to his momentary pleasure. But it is often simpler and more agreeable to please him in a manner that is positively injurious. Of this the most striking illustration will be found in the case of indiscriminate charity. Some people are fond of almsgiving, but they are too indolent to investigate matters and to seek out deserving cases. Their charity is therefore only a form of selfishness. To give money unless you are sure it will be well spent, is really to be guilty of an unkindness. I knew a person who was in the habit of bestowing a penny on every beggar woman who called at the door, and an extra penny if she had a child. The lesson of course was readily learnt, and soon all the women came as mothers. The chief result, therefore, of that person's charity, was the creation of a large number of liars. Or take another illustration. Miss Muloch very truly observes, "Woman's devotedness may be carried too far: a mother, by overweening indulgence, may make her son into a scapegrace; or a wife, by cowardly subservience, may convert her husband into a selfish brute." To yield in such cases is generally easier than to resist; but resistance is a duty, yielding is a sin. To sacrifice rights that ought to be insisted upon, merely for the sake of what is called peace, is manifestly a kind of selfishness; for it is the choice of a smaller self-denial when duty demands a greater.

So common is selfishness in one form or another that many philosophers — notably Mandeville — have regarded it as the only motive of human actions. They have maintained that we are unable, by our very constitution, to take any pleasure in the welfare of others except in so far as it directly increases our own. This is not true. The acutest students of human nature, as for example Hume, have held that (notwithstanding exceptional cases) men do, speaking generally, possess a faculty of disinterested affection, or at any rate the rudiments of such a faculty. Its occasional absence no more proves its non-existence, than the blindness or ugliness of some human beings proves the whole human race to be destitute of sight and beauty. Most of you take, do you not, some pleasure in the pleasure of others, apart altogether from any benefit you yourselves may derive from it? If so, there is within you a principle of benevolence as well as a principle of self-love.

Selfishness. 149

Now it was the one great aim of Christ—the purpose for which He lived and died—to induce men to cultivate the comparatively feeble sentiment of benevolence, till it became as potent and influential as self-love, till there should be no object in life which they had more at heart than the wellbeing of their fellow-men. Christ sought to develop the sentiment of benevolence into an enthusiasm, which would not be satisfied with refraining from injuring, but would manifest itself in deeds of kindliness and love. It was just this substitution of a positive for a negative standard of duty, which was needed to perfect the human character, or, in Scriptural phraseology, to save the human soul. Working out your salvation is learning to be kind. Mark you, this is no Broad Church theory. If there is the slightest reliance to be placed on the writings of the evangelists, it is the distinct and unmistakable doctrine of Christ. " Come, ye blessed of my Father, inherit the kingdom prepared for you : for I was hungry, and athirst, and naked, and a stranger, and sick, and in prison, and ye ministered unto me."

We profess—you and I—to be disciples of Christ. Let us ask ourselves, then, do we take a hearty and a constant pleasure in the happiness of others ? Does their welfare form part of our aim in life? Has the sentiment of benevolence been developed within us into enthusiasm? Is our home happier, purer, more homelike, because we live there? Do our servants reap the benefit of the lessons that we have learnt from Christ? Are those whom we meet in society better or worse for knowing us? Do we gladly seize opportunities,—do we go out of our way to make opportunities,—for conferring happiness or doing good?

If not, I fear me we are laying up for ourselves the bitterest remorse. Memory and imagination may not only continue beyond the grave, but their power may be intensified. You know Hood's poem called "The Lady's Dream," and how he represents those whom she might have befriended as passing before her in a long and ghastly procession. She exclaims in passionate despair—

> "The wounds I might have healed!
>   The human sorrow and smart!
> And yet it never was in my soul
>   To play so ill a part:
> But evil is wrought by want of thought,
>   As well as want of heart.
>
> Each pleading look that long ago
>   I scanned with heedless eye,
> Each face was gazing as plainly there
>   As when I passed it by.

> Woe, woe for me if the past should be
> Thus present when I die!
>
> No need of sulphureous lake,
>   No need of fiery coal,
> But only that crowd of human kind
>   Who wanted pity and dole,
> In everlasting retrospect
>   Will wring my sinful soul."

But I must not leave you with so sad a thought. You may live, if you please, a godlike life, the memories of which will hereafter afford you unspeakable joy. Take up the great life of humanity into your own. And don't fancy, if you are unable to accomplish much, that it is therefore useless to try and accomplish anything. There is a pretty legend in the Talmud to the following effect: A sage, while walking in a crowded market-place, suddenly encountered the prophet Elijah, and asked him who out of that vast multitude would be saved. Whereupon the prophet first pointed out a weird-looking creature, a turnkey—because he was merciful to his prisoners; and next, two common-looking tradesmen, who were walking through the crowd pleasantly chatting together. The sage instantly rushed after them and asked what were their saving works. But they, much puzzled, replied, "We are but poor workmen who live by our trade.

All that can be said for us is, that we are always of a cheerful spirit and good-natured. When we meet anybody who seems sad, we join him, and we talk to him, and cheer him till he forgets his grief. And if we know of two persons who have quarrelled, we talk to them, and persuade them till we have made them friends again. This is our whole life."

And was it not enough? Little kindnesses are of enormous value. Most true is the exclamation of Browning—

> "O the little more, and how much it is!
> O the little less, and what worlds away!"

Sir! Madam! be kind as you have opportunity, and you may say with truth, "For me to live is Christ."

Common Sins.

II.

BAD TEMPER.

"Let every one be slow to wrath : for the wrath of man worketh not the righteousness of God."—JAMES i. 19, 20.

IT is a common saying that every one has a temper but a fool. Certainly he who sees wrong done without feeling angry must be either a fool or a knave. The capability of anger is one of our most valuable endowments. The Stoics, I know, maintained that we ought to eradicate it; but it has a most important function to fulfil. The emotion of anger in the moral sphere, just like the sensation of pain in the physical, is intended to warn us that something is wrong. Anger, to use Locke's words, "is an uneasiness or discomposure of the mind" which springs up when injury has been done to ourselves or to others; and its purpose is to stimulate us to a remedial course. The protective power of this passion is very great. "Without any other armour," says Horace Smith, "than an offended frown, an indignant eye and a rebuking voice, decrepit age, timid womanhood, the weakest of our species, may daunt the most daring; for there is something formidable in the mere sight of wrath, even when it is incapable of inflicting any chastisement on its provoker. It is a moral power which tends to repair the inequality of physical power, and to approximate the strong and the weak towards the same level."

But, however useful and necessary, the passion of anger becomes very dangerous when it is not criticised and controlled by reason. Feeling and emotion may constantly mislead us; and therefore their promptings should never be unreflectingly obeyed. For example, the instinctive suggestions of pleasure and pain always require to be interpreted by thought. It is a common thing for a man to feel pain, or rather to fancy he feels it, in a limb that has been amputated; and again, conduct which will result in mischief, may be for a time highly pleasurable. Similarly the mere fact that anger exists in our minds is no proof that the anger is legitimate;

still less does it warrant us in thoughtlessly manifesting the anger, and manifesting it in proportion as it is felt. We are only at liberty to yield to the emotion if, and so far as, reason allows. When we yield without reflection, anger degenerates into bad temper—into what our text calls "the wrath of man."

Let us look into this.

(1.) Reflection may show us that we have no right to be angry at all. Circumstances may often arise at which we cannot help feeling vexed or annoyed, but in which nevertheless there is nothing to justify the emotion of anger. However disagreeable, for example, the weather might be, we should never dream of getting angry with it. It is only children and savages whose anger is excited by inanimate objects. But whenever anything is said or done by a human being contrary to our desires and tastes, we are all of us more or less apt to feel enraged. And yet a little reflection may show that this feeling of anger is unreasonable. People do not exist for the sole purpose of furthering our wishes. We have no business to feel angry with them, unless they have encroached upon our rights, unless they have violated a moral obligation. For example: a man says to me, "Sir, I don't like your style of preaching." Should I be justified in being angry with him? Certainly not. In disliking it, he only exercises a right of his own; he does not violate mine. Or, to take another equally simple illustration: suppose, in the course of an argument with your friend, you insist strongly upon some view of which he disapproves. He will very probably lose his temper; but has he any right to do so? Surely not. You are under no moral obligation to agree with him. You have as much right to your opinions as he has to his. Manifestly then, in all such cases, if the feeling of anger arises, it ought instantly to be crushed. Wrath is only righteous when applied to moral wrong. St Chrysostom truly says, "Anger is a sort of sting implanted in us, that we might therewith attack the devil, and not one another." In this matter, as in all others, Christ should be our example. How often must He have been grieved, disappointed, and vexed at the unsympathetic conduct of His disciples. Yet He was never angry with them. If the feeling ever arose in Him, it was never manifested. His anger was exhibited only against the mischievous cant of the Pharisees and Scribes.

(2.) Reflection may show that, though we may have cause for anger, yet our anger is excessive.

Bad Temper.

There are persons who are almost always out of temper, who will get in a rage at anything, or even at nothing. If we inquire into the cause of their wrath, in nine cases out of ten it turns out to be some petty personal annoyance. They are more enraged at the thwarting of their smallest whim, than at the most flagrant act of injustice inflicted upon any one else. I know a man—you know him, too, very likely—who is thrown into a paroxysm of fury if the match-box has been removed from its customary place. Now it is true that any one in the position of a master or father has a right to expect that even his slightest wishes should be regarded. But manifestly no one has a right to be as angry at the thwarting of a whim, as at the violation of an eternally binding moral duty. All such excessive manifestations of anger may be cured by thought. For our anger spontaneously subsides, when we become convinced that there is no real ground for it.

(3.) Reflection may suggest that though the feeling of anger is unavoidable, and though its manifestation would be legitimate, it will be better for us, under the circumstances, not to show it. The finest illustration of this will be familiar, no doubt, to many of you. It occurs in Victor Hugo's most celebrated novel, and it deserves to be written in letters of gold. You remember how Jean Valjean, who had been known to himself and others for the last nineteen years as No. 5623, and who has at last been dismissed from the galleys on a ticket-of-leave—you remember how he walks wearily along in the dust and heat, how he is turned out of the various inns, repulsed from every door, and even chased from an empty dog-kennel into which he has crawled for shelter. He wanders on again, saying despairingly to himself, "I am not even a dog." By-and-by he comes to the house of the good old Bishop Myriel. He knocks and enters, and tells his story. The Bishop, to the great discomposure of his housekeeper and the utter bewilderment of Valjean, orders a bedroom to be prepared for him, and invites him in the meantime to take a seat at the supper-table. After supper, the Bishop conducts him to his room, and the poor man lies down and falls asleep. In the middle of the night he wakes and begins to think; and the result of his thinking is, that he will get up and make off with the silver dishes which he had seen on the table the previous evening. He does so, but is soon captured by the police and brought back. The Bishop dismisses the gendarmes, pretending that he had made the man a present of the silver, and asking him why he had not taken the candlesticks as well. When they were left alone together, he says to the astonished thief, " Jean Valjean, my brother, never forget you have promised to employ this silver which I have given you in becoming an honest man. You belong no more to evil, but to good. I have bought your soul. I reclaim it from black thoughts and the spirit of perdition, and I give it to God." You know the result. From that day Valjean was a changed man. He became one of the noblest characters in the whole range of the world's fiction. Fiction ? Yes; but fiction that is true to fact.

Now please don't misunderstand me. Don't imagine that I am a weak sentimentalist who would do away with punishment. But there are times and cases, as in this instance, where punishment fails. Valjean, after nineteen years on the galleys, came away worse than he went. There was but one method untried—the method of the Bishop. And in our own experience, it may be, cases will sometimes arise when, by restraining an anger perfectly legitimate and withholding a punishment perfectly merited, *we may save a soul from death.*

(4.) Reflection may show us that though the

feeling of anger was legitimate, and though it was right and desirable to manifest it, yet the feeling has lasted long enough and may now be dismissed. "Anger resteth," says the author of Ecclesiastes, "in the bosom of fools." It arises in the bosom of wise men, but it remains only in the bosom of fools. There is no surer sign of a weak mind than what is called a sulky temper,—a temper which broods over its injuries and nurses its ill humours, steadily refusing to respond to expressions of repentance and overtures for forgiveness. The wise man—the man who thinks—knows both the time to be angry and the time to cease from anger.

From all this, you will see, it follows that if we treat men according to the first promptings of anger, we shall almost always do them wrong. It is important that we should pause and reflect, whenever we have it in our power to inflict punishment. "There is no passion," says Montaigne, "that so much perverts men's true judgment as anger. Why, then, should fathers and schoolmasters be allowed to whip and chastise children in their rage? This is not correction, but revenge. Chastisement is instead of physic to children; and should we bear with a physician who was exasperated and enraged with his

Bad Temper. 161

patient?" "If we would do well," continues Montaigne, "we should never lay a hand upon our servant whilst our anger lasts. While the pulse beats high and we feel an emotion in ourselves, let us defer the business; for it is passion that commands and passion that speaks then—not we. But faults, seen through passion, appear much greater to us than they really are, just as bodies do being seen through a mist." And then Montaigne relates some stories in point. How, for example, Plato on one occasion, being highly incensed against a servant, asked a friend to chastise him, excusing himself from doing it on the ground that he was in anger. And how Carillus, a Lacedemonian, said to a slave who had been insolent to him, "If I were not in a great rage I would cause thee to be put to death."—We may lay it down then as a general rule that the more eager we are to inflict immediate punishment, the more necessary it is for us, if we would avoid sin, to pause and reflect.

So far I have been endeavouring to show that bad temper—*i.e.*, the thoughtless yielding to the first promptings of anger—is wrong. Now let me point out that it is also impolitic. It is our interest, as a rule, apart altogether from moral considerations, to keep our anger under the control of our reason. An exhibition of bad temper is the very last thing in the world by which to get one's self better treated. Everybody is pleased to meet, and glad to serve, the good-tempered man; but as for the bad-tempered man, people are perfectly satisfied if they can only manage to keep out of his way. The bad policy of ill temper was very neatly pointed out by Queen Elizabeth. There was a certain hot-tempered courtier on whom her Majesty had not yet bestowed the promotion which she had promised. Meeting him one day, she asked him, "What does a man think of when he thinks of nothing?" "He thinks, Madam, of a woman's promise," was the reply. "Well," said the Queen, walking away, "I must not confute you. Anger makes men witty, but it keeps them poor."

It must be confessed, however, that there is one place where bad temper may be considered in a sense useful, and that is in a home. There are homes—no, I mean houses—cursed by the presence of a domestic tyrant, generally a man, but occasionally, sad to say, a woman; and in such a house every one is kept in a constant state of terror, lest something should happen to rouse the despot's wrath. The smallest trifle may produce a paroxysm of fiendish rage. And therefore all those whose evil destiny it is to live with him, are slavishly careful to avoid everything that might lead to such an outburst. Those who have the opportunity and ambition to play this kind of part in life may find bad temper a useful quality; but for others it is, as I have said, useless or even injurious.

But once more, bad temper is exceedingly unbecoming. In this respect it may be distinguished from anger. As I pointed out before, legitimate manifestations of anger are impressive and awe-inspiring,—so much so, that they frequently enable the weak to offer a successful resistance to the injuries with which they are threatened by the strong. But the person who is, as we say, "in a temper"—that is, in a bad temper — always appears ridiculous. Jeremy Taylor says—"It makes the voice horrid, the eyes cruel, the face pale or fiery, the gait fierce, the speech clamorous and loud, and the whole body monstrous, deformed, and contemptible." I am sure that those who are at all particular about their personal appearance, might be cured for ever of their bad temper, if only they could be induced, during some violent paroxysm, to gaze into a looking-glass. They would receive a shock that would make them changed characters for the rest of their lives.

But permit me to add one warning. I have spoken strongly—as I generally speak. I believe that there is nothing more contemptible, and few things more mischievous, than bad temper. But though I would have you very strict and inexorable in judging yourselves, I would have you very gentle and lenient in judging others. Take care lest you mistake for bad temper what is only the involuntary manifestation of physical pain. You would not expect any one, during a violent attack of neuralgia, to look or to speak very good-humouredly. But in the present day, besides neuralgia, there are a whole host of nervous diseases, which go under the general name of neurasthenia. They seem to be a comparatively modern class of ailments. Whether they arise from the high pressure at which we live, I do not know. But here they are, and we must make allowance for them in our estimation of character. An invalid, for example, once told me that her nearest approach to comfort consisted in being only a little uncomfortable. Now this chronic presence of pain should cover a multitude of seeming sins. If, then, you are uncertain whether any one's hastiness of speech and

Bad Temper. 165

manner be ill temper or not, whether it be the expression of a bad state of heart or only a bad state of health, give them the benefit of the doubt —deal very gently with them, I beseech you, for Christ's sake.[1]

[1] After preaching this sermon, I received the following anonymous letter: "Sir, if I were in the habit of betting, I would lay any odds that no congregation ever went away so enraged as your congregation this morning. Your sermon consisted only of commonplace platitudes, that would have disgraced a school-boy's essay. I pray God that He may raise up more preachers of the mental calabre of —— and ——." A writer possessing such originality as to spell calibre with two a's, and such versatility as to conclude with a prayer when he had begun with a bet, should not be unknown to fame. I therefore take this opportunity of introducing him to the public.

Common Sins.

III.

EVIL-SPEAKING.

"Let all evil-speaking be put away from you."—EPH. iv. 31.

BY one of the strange perversities of human nature we attach no importance to common things. Actions we are always performing are, just because of this frequency, the most important actions of our lives. And yet we keep on performing them day after day, never asking whether we are doing them well or ill, never stopping to inquire what will be their effect upon ourselves and others. I suppose one-third, at least, of our waking hours is spent in talking. Every week we say enough to make a three-volume novel. And yet some of us have never once, in the whole course of our existence, paused to investigate the quality of our talk.[1]

[1] See also a sermon on little sins in my 'Origin of Evil.'

There is nothing, perhaps, of which the human race has more reason to be ashamed than its conversation. "If," says La Bruyère, "we were to pay serious attention to all the dull, silly, and puerile observations that are made in ordinary conversation, we should be ashamed to speak or to listen, and should perhaps condemn ourselves to unbroken silence." While, on the one hand, the faculty of speech is a distinguishing excellence of the human race, on the other hand there is nothing which shows its pettiness and meanness and wickedness so clearly as the extent to which this faculty is abused. How many men and women there are who usually talk nonsense —nay, how many there are who usually talk what is worse than nonsense, whose favourite amusement is disparaging or calumniating their neighbours, and whose presence in the world would have been far more endurable if they had been born dumb! Evil-speaking is a vice common to all sorts and conditions of men. It is to be found among the upper classes as well as among the lower. It infests the quiet country village no less than the busy bustling town. You remember Tennyson's words:—

"Below me there is the village, which looks how quiet and small,

And yet bubbles o'er like the city with gossip and scandal and
    spite.
. . . The long-necked geese of the world are ever hissing
    dispraise,
Because their natures are little. . . . Whether he heed it
    or not,
Each man walks with his head in a cloud of poisonous flies.
. . . We cannot be kind to each other here for an hour;
We whisper, and hint, and chuckle, and grin at a brother's
    shame.
. . . We men are a little breed."

Evil-speaking is a vice which seems almost universal. "Half the world," says Horace Smith, "takes pleasure in inventing scandal, and the other half in believing it."

Neither education nor civilisation has succeeded in diminishing the prevalence of scandal. On the contrary, men seem to get fonder of it as the world grows older. Among the early Romans there was a legal system called the twelve tables, which was promulgated by the decemvirs, and which was long regarded as the foundation of all law. In this system, and indeed throughout the whole history of Rome, we find libel dealt with as a very serious crime. The authors of libels, and even the persons who disseminated them, were punished by exile and confiscation of property. Had the proprietors, and editors, and contributors of some of our society and religious newspapers lived in those good old times, it would have gone, I suspect, rather hard with them. There are journals in the present day which exist solely for the purpose of systematically spreading scandal. With a direr plague the world was never smitten. If anything can be heard, or surmised, or invented that is likely to be injurious or distressing to public characters or to persons well known in society, it is instantly seized upon by these unscrupulous journalists, and disseminated over the length and breadth of the land. And the so-called religious newspapers, with one or two honourable exceptions, are worse than the society journals. Both are lavish in their vilification, but the religious newspapers vilify in the name of Christ. If you were to ask me where you would find the grossest instances of envy, hatred, malice, and all uncharitableness, I am afraid I should be obliged to say, in the rival columns of certain ecclesiastical newspapers. Alas for the right-minded pagan who should get his notion of Christianity from their unhallowed columns! With loathing and disgust he would exclaim, "See how these Christians hate one another!"

There can be no doubt, of course, that printed vituperation has been published with malice aforethought. There is, moreover, a good deal of unprinted scandal, about which we may feel almost as sure that it has been uttered for the express purpose and with the direct intention of injuring those to whom it refers. "There are persons," says Steele, "who would be too lazy to go out of their houses, or to open their lips in conversation, were it not for the pleasure they find in speaking ill of their neighbours." "The poison of asps is under their lips." Every word they utter injures somebody, and is distinctly intended to do so. The more damage they can inflict upon those who have the misfortune to be acquainted with them, the better pleased they are.

But there is a larger class of persons who do almost as much mischief unintentionally. They indulge in evil-speaking rather from stupidity and thoughtlessness than from baseness of heart. They do their best to ruin their neighbours' reputations, and it never occurs to them that their neighbours will be any the worse for it. They make their disparaging remarks, not for the sake of injuring the persons disparaged, but merely that they may amuse themselves and their auditors. Such remarks are almost certain to be well received. As the proverb has it, scandal is the best sweetener of tea. This is the reason which induces many persons to talk it. Evil-speaking is the readiest and most effective method of making themselves agreeable. They may be in other respects good-hearted, and even generous. You remember what Cowper says of Flavia—

> "Her superfluity the poor supplies ;
> But if she touch a character, it dies."

Such persons do not realise the misery that is caused by their careless words. But why do they not realise it? Why do they not reflect before they speak? Why do they not use their minds? They have minds, I suppose,—for they would be very much offended with me if I said they had not. But what is the use of having a mind unless you use it? A little thought would put a stop to nine-tenths of the scandal with which human intercourse is disgraced.

In addition to downright scandal and calumny, which consists in remarks affecting men's moral characters, there is another common form of evil-speaking, in which, though nothing is said against his character, the subject of conversation is held up to ridicule. His little foibles and peculiarities and weaknesses are specified and commented on, not to say exaggerated. A laugh is raised at his expense; and those who have joined in it will never think quite so well of the unfortunate man again. It is really terrible to remember how much of our social intercourse is wasted—nay, worse than wasted—prostituted in this kind of conversation. It is scarcely necessary to point out that evil-speaking may be, and sometimes is, carried on without the aid of words. Swift talks of those who can "convey a libel in a frown, or wink a reputation down." For depreciatory purposes, a shrug of the shoulder is more effective than a torrent of words.

Now, evil-speaking — in its grosser form of calumny, at any rate—is one of the worst, one of the most inexcusable of sins. The Greek word διάβολος means—first, a slanderer; and secondly, a devil. The Greeks considered the two terms synonymous; and not unjustly. A calumniator is far worse, for example, than a thief. This would probably be admitted by the slanderer himself in his own individual case. If he had a character to lose, and any one took it away, he would quote with approval Shakespeare's words:—

"Who steals my purse steals trash. 'Tis something, nothing.
'Twas mine, 'tis his, and has been slave to thousands.
But he that filches from me my good name,
Robs me of that which not enriches him,
And makes me poor indeed."

In the case of calumny, the robber steals for the

pure pleasure of stealing; he takes what to himself is worthless from its possessor, for whom its value is absolutely priceless. And evil-speaking, even in the milder form which consists merely in ridiculing or laughing at others—even in this form evil-speaking is a distinct and flagrant breach of the golden rule. If any one says, Well, other people talk against me, so I may as well talk against them—I venture to suggest that this is scarcely a maxim of which Christ would have approved. It shows what a difference there is between professing and practising Christianity, that numberless persons indulge unceasingly and remorselessly in evil-speaking, yet call themselves Christians, and, what is still more curious, actually believe that they are Christians.

It must be admitted, however, that evil-speaking, bad though it be, is of all others the sin by which, in social life, we may be most readily overtaken. If we would avoid it, there are three things which we must do.

(1.) We must learn to talk. Talking is an art. It would be a good thing if there were professors of conversation. I suppose, however, that they would have but few disciples, as most people imagine themselves able to converse without assistance or instruction. And yet if we use conversation in the best sense of the word, it is surprising how few are capable of it. Good conversation should be instructive, yet not dry; entertaining, yet not uncharitable. But no one will reach this ideal standard without much thought and care and practice. Time would not allow me, nor is it exactly my business here, to attempt to formulate the rules which we must observe if we wish to become good talkers. But there is one rule which falls strictly within the province of the pulpit, and it is this—learn to talk about things and events, rather than about persons. Conversation about persons is almost sure, sooner or later, to take an uncharitable turn. It is easier, no doubt, to talk about persons, because so many disagreeable remarks spontaneously occur to one. It is more difficult to talk about things and events, because this requires a certain amount of intelligence and reflection and information. If we are to talk of things, we must know something about them. And it is our duty to see that we do. We owe it to society to take care that we are well informed on topics of general interest. You sometimes meet with clever men — men who are great authorities on electricity, or steam-engines, or caterpillars; but outside of their own subject they have not a word to say for themselves. They are above scandal: so far well. But they are incapable of joining in any general conversation; and so far it is not well. Since in our daily life we are constantly being placed in circumstances where we are expected to converse, and where we ought to converse, it is evidently incumbent on us to prepare ourselves for conversing well.

(2.) We must learn to be silent. And this, if persons are unaccustomed to it, is by no means an easy lesson. A chatterbox once applied to Socrates to be taught rhetoric. Socrates told him he must pay double the usual price, for it would be necessary to teach him first to hold his tongue. Now there are persons who have never been known to keep silence, when it was possible for them to speak. From morn till dewy eve, so long as any one will listen, and even longer, they will talk. Now of course such persons, who never pause for an instant to collect their thoughts, are bound to talk badly. There are others who are afraid to be silent, who look upon a lull in conversation as a catastrophe which must, at all hazards, be averted. At such moments they will say anything rather than say nothing. It is not surprising if what is said under these circumstances had better have been left unsaid. "It is never more difficult to talk well," says La Rochefoucauld, "than when we are ashamed of our silence." When we feel that we must speak, we say anything that first occurs to us; and what first occurs to us, under these unfavourable auspices, is not likely to be worth saying at all. Now we must learn that there is no necessary disgrace in silence; that, on the contrary, there are occasions when it may be more eloquent than speech; and that at the worst, silence, even when inopportune, is better than inopportune speech. It is related of Isocrates, that on one occasion, when dining with the king of Cyprus, he was asked why he did not join in the discourse of the company? He replied, "What is seasonable I do not know, and what I know is not seasonable." If we would avoid talking ill, we shall often have to follow the example of Isocrates. When evil-speaking is going on around us, or when we can only contribute to the general conversation something that ought not to be said, we must be content to sit in silence.

(3.) Lastly, and specially, we must learn to reverence humanity. In Kant's System of

Ethics it is justly laid down as a maxim of universal obligation, that every human being is to be regarded and treated by every other human being as an end in himself; neither is to use the other as a mere means to his own aggrandisement or pleasure. All evil-speaking is a violation of this maxim. We too often treat our fellow-creatures like so many conversational ninepins. We make havoc of them just for our own amusement. We turn them into ridicule in order that we may look clever. We darken their characters that our own may appear the brighter. The real explanation of the fact that disparaging remarks are so universally popular, is this; in lowering others we seem to be raising ourselves. When we say that So-and-so is a very immoral man, we of course imply that we are very moral—that we belong to a small minority, which our last statement has still further reduced. When we say that So-and-so has certain ridiculous habits or foibles, we of course imply that we have none. We seem to be killing two birds with one stone. In degrading him, we fancy that we are at the same time elevating ourselves. But what business have we to use our fellow-creatures for our own selfish ends? We have no more right to try and win esteem at the expense of another's reputation, than to enrich ourselves out of another's pocket. No more right, did I say? Nay, much less; for money is of incomparably lower value than reputation.

Like all other sins, evil-speaking carries along with it its own punishment. For though by pandering to their love of detraction we may win a momentary popularity among second-rate people, we at the same time inflict upon ourselves a permanent and ineffaceable injury. To speak evil of others is to be petty, mean, selfish, and dishonourable; and the oftener we yield to this temptation, the more likely we are to become essentially and irretrievably bad. In dishonouring our neighbours, therefore, we dishonour ourselves still more. We are not in reality benefited at their expense. Instead of elevating ourselves, as we fancy we are doing, by the attempt to depreciate others, we are most effectually accomplishing our own degradation. In *speaking* ill of them, we are *doing* ill to ourselves.

But perhaps there is nothing more serious about the sin of evil-speaking than the fact that it is so catching. The scandal-monger will always find listeners, who will be sure to repeat, and very likely to exaggerate, his stories. By his scandal, therefore, he not only degrades himself,

Evil-Speaking.

but helps to degrade the innumerable persons who come directly or indirectly under his influence. One ill-spoken word may give birth to many, and they to many more, until at last thousands and thousands of men and women shall have been infected and polluted by the pestilent contagion.

So if you would live a worthy life, if you are in the least degree anxious to do what Christ will approve, if you care in any measure for the welfare of your fellow-men, there is no precept in the Bible which it is more important to lay to heart than the precept of our text—" Let all evil-speaking be put away from you."

Common Sins.

IV.

CANT: HYPOCRISY TOWARDS MEN.

" Be not ye like the actors."

I WISH to speak to you this morning about hypocrisy, or, as it is commonly called, cant.

The word cant is said to have been originally the name of a Cameronian minister, whose preaching was quite unintelligible except to the members of his regular congregation. The difficulty of understanding him was looked upon by his followers as a proof of his extraordinary piety. I do not know whether the gentleman himself mistook his obscurity for inspiration; but if he did, he may not unjustly be regarded as a type of those who claim to be considered virtuous or religious, simply because they repeat certain stock phrases or perform certain stock ceremonies, which have no necessary connection either with morality or with worship.

Professor Skeat, however, derives the word cant from the Latin *cantare*, to sing, and says that it originally meant a beggar's sing-song whine. This derivation is most probably correct. The professional beggar affords a good illustration of cant. You can never tell by the tone of his voice how much money there is in his pocket. Very likely there is a good deal; but he always addresses you in melancholy accents, as if he were in the last stage of starvation. Similarly with many persons who are not beggars, there is the same want of connection between their outward demeanour and their inward state. A careless observer may think them models of virtue and of religion, but in their hearts they hate both. Their semblance of morality, their profession of religion, is an impertinent mockery, as false and deceitful as a beggar's whine.

About the derivation of the word hypocrite there can be no mistake. It comes from a Greek word which signifies to act a part—first, legitimately as an art; and second, illegitimately as an artifice. The hypocrite is not what he seems to be. He is always acting. He constantly endeavours to appear that which he is not. At last he may even deceive himself. He may come to believe that he actually *is* what he has always been trying to appear to be. It is said that if actors were to play continually the same part night after night for many years, their minds might possibly become affected, so that at last they would get confused about their own identity, and scarcely be able to tell whether they were themselves or the characters they represented. And since the hypocrite acts not only in the evening, but all day long as well, there would seem to be even more likelihood of his being overtaken by a similar catastrophe. But in what number of cases this result is reached, it does not concern us now to inquire. Hypocrisy is the systematic attempt to impose upon others, and I am afraid that those who practise it form a considerable proportion of the human race.

There is one kind of hypocrisy on which I need not dwell—viz., the simulation of wickedness. We have all met with young gentlemen who pretended to be much worse than they really were; who tried to persuade us that they were terrible fellows, accustomed to ride rough-shod over divine and human laws, and not caring either for God, man, or devil. I say I need not dwell on this form of hypocrisy; for it is a kind of disease which only attacks persons of weak intellect, and even they generally manage to outgrow it. As they get a little wiser, or—if that never happens—as they become a little older, they make two simple discoveries: first, that they were not believed when they asserted themselves to be such monsters of iniquity; and secondly, that if they had been believed, things might have gone rather badly with them. They find that the simulation of extraordinary wickedness can never do them any good, and may do them much harm.

Most men have wit enough to avoid such a mistake from the very first. Hypocrisy, as a rule, consists in the simulation of goodness. Men generally pretend to be better than they are. In doing so, they are influenced by a variety of motives; but all these motives, in the last resort, resolve themselves into some form of selfishness.

In the first place, a man may be a hypocrite for mercenary purposes. He may hope by his professions of piety to enrich himself all the more rapidly at the expense of his neighbours.

This kind of hypocrisy is well illustrated by an ancient fable. Once upon a time a rat in his declining years called his children around him, and delivered to them the following address:

"My dear children," he said, "the infirmities of age are pressing so heavily upon me, that I have determined to devote the short remainder of my life to mortification and penance, in a narrow and lonely cell which I have recently discovered. But I do not wish to interfere with your enjoyment: youth is the season for pleasure, and I should like you all to be happy. My only injunction is, that you never attempt to discover my retreat. Leave me in peace, and let me pursue my meditations undisturbed." The old rat, who seemed deeply affected, then said good-bye, and was seen no more for several days. But by-and-by his youngest daughter became so anxious about his welfare, that she could not resist trying to find out his cell of mortification. At last she discovered it. It was a hole made by his own teeth in a large Cheshire cheese! I see you smile at the conduct of this hypocritical rat; yet it was terribly human. He is a true type of many of the so-called lords of creation. The rat wanted to keep the whole cheese to himself, and he imagined his best plan would be to pretend that he had lost all taste for earthly enjoyments. Whichever way his family might go in their search for food, he thought to himself they would be sure to avoid the direction in which they had seen their father depart upon his lonely pilgrimage. And if they had all been as selfish as he imagined, his calculations would not have been upset.

In the same way the human hypocrite frequently assumes the outward demeanour of piety, because he thinks it will enable him more easily to overreach his neighbours. Knowing himself to be a rascal, he pretends to be pre-eminently religious, hoping in this way to conceal his rascality, and at the same time to win all the more readily the confidence of his dupes. He has set his heart upon acquiring money, or power, or social advancement, which he sees no prospect of obtaining except by dishonest means; and in order to prevent his dishonesty from being suspected—in order that his victims may be thrown off their guard—he makes loud professions of his great love for virtue and his extraordinary zeal for religion. You remember, for example, the soliloquy which Shakespeare puts into the mouth of the Duke of Gloucester, who afterwards became Richard III.:—

> "I do the wrong, and first begin to brawl.
> The secret mischiefs that I set abroach
> I lay unto the grievous charge of others.
> Clarence, whom I indeed have laid in darkness,
> I do beweep to many simple gulls,

> And tell them 'tis the queen and her allies
> That stir the king against the Duke my brother.
> Now they believe it, and withal whet me
> To be revenged on Rivers, Vaughan, Grey.
> But then I sigh, and with a piece of Scripture
> Tell them that God bids us do good for evil.
> And thus I clothe my naked villany
> With old odd ends stolen forth of holy writ,
> And seem a saint when most I play the devil."

Among commercial swindlers, again, we very often find examples of the same sort of pious knavery. They existed in the time of Christ. He describes them as persons who for a pretence make long prayers, and as soon as their prayers are over, proceed to devour widows' houses. Alas, they are still as numerous as ever! Men of the world, students of human nature, can generally see through them. But they always find people weak enough to believe in their professions, and to trust them on the strength of their supposed piety. Tennyson has once and for ever described this kind of creature:—

> "With his fat affectionate smile
> That makes the widow lean. . . .
> Who never naming God except for gain,
> So never took that useful name in vain;
> Made Him his catspaw, and the Cross his tool,
> And Christ the bait to trap his dupe and fool."

For all such persons Christ expressed the most unmitigated scorn. And we cannot wonder at it. Professing an interest in others merely that they may advance themselves, pretending to be religious only for the sake of drawing away attention from their rascality, using the very name of God as an instrument for the furtherance of their own iniquities, they have sunk to the lowest depths of degradation. Gentle, forgiving, tolerant as the Saviour was, He denounced them with the utmost vehemence. "Woe unto you, Scribes and Pharisees, actors, ye shall receive the greater damnation."

Secondly, there is another and much less infamous class of hypocrites, who are quite satisfied if they win the esteem of their fellow-men. They do not desire to defraud their neighbours out of anything but their good opinion. They know that men admire genuine religion, and they fancy that, by merely appearing religious, they may secure the admiration they desire. Many of the Pharisees and Scribes in the time of Christ were hypocrites of this kind. They did not love religion for its own sake; they did not love it at all. They used it merely as a means, a somewhat tiresome means, for securing that which they did love—viz., notoriety.

But though less degraded than the mercenary class of hypocrites, Christ seems to have regarded them with almost equal detestation. Even this less abhorrent form of cant He denounced in the strongest possible terms, and was never tired of warning His disciples to avoid it. "When ye give your alms," He said to them, " do not sound a trumpet before you as the actors do, that they may have glory of men." The true end of almsgiving is the benefit of the receiver. If, therefore, we bestow our bounty in order to benefit ourselves, we are hypocrites, playing a dishonest part. Christ wanted His disciples to make quite sure of the purity of their motives, and so He advised them to give their alms in secret. In that way the true end of almsgiving would be attained, and the false end would be avoided. Similarly in regard to prayer, He said to them, "When ye pray, ye shall not be as the actors, who stand in the synagogues and in the corners of the streets, that they may be seen of men." What the actors wanted was merely a reputation for piety. Prayer with them meant, not communion with God, but the appreciation of the gaping mob. Here, again, Christ tells His disciples, in order that they may be quite sure of the honesty of their intentions, to avoid the crowd, and to go into some secret place where they can be seen by none but God. Then, and only then, can they be sure that their prayer is a genuine act of worship. And once more Christ said, "When ye fast, be not as the actors, of a sad countenance; for they disfigure their faces, that they may appear unto men to fast." The actors did not fast in order that their bodies might be made healthier, that their minds might be cleared, that their spiritual nature might be quickened. All they wanted was human applause, and so they would endeavour to increase the visible effects of their abstinence by leaving their hair unbrushed and their face unwashed, hoping that men might regard their leanness and untidiness and dirt as the signs of peculiar sanctity. "But thou, when thou fastest," said Christ, "anoint thy head and wash thy face, that thou appear not unto men to fast." Do not tell your neighbour anything about it. It is no concern of his. It is better that he should not know. By keeping the matter to yourself you avoid all risk of acting. Lastly, when the actors professed love of goodness and hatred of wickedness, it was all talk, mere stage-play. This was proved by the fact that while they seemed very anxious to make other people better, they never tried to improve themselves. They were severe upon the peccadilloes of their neighbours, and unmindful of their own crimes. This showed conclusively that they professed what they did not feel. They had no real love for goodness. They wanted to establish a reputation for righteousness, without the trouble of being righteous. "You actors," said Christ to them, "if you really hated sin, you would try to eradicate your own. If you really loved righteousness, you would be supremely careful that your own conduct was righteous. It is all nonsense to try and pull the mote out of your neighbour's eye, when behold all the while a beam is in your own eye! Nay, it is worse than nonsense; it is acting, it is a lie!"

The same sort of hypocrisy, which was so prevalent in the time of Christ, exists among us to-day, though in a somewhat modified form. It would not now be considered fashionable to say one's prayers at the corner of the street, nor to go about with a dirty face, nor to find fault with people's conduct—except behind their back. Still, certain religious observances are fashionable even yet, and in particular that of going to church. What the actor wants in the present day is not so much notoriety as respectability. And to be respectable one must appear religious:—

> "At church on Sunday to attend,
> Will serve to keep the world our friend."

There are many persons who find themselves

much bored by the routine of Sunday morning, but who go through it systematically, simply because society has so ordained. Horace Smith sarcastically defines a congregation as "a public assemblage in a spiritual theatre, where all the performers are professors, but where very few of the professors are performers." And no doubt, in every church and at every service, there are many persons present assuming a devotional attitude and repeating devotional words, who feel no devotion in their hearts, and who, if the fashion were to change to-morrow, would experience a sense of relief. Now it is needless to say that no one has a right to be in church during the prayers who does not at least *desire* to worship. To sit or kneel there when the heart is far away, is a dishonest piece of acting.

Into this kind of hypocrisy we are all more or less apt to glide. Our profession of religion was, in the first instance perhaps, genuine and true; but our original ardour has cooled, and we are tempted to keep on practising the same outward observances, though they may now have lost all, or nearly all, their meaning. We do so either for the sake of appearances or from the mere force of habit. And the best of us, even those who come into church with a sincere wish to worship, are apt in a few minutes to grow lukewarm and indifferent. It is only a small part of the service that we really follow and feel. For the rest of the time we are but actors. Our inward thoughts do not accord with our outward attitude. And surely, in the eyes of the all-seeing Father, there can be no sadder sight than the religious performances of those who do but insult Him by a false show of worship. Let us never hereafter come into the house of God without thinking of the Master's words, "Be not ye like the actors."

Common Sins.

V.

CANT: HYPOCRITICAL CHURCH-GOING.

"Be not ye like the actors."

WE are engaged in considering the subject of Cant. The Greek word of which "hypocrite" is a translation, means, as we saw, an actor: and it is used, primarily, in a good sense, for one who plays a part legitimately on the stage; and secondarily, in a bad sense, for one who, with intent to deceive, plays a part in actual life. At the close of my sermon last Sunday, I was directing your attention to a class of actors who, in the present day, attend church simply for the sake of appearing respectable. Society has declared it to be the correct thing; and that is their reason for going. They seem to be worshipping God, but they are in reality worshipping society. And with reference to this class of hypocrites I said, that no one had a right to be in church *during the prayers* who did not at least desire to worship.

During the week I have received a very interesting and suggestive letter, in which hypocritical church-going is defended, on the ground that it is better than nothing—better than staying away altogether.

"My plea for the hypocritical church-goer is based on two counts. First, there is merit in observing the decent *convenances* of life, — in doing what is considered respectable and avoiding the opposite. The entire wellbeing of society depends on such observance. It prevents the inevitable disintegration which would be consequent upon each man living as he himself sees fit. The acquaintance who meets you with a 'How are you? I hope you are well?' probably does not care a jot whether you are fit to climb the Matterhorn, or are creeping through life with your cloak drawn over a wolf that is gnawing at your vitals and drawing the life out of you. Never mind. That casual acquaintance is imperceptibly the better for putting himself into a sympathetic attitude, and you are the better for even his simulated interest. Therefore I plead for more mercy than you showed for the social hypocrite, who cleans the outside of cup and platter, puts on his Sunday hat, goes to church, and maintains at least a quiet decent attitude. He has a vague feeling he goes there because he used to do so as a child, with father and mother and sisters. He is still holding, albeit feebly, to the old cords that bound him—bound him all too tightly, he once thought; but now, though he might cut himself adrift, he cannot make up his mind to do so. The restraint of Sunday, which was once very irksome to him, has become almost pleasant because of old memories and associations. Though he may banish serious thought during the work-days, Sunday morning reminds him that there is something beyond this life; and perhaps he feels that those whom he has loved and lost are not altogether out of reach. He goes to church from old habit; and it is better that he should, than, with brutal honesty, to avow he has nothing to do with religion and its stereotyped observances. I am certain that it is this hypocrisy that often brings to church the poor masher, with his agonising collar and his book held upside down; Anonyma, with her toned-down appearance; and even the man in the big white waistcoat, who is secretly uneasy in regard to the honesty of his late city transactions. In church—poor stuff as church too often is—they have a chance of hearing some helpful word; a crumb or two may fall upon their atrophied souls. Instinctively and ignorantly, but still actually, they are waiting upon the Lord. It has been proved in the colonies that rapid social retrogression follows upon local inability to go to church. If the settler's 'grant' be so remote that church is now an impossibility, he gradually ceases to miss it, abandons the weekly burnishing and decorum, and then the rest follows. An intelligent colonist told me that when the church is so far off as to be a physical impossibility, low morals, low behaviour, general brutality, very surely become the fashion of that station. For these reasons it seems desirable that those who are indifferent, or almost indifferent, to religion, should still, in spite of the hypocrisy it implies, persistently go to church.

"But secondly, church-going is a commendable practice, not only in the case of those who are indifferent to religion, but even in the case of those who are positively antagonistic to it, whose hearts are in a distinctly *irreligious* condition. However much a man may dislike coming, it is better for him to come than to stay away. The soul is often so sick, so bewildered, that, like a disordered stomach, it loathes man's ordinary meat. 'I hate it all. I am weary of it all. I would rather kick over trace and barrier, and show myself what I really am. As for this cumbersome liturgy, this man who, by standing a few feet above me, presumes to drone out his platitudes —away with it all! I cannot endure the miserable farce it is to me!' And yet if the poor hypocrite goes up with the multitude to the house of God, he may perchance find Him,—at least he has put himself into the right attitude. There are times when even private prayer is impossible, when one's whole nature is topsy-turvy, so that even to tell the Father about one's trouble is only to put one's wickedness in a terribly tangible shape. Still it is good to kneel— to kneel without one expressed word or thought. Therefore I would not have you be so hard with all forms of hypocrites, and discourage them from putting in an appearance at church. By being so discouraged, they might be made to lose even the little grain of goodness which they have."

Now this letter shows me that part of my sermon last Sunday may have been very generally misunderstood; and it also suggests several considerations to which I had not sufficiently attended, and which ought to be taken into account in a discussion of the subject of cant.

But there seems to me some little confusion in the writer's mind, to which I must allude. My correspondent begins the defence of hypocritical church-going by saying that there is a merit in observing the decent *convenances* of life, and then, *under the same head*, proceeds to give a description of those who are instinctively impelled to religious observances, not by fashion, but by recollections of their early years and by memories of the loved ones they have lost.

It seems to me that we have here two totally different classes of people, and that it is most important for us to distinguish them from one another. After careful consideration, I still think that persons who belong to the first class, who go to church merely from motives of fashion, have no right to be there at all. Let me try to be very accurate. In this class I do not mean to include those whose motives are mixed, nor yet those whose motives are vague and undefined, but only those who know perfectly well that their sole motive is the desire to appear respectable,—who attend church just as they conform to any other social *convenance*. Now respectability is a very good thing. The observance of social *convenances*, even though they may sometimes be tiresome or absurd, is also, as a rule, a very good thing. Saying "How do you do?" for example, to one's neighbour, even though one may not be much interested in the reply, is certainly better than treating him with the outward indifference of a savage. But going to church surely stands in a different category from an ordinary matter of etiquette.

In the first place, it is not one of those *convenances* which are necessary to keep society from disintegration. There are many men in the present day, occupying high positions in the world of science or art or literature,—honourable, pure-hearted, noble-minded men,—who are never seen in a place of worship. And if society were entirely composed of men like themselves, there would not be the slightest fear of its disintegration. While I much wish that they could honestly come, I cannot help thinking that, while they feel as they do, it is better for them honestly to stay away. Their presence would only remove them farther from God. It is better honourably to incur the bad opinion of our neighbours, than dishonourably to court their good opinion. Society, I think, is much less likely to be disintegrated by sincere infidels than by so-called Christians who have dishonestly assumed that name.

And, in the second place, not only is a conventional attendance at a place of worship unnecessary for the preservation of society, but if it be merely conventional, if it be merely the outcome of a desire to conciliate society, it is nothing short of an act of blasphemy. Some people take a pew in church on the same principle as others take a box at the opera—viz., for the sake of standing well with the world. And I say that nowhere in the universe is a man so far from God as in a pew which he occupies for this irreligious purpose. Going to church merely for the sake of respectability, seems to me precisely analogous to that fasting and praying and almsgiving for the sake of notoriety, which the Saviour so vehemently condemned. Acting religion, putting on a false appearance of religiousness, is bad everywhere and under all circumstances, but in church it is worst of all. To be an actor there, is to turn the temple of God into a playhouse. I cannot believe that persons who deliberately come for this express purpose will ever receive anything but a curse for their impudent attendance on the means of grace. Christ Himself turned out of

Cant: Hypocritical Church-Going.

the Temple those who used it as a place for merchandise; and the attempt to earn a reputation there is not less a prostitution than the attempt to earn an income. It is impossible that any one can be spiritually benefited by the endeavour to make a convenience of the Almighty. It would be better that he should violate every social *convenance* than systematically insult God for the sake of pleasing man. But if men honestly stayed away from church while they felt it was a mockery to be there, a time might come when, as my correspondent so well puts it, the recollection of their early years, and of loved ones who had died, might excite in them a vague longing after the unseen and eternal. And if they come in any degree impelled by such an impulse as that, —no matter though the impulse be feeble and indefinite,—its existence distinguishes them most completely from the persons who come simply to win the good opinion of their neighbours.

There can be no doubt that thousands of persons go to church from a vague sense—often very vague indeed—of their need for something which they do not find in the routine of their daily life. God forbid that I should say anything to induce them to stay away. If, as we attempted to enter this chapel to-day, we had been stopped by some supernatural being who could see into our hearts, and who allowed none to pass but those who were thoroughly and profoundly and enthusiastically religious, I might have been preaching at this moment to half-a-dozen persons; or there might have been no sermon—he might have excluded me. We do not come because we are perfect, but rather because we are imperfect. We seek some help and stimulus which we cannot find elsewhere. Our sense of imperfection may be weak, our desire for improvement may be feeble, our faith in the unseen may be fitful; but all this Christ can tolerate. The words of Isaiah have from time immemorial been applied to Him: "The bruised reed He will not break: the smoking flax He will not quench." The feeblest yearning heavenwards entitles a man to a place in the house of God; and in coming to it, he puts himself, as my correspondent most truly says, into the right attitude—into perhaps the best attitude —for receiving the blessing which he dimly, it may be almost unconsciously, desires.

Let me now say a word or two about the second part of the letter. Under this head, again, it seems to me that there is an important distinction to be made.

No doubt there are times when the soul is so sick and so bewildered that it loathes its ordinary food. Owing to some grievous disappointment or bereavement, or on account of some mental perplexity that persistently refuses to be unravelled, our whole nature is occasionally convulsed, and words are equally powerless to express what we feel or to afford us the slightest consolation. At such times the best liturgy may seem meaningless and the best sermon twaddle. And yet, as my correspondent says, at such a crisis of our life it is good to kneel, either in church or out of it, even though we cannot speak, even though we cannot think. To kneel is to place ourselves in an attitude of resignation and faith; and to do that is to do our best.

But there are persons who, *in their natural and normal state*, find the services of the Church tiresome and profitless, and yet they continue to attend month after month and year after year. Such persons, it seems to me, would do better to stay away. There is no religion in their sitting or kneeling while the liturgy is being said, nor even in their thoughtlessly repeating it. On the contrary, the oftener they do this the more injury they inflict on themselves. If they came less frequently they might get some good. The sincerest worshipper finds it difficult to resist the monotony of constant repetition. What, then, must be the paralysing and deadening effect of this monotony upon those who never attempt to resist it? Their systematic attendance on the means of grace is but the systematic deterioration of their spiritual nature. Every time they come their hearts are rendered *less susceptible* to the influences of the spirit of God.

And with regard to the sermon, it must be even more apparent that there is no merit in merely sitting it out. If you continually regard the preacher as a man who, " because he stands a few feet above you, presumes to drone out his platitudes," you would be as well, or better, away. Even listening to a sermon and appreciating it, however commendable, is not a distinctly religious act. Though unfortunately sermons sometimes lead to the worship of man, they form no part of the worship of God. I think the custom we have here is a very good one, and I should like to see it adopted everywhere—the custom, viz., of allowing those persons who do not want a sermon to go away without one. If I may speak for myself, I would say it is certainly no kindness to the preacher to remain, if you are all the time wishing him to get it done. Occasionally when I have been preaching, I have caught sight of a face upon which was depicted so much weariness, not to say woe, that I have been half induced to pronounce the ascription on the spot, and release the poor sufferer from his martyrdom. But one is expected to go on till one has finished, and so I have gone on; though to proceed after such a damper involves much difficulty and discomfort.

In a word, then, it seems to me that those who never take, and never expect to take, any interest in the prayers, ought not to attend them; and that those who are always bored, and always expect to be bored, by the sermon—though they are committing no particular sin by sitting it out—would be acting much more wisely if they remained away.

Whether my correspondent will agree—whether you will agree—with what I have said this morning, I do not know. But at any rate there is a point in regard to which we shall all, I think, be at one—the point, viz., to which the letter I read you so admirably directs our attention. Whoever looks back regretfully to the innocence of childhood—whoever thinks tenderly of some departed friend—whoever has the faintest spiritual desire, the feeblest belief in an unseen world, the weakest yearning after something higher, stronger, better than himself—whoever is in the slightest degree grateful for the joy of life—whoever feels wretched, helpless, perplexed, undone,—has a right to come into the house of God; and if he come, assuredly he will not be sent empty away.

Common Sins.

VI.

CANT: HYPOCRISY TOWARDS GOD.

"Be not ye like the actors."

WE are engaged in considering the subject of Cant. The Greek word of which hypocrite is a translation meant an actor—one who plays a part or assumes a character. There are, of course, two classes of actors: first, those who act legitimately—those who, for the sake of affording amusement or instruction, play a part upon the stage; and second, those who, with the intent to deceive their neighbours, play a part in actual life. In modern English the word actor is restricted to the first class, and the word hypocrite to the second class. And as hypocrite is only used in a bad sense, its original signification of playing a part or assuming a character has been forgotten.

It has sometimes been said that every one is an actor.

"All the world's a stage,
And all the men and women merely players,"

exclaimed the melancholy Jacques. But by this statement he meant to refer rather to the vanity of human life than to the dishonesty of human beings. There is no more in our existence, he means to say, than in a mere piece of acting. Every one must play the part which has been assigned to him, and soon he will have to make his exit — soon the curtain will fall upon the whole performance, and the human race will be as if it had never been. "We spend our years as a tale that is told; we walk constantly in a vain show." The end of it all is vanity. Life is essentially evanescent, and after it comes the grave, where there is neither work, nor device nor wisdom, nor knowledge. This pessimistic doctrine, according to which our earthly existence is a mere stage-play, we cannot now stop to investigate.

Cicero, however, has almost gone so far as to declare that every man is a hypocrite. "Few," he says, "are endowed with virtue in comparison with the number of those who wish us to believe that they possess it. Every man's nature is

Cant: Hypocrisy towards God. 209

concealed with many folds of disguise, and covered as it were with various veils. His brows and eyes and very often his countenance are deceitful, and his speech is most commonly a lie." Now it seems to me this is somewhat of an exaggeration. It is true that we do not know all about one another; but there is no hypocrisy necessarily implied in this. A man is not a hypocrite for trying to conceal his bad qualities. He may be partly induced to do so because he is really ashamed of them. A man is not a hypocrite for endeavouring to show himself to others at his best. He may be in some degree impelled to this by a sincere respect for virtue. A man is not a hypocrite for refusing to turn his heart inside out for the inspection of a curious public. No one but a fool blurts out his inner and most sacred experiences. There are many of our thoughts and feelings which a stranger has no right to know, and which we have no right to reveal. A man is not a hypocrite for keeping silence about his sins. It is bad enough to commit them; but to talk of them, to make them public, would be to enhance their mischievousness a thousandfold. Such a morbid self-revelation, for example, as that contained in the confessions of Rousseau is a sign, not so much of honesty, as of indifference to the opinions and feelings and wellbeing of mankind. And lastly, a man is not a hypocrite for desiring the esteem of his fellow-men, and for trying his hardest in any honest way to obtain it. This desire is a divinely implanted instinct; and it is one of the most powerful aids to virtue. The hypocrite, properly so called, is the man who professes what he does not feel; who assumes a character outwardly to which there is nothing in his heart that corresponds; whose life is a deceitful simulation, an imposition, a sham.

We have already noticed two classes of hypocrites. To the first class belong those who pretend to be virtuous or religious, for the sake of concealing their rascality, and with the deliberate intention of abusing the confidence which they expect their simulated goodness will inspire. Christ referred to them as persons who devoured widows' houses, and for a pretence made long prayers. And in modern times they are exemplified by many a pious scoundrel in the commercial and professional worlds. Hypocrites of the second class are content if they secure the good opinion of their neighbours; they have no *ulterior* aim. This class finds illustration among Pharisees, ancient and modern. The former, by their almsgiving and penances and long prayers, catered for public notoriety; and the latter, the Pharisees of the present day, who aim at being respectable rather than notorious, endeavour to attain this object by persistently going to church, in the services of which they take not the slightest interest.

So far we have been engaged with the attempt to deceive man. Now let us look at another class of hypocrites—namely, those who try to deceive God. As the author of 'Ecce Homo' has well pointed out, a new phase of hypocrisy arose through a misunderstanding of the teaching of Christ Himself. The hypocrites of Christ's age, just like the modern hypocrites we have already discussed, wanted simply to make money, or to be highly esteemed among their fellows. Their hypocrisy was the means they employed for the attainment of their end. But in that end itself there was nothing peculiar. The aim of all those whom Christ addressed, no matter how they sought to reach it, whether by hypocrisy or by any other means, was identical. What they all sought for was present gratification and personal aggrandisement. So far as his ultimate object was concerned, the most accomplished of the Pharisaical hypocrites was indistinguishable from the ordinary vulgar boor. They all lived simply and exclusively for self. Now Christ endeavoured to cure men of their vulgar selfishness, by telling them of other riches and another happiness laid up in heaven, which were to be the rewards of self-denial. But many of his professed followers failed to catch the spirit of His exhortations; and instead of being cured of their avarice and sensuality, merely transferred them to new objects of desire. They were as selfish in seeking for the happiness of heaven as they had formerly been in seeking for the happiness of earth. They merely exchanged their worldliness for otherworldliness. "Shrewd enough to discern Christ's greatness, instinctively believing what He said to be true, they would set out with a triumphant eagerness in pursuit of the heavenly riches, and laugh at the short-sighted and weak-minded speculator, who contented himself with the insignificant profits of a worldly life. They would practise assiduously the rules by which Christ said heaven was to be won. They would patiently turn the left cheek, indefatigably walk the two miles; they would bless with effusion those who cursed them, and pray fluently for those who used them spitefully. To love their enemies, to love any one, they would certainly find to be

Cant: Hypocrisy towards God. 213

impossible; but the outward signs of love might be easily learnt. And thus there arose a new class of actors, not, like those whom Christ denounced, exhibiting before an earthly audience and receiving their pay from human managers, but hoping to be paid for their performance out of the incorruptible treasures, and to impose by their dramatic talent upon their Father in heaven."

The motive which influences this third class of actors, you see, is neither the desire for earthly happiness nor the desire for the esteem of their fellow-men, but the desire for heaven. The sole reason why they want to go there is because they regard it as a more comfortable place than hell. Like the other hypocrites, they are selfish; only their selfishness seeks its gratification not in this world, but in the next. But because they aim exclusively at *future* happiness, they fancy they are Christians.

But they are not. For the essence of Christianity is unselfishness; and attempting to do right for the sake of heavenly happiness is not one whit less selfish than attempting to do right for the sake of earthly happiness. It is true that a pious and devout life will win for a man the reverence of the multitude; and yet Christ tells us that when we pray we are to think of God, and not of the credit we may gain. It is true that by loving our neighbours and our enemies we shall win heaven; and yet we are not to think of the heaven we shall win, we are to think of our neighbours and our enemies. It is true that future happiness is promised to those who do their duty; and yet the very nature of duty, as Christ understood it, forbids that it should ever be performed by those who regard it as a means to an end. In order to do it at all, we must look upon it as an end in itself. Christ summed it up in the word love, and we cannot love for the sake of what we are to gain by it. We may, for the sake of gain, pretend to love. But Christ is not to be put off with mere pieces of acting, out of harmony with the wishes and feelings of the heart. "The vehemence with which He denounced all insincerity and hypocrisy, sufficiently shows with what horror He would have regarded any interested benevolence or calculating philanthropy which may usurp the name of love." Our acts and words and inmost desires must all correspond. Our very wishes and inclinations must be in harmony with the maxims by which we say that we are guided. It is not enough to act as if we loved our neighbours; we must really love them. It is not enough to act as if we were doing our duty; we must absolutely do it. It is not enough to be unselfish as far as this world is concerned; we must be unselfish even in regard to the next.

This is the paradox and the stumbling-block of Christianity. Happiness is in store for the good; but those who think only of happiness can never become good, and can never therefore win the happiness. The virtue of unselfishness is to be rewarded; but to think only of the reward is to miss it through the vice of selfishness. Selfishly aiming at the reward of goodness is one of the ways by which men bring upon themselves the punishment of wickedness. Selfishly seeking for heaven is one of the ways by which men fit themselves for hell. The Almighty, unto whom all hearts are open, all desires known, and from whom no secrets are hid, will not be deluded by mere outward acts. He is not to be cajoled by stage play.

There is another form of this attempted cajolery much in vogue in the present day. Many persons seem to think that the practice of religious observances will answer the same purpose as being really religious. They imagine that by the performance of certain ceremonial acts, which have no connection with their daily life and conduct, they become inheritors of the kingdom of heaven. They fancy that they will pass muster with the Almighty as devout, if they merely assume the attitude and repeat the words of devotion. There is a story told of a church-going gentleman who, before putting a three-penny-piece into the plate, carefully examined it so as to make sure of its not being a fourpenny-piece, singing all the while with great apparent zeal the words of the hymn :—

> " Were the whole realm of nature mine,
>   That were a present far too small;
> Love so amazing, so divine,
>   Demands my love, my life, my *all*."

Similarly there are persons who imagine that God will regard them as religious because they attend an early celebration of the Communion, and that He will pay no attention to the fact of their afterwards making themselves disagreeable at the breakfast-table. They imagine that God will regard them as very religious because on what they call the Sabbath they refrain from doing certain things which are perfectly legitimate, and that He will pay no attention to the fact of their spending a great part of the day they think so sacred in doing what would be wrong on any day—namely, in the slanderous and scandalous attempt to damage their neighbours' reputations. They imagine that God will regard them as very religious because they punctiliously bow low at the name of Jesus, and that He will pay no attention to the fact of their systematically ignoring the new commandment. I know men — I daresay you know them too—who, because they rent a pew in a place of worship and are regular communicants, look forward to conspicuous positions at the right hand of God; and yet, by their paroxysms of horrible rage, they convert, for all those who have the misfortune to live with them, what should be home into a very hell. They seem to think that God is indifferent to everything but what is done in church; that He attends there as at a theatre, to enjoy their acting; and that if they perform well, He will reward them for their pains!

I suppose no one could believe this if he took the trouble to reflect. But the mischief of it is, there are so many persons who never will put themselves to that inconvenience. A very little reflection might suffice to show that the services and sacraments of the Church are intended to quicken within us the spirit of Christ; and that unless they do so, our participation in them is a mere piece of acting. "If any man have not the spirit of Christ, he is none of His." We may have been baptised almost as soon as we were born, we may have learnt the Catechism almost as soon as we could speak, we may have been confirmed in early youth, and communicated regularly ever since; but unless all this has had a good effect upon our hearts and lives, it has been but stage play. It may deceive our fellow-men into the belief that we are pious; but foolish indeed must we be if we imagine that it will deceive God. So far from deceiving Him or conciliating Him, He will visit us on account of it—if we are to believe the words of Christ—with the extremest punishment. "Woe unto you, Scribes and Pharisees, actors! ye shall receive *the greater* damnation."

Common Sins.

VII.

BIGOTRY: ITS PREVALENCE.

"Our fathers worshipped in this mountain; and ye say, that in Jerusalem is the place where men ought to worship."—JOHN iv. 20.

THE word bigot is very often derived from an incident said to have occurred to Rollo, Duke of Normandy. When he was about to marry the daughter of Charles the Foolish, he refused to perform the usual ceremony of kissing the king's foot; and, on his friends urging him to comply with the custom, he replied, "Ne se, by Gott"—that is, Not so, by God. The courtiers thereupon, converting the last two words of his answer into an epithet intended to be opprobrious, derided him and called him bigot. This story is related by Camden; but whether it be true or not, it is impossible now to say. Certainly it seems rather hard upon Rollo if, on account of his honourable pride, he is to be regarded as akin to those who are now called bigots.

A more likely derivation of the term is from the Spanish word *bigote*. In modern times *bigote* means merely a moustache. But formerly the torturers, executioners, and other officials of the Inquisition were called *los bigotes* or *los bigotados*. They were so designated on account of the enormous hirsute appendages which they wore to conceal the lower half of the face, the upper part being hidden by the half mask. A complete disguise was necessary, for many of these officers were amateurs, receiving no pay, and doing what they did either out of spite, or because they "sought to merit heaven by making earth a hell." And in such cases it was desirable to preserve a strict incognito. A gentleman who was kind enough to write to me a year or two ago after I had been preaching on this subject, informed me that in some of the South American republics, where the hand of the Inquisition fell heaviest, the name "bigotes" or bigotados" survives to this day, and is given to certain individuals who, in fulfilment of vows or as a penance, carry their candle in the processions of Holy Week, dressed in a tight-fitting costume of black serge, high black sugar-loaf hat, and having their faces concealed partly by the half mask and partly by the "bigotes."—This certainly seems a much more satisfactory derivation than the old one from Duke Rollo's oath. The Inquisitors and their assistants, if somewhat extreme, were still typical bigots, and may therefore well be looked upon as the spiritual ancestors of all those who are now called by that name.

A bigot may be defined as a man who worships his own creed. He regards it as infallible, and necessary for salvation; or at any rate he believes that other men will find favour with God just in proportion as their opinions agree with his own.

The sincere and conscientious bigot generally —if he can—makes men suffer for what he conceives to be the erroneousness of their opinions, in order that they may thereby be stimulated to the adoption of more orthodox views. He tortures their bodies in order that he may save their souls. Persecution, you will observe, is not necessarily a proof of the bigot's cruelty or badness of heart, but rather the contrary. No doubt men have sometimes persecuted merely because they took delight in causing pain, and sometimes in order, as they thought, to curry favour with God by punishing those whom they regarded as His enemies. But still more frequently, I apprehend, persecution has arisen from a sincere desire to promote the spiritual wellbeing of mankind. Of two bigots, the one who persecutes is, as a rule, a more estimable person than the one who does not. For if a man thinks that others can only be saved by agreeing with himself, it is surely his duty to try by any and every means to bring about this agreement. The bigot who does not persecute, who does not try to lead others to an orthodox and saving faith, must be altogether indifferent regarding their welfare. He is probably rather pleased at the idea that future happiness will be restricted to himself and a few kindred spirits. But the persecutor is generally a man of wider sympathies. The Inquisitors were not the worst members of the Church of Rome, but perhaps, on the whole, the best. Llorenti, the great historian of the Inquisition, does not even insinuate a charge against their moral character. While he execrates the seeming cruelty of their conduct, he cannot deny the purity of their motives. Similarly Townsend, an English clergyman, in describing the Inquisition at Barcelona, which was one of its most important centres, admits that all its members were men of worth, and most of them distinguished for humanity.

Now I want, in the first place, to draw your attention to the commonness, to the almost universal prevalence, of bigotry. It is often thought that bigotry is peculiarly a characteristic of the Romish Church. But this is a mistake. If the Roman Catholics have persecuted more than other sects, it has been partly because they had more power, and partly because they were more sincere. But, as a matter of fact, Protestants have usually been no less intolerant of heterodoxy than Roman Catholics; sometimes they have carried off the palm. The intolerance of different sects does not depend upon their avowed tenets, but on the circumstances in which they are placed, and the amount of power of which they are in possession. Strictly speaking, Catholics, who believe in an infallible Church, ought to be—might be expected to be—more intolerant than Protestants, who believe in the right of private judgment. But Buckle truly says, whoever has read the works of the great Calvinist divines—and, above all, whoever has studied their history—must know that in the sixteenth and seventeenth centuries the desire of persecuting their opponents burnt as hotly among them, as among any of the Catholics even in the worst days of the Papal dominion. And even now there is more bigotry among the lower orders of Scotch peasantry than among the lower orders of French Catholics. History contains many instances of the curious fact, that though Catholics are theoretically, owing to their dogma of infallibility, more bigoted than Protestants, Protestants have frequently been in practice more bigoted than Catholics.

There is one very remarkable example of this, on which Buckle dwells at some length. The Edict of Nantes was passed by a Catholic king, for the sake of protecting the rights of Protestants. But these Protestants were not content with the liberty to enjoy their own religion. They no sooner became tolerated than they set about trying to weaken the religion of that very party to whom they owed their freedom. They asked the Government to put a stop to Catholic processions; and as this was not done, they took the law into their own hands, attacked the processions whenever they met them, subjected the priests to personal insults, and even endeavoured to prevent them from administering the sacrament to the sick. They attended Catholic

Bigotry: its Prevalence.

funerals for the purpose of drowning by their clamour the voice of the clergyman, and turning the ceremonies into ridicule. They declared that they would withhold the sacrament, not only from those of their number who married Catholics, but even from those whose children were guilty of this heretical union. In some towns where their influence was supreme, they would not allow the Catholics to have a single church, in which to celebrate what for centuries had been the sole religion of France and was still the religion of an enormous majority of Frenchmen. When Louis XIII. visited Pau in 1628, although he had favoured the Protestants by confirming the Edict of Nantes, he was treated by them with indignity on account of his Catholicism, and he found that they had not left a single place in which the King of France, in his own territory, could perform those devotions which he believed necessary to his future salvation. This was the way, says Buckle, in which the French Protestants treated the first Catholic Government which abstained from persecuting them—a Government which had not only allowed them the free exercise of their religion, but even advanced many of them to offices of trust and honour.

And the history of our own Church is not

without some suggestive illustrations of bigotry. When James II. came to the throne, the English clergy rallied round him in spite of his being a Roman Catholic, for they greatly admired his reverence for the priesthood, and hoped that eventually his affections might be transferred from the Romish Church to their own. This curious alliance between a Protestant hierarchy and a Popish king continued as long as he allowed them the privilege of persecution; but as soon as that privilege was withdrawn the alliance came to an end. You remember that by the Test and Corporation Acts, passed in the previous reign, all persons employed by Government were compelled under a heavy penalty to receive the sacrament according to the rites of the Church of England. King James's Declaration of Indulgence announced the suspension of these laws. At once the clergy turned against him. In their eager desire to punish the monarch who had now become repugnant to them, they actually applied for aid to the very Dissenters whom only a few weeks before they had hotly persecuted. And the result was that singular coalition between Churchmen and Dissenters which ended in the overthrow of the King. Now, notwithstanding all that we owe to the Revolution, we must not allow ourselves to ignore the significance of the fact that it was hastened on by the Declaration of Indulgence, and the clerical hostility which that Declaration excited. The first and only time the Church of England ever made war upon the Crown, was when the Crown had declared its intention of tolerating, and in some degree protecting, the rival religions of the country.

And even yet, in this comparatively advanced age, we not unfrequently meet with startling examples of narrow-minded intolerance. A year or two ago, as I daresay many of you remember to have read in the newspapers, an English clergyman refused to allow the funeral of a Dissenter to pass through the gates of the cemetery. He directed the relatives of the deceased to make a hole in the wall, as far as possible from the main entrance, and through this hole he allowed them to drag their dead. Even at the very portals of the unseen world this officious priest must interfere, and try to separate his own followers from the rest of mankind. He would carry, we may be sure, his impertinent self-complacency with him to the very judgment-seat. Methinks I see him stalking up to the eternal throne, in the full assurance of his insufferable pride, waving aside in haughty scorn every one whom he does not recognise as an orthodox Episcopalian.

And bigotry is not confined to great national Churches, but is to be found in the smallest sect. Every denomination in Christendom has had its little pope—some writer or preacher whom it has regarded as infallible. Every denomination has had its little systems of inquisitorial surveillance and excommunication and persecution, by which it has sought to make things unpleasant for those who did not hold its views. And the majority of the members of every denomination, till quite recently at any rate, have been in the habit of regarding themselves as the sole and exclusive possessors of perfect truth. In that very interesting and instructive novel, 'We Two,' Mr Fane-Smith is a typical specimen of a very common character. You remember he had read ecclesiastical history, and he had extracted from it several convenient epithets with which to condemn his neighbours and acquaintances. He used to call people Photinians, Noetians, Socinians, and so forth—which was at once a learned and disagreeable way of saying that their theological opinions were not the same as his own. He, Mr Fane-Smith, says the author, had exactly grasped the whole truth, and whoever swerved to the right or to the left, if only by a hair's-breadth, was, he considered, in a lamentable and dangerous condition.

Now this eternal popery of the human heart —as it has been well called—though so common throughout Christendom even amongst the professed opponents of Popery, is supremely un-Christian. Another day I shall point out to you the inherent absurdity and the terrible mischievousness of bigotry. But time will only permit me now to call your attention to the fact that it was most clearly denounced by Christ. Here we have one of those remarkable contrasts, of which unhappily there are so many, between the Christianity of Christendom and the Christianity of Christ. I remember when I was a student in Edinburgh hearing the late Dean Stanley preach, in Old Greyfriars' Presbyterian Church, upon the Saviour's new commandment that we should love one another. The Samaritans, he said, had laid down an eleventh commandment, "Thou shalt build an altar on Mount Gerizim, and there only shalt thou worship;" and the sects and Churches of Christendom have usually followed the spirit of the Samaritan, rather than of the Christian, rule. Thou shalt worship God, they have said, thus and only thus. They have believed in the exclusive sacredness of this or that place, this or that doctrine, this or that institution, this or that form of worship; and they have maintained their belief, often at the point of the sword, but always with bitterness and acrimony. Instead of showing love to their fellows according to the eleventh commandment of Jesus, they have shown hatred according to the eleventh commandment of their own. And strangely enough, they flattered themselves that they were eminent and exemplary Christians, just in proportion as they manifested their un-Christian and anti-Christian zeal. But a little reflection should suffice to show that the bigot's zeal is out of harmony with the genius of Christianity. Christ never said a word to justify it. On the contrary, He was always condemning and denouncing it. He did not require men to accept a complicated theology. He did not bid them perform an elaborate ritual. How far these things may be useful is a matter of opinion, but to say they are necessary to salvation is to give the lie to Christ. Though brought up under the influence of Jewish pride and exclusiveness, He declared on one occasion that there was more faith, more genuine religious feeling, in a Gentile whom his hearers regarded as a spiritual outcast, than He had ever found among themselves. When John said to Him, "Master, we saw one casting out devils in Thy name, and he followeth not us; and we forbade him, because he followeth not us," Jesus replied, "Forbid him not; . . . for he that is not against us is on our part." In the Sermon on the Mount, which so many professing Christians appear never to have read, Christ declares, "Not every one that saith unto me, Lord, Lord,"—not every one who uses a certain form of words or professes a certain form of belief,—"shall enter into the kingdom of heaven, but he that doeth the will of my Father." And to the woman of Samaria, puzzled over the theological controversies of the day, he explained that they were altogether matters of indifference. The Samaritans were wrong in asserting the peculiar sacredness of Mount Gerizim. And His own countrymen were no less wrong, He acknowledged, in claiming a similar distinction for Jerusalem. The Father seeketh, He said, spiritual worshippers. Christ Himself went to the Temple and conformed to the usages of the synagogue. But it was not in such conformity, He taught, that real religion consisted. A man may fulfil all the ecclesiastical requirements of his age and country, and yet be essentially irreligious. The Father seeketh spiritual worshippers,—not the recitation of creeds, not the performance of ceremonies, but the adoration and affection of the heart. To worship the Father in spirit and in truth, it is not necessary to enter into any particular temple, nor to kneel at any particular shrine. The holy of holies is within us. To worship in spirit and in truth is to realise the weakness and finitude of one's own nature, and to give one's self up to be possessed and suffused by the infinite love of God.

Common Sins.

VIII.

BIGOTRY: ITS IRRELIGIOUSNESS.

"Our fathers worshipped in this mountain; and ye say, that in Jerusalem is the place where men ought to worship."—JOHN iv. 20.

A BIGOT, as I said last Sunday, is a man who worships his own creed, who fancies himself pre-eminently acceptable to God because of certain opinions which he holds, and who believes that those whose views are different from his own are in danger of being ultimately lost, or at any rate that they are less acceptable to God than himself. I pointed out to you how distinctly and constantly this bigoted state of mind was condemned by Christ. Neither Mount Gerizim nor Jerusalem, He said, was peculiarly the dwelling-place of the Almighty. The favour of

God was to be won, not by saying Lord, Lord, but by doing right. In other words, the outward forms and expressions of religion are matters of comparative indifference. "The Father seeketh *spiritual* worshippers." True religion consists in the affection of the heart and in the consecration of the life—which affection and consecration are compatible with totally dissimilar creeds and ceremonies.

Plain and distinct, however, as was Christ's teaching on this subject, it has been but seldom understood—which is the more remarkable since it is insisted upon throughout the New Testament over and over again. St Peter, for example, who was originally as bigoted as any of his race, at last discovered his mistake. In his speech to Cornelius he said, "God hath showed me that I should not call any man common or unclean. Of a truth I perceive that God is no respecter of persons: but in every nation he that feareth Him and worketh righteousness is accepted with Him." And this lesson once learnt, St Peter never forgot. He strenuously opposed the Pharisaic section of the early Church. The Judaisers—those who wanted perfect uniformity of rites and observances—said, "Except ye be circumcised after the manner of Moses, ye cannot be saved."

St Peter declared, on the contrary, that this ancient rite was a matter of no consequence whatsoever. "God, who knoweth the heart, gave the Holy Ghost to the Gentiles, even as He did unto us; and put no difference between us and them, purifying their hearts by faith." St Paul too, in his elaborate Epistle to the Romans, argues that the important thing in the sight of God is, not a man's country, nor his creed, nor his mode of religious observance, but his life. "Not the hearers of the law are just before God, but the doers of the law shall be justified." In other words, God considers men good, not because they are in reception of an orthodox creed, but because their actions are in harmony with the dictates of their conscience. "For when the Gentiles, which have no law, do by nature the things contained in the law, these, having no law, are a law unto themselves." They have a measure of light, in accordance with which they ought to act. "Circumcision verily profiteth if thou keep the law any better for it: but if thou be a breaker of the law, thy circumcision is made uncircumcision. Therefore if the uncircumcision keep the righteousness of the law, shall not his uncircumcision be counted for circumcision? And shall not the uncircumcision which is by nature, if it fulfil the law, judge thee, who by the letter and circumcision dost transgress the law?" That is, he who merely keeps the letter of the law shall be condemned and dishonoured by him who actually keeps its spirit. To be orthodox in ritual is nothing; to be orthodox in conduct—to do right—is everything. "For," continues St Paul, "he is not a Jew which is one outwardly; neither is that circumcision which is outward in the flesh." Every outward and visible rite—if it is to be anything but nonsense—must lead to some inward and spiritual grace. "He is a Jew which is one inwardly; and circumcision is that of the heart." Whether a man's ritual be elaborate or meagre does not matter in the very least. The only thing of supreme importance is that his heart should be pure. What God wants in men is not uniformity of creed or of ceremony, but moral conduct and a religious life.

Now for us who profess and call ourselves Christians, it should be sufficient condemnation of bigotry that it was discountenanced by Christ and His immediate followers. It may be useful, however, to look into this subject somewhat more deeply. I propose to show you this morning that bigotry is incompatible, not only with Christianity, but with any real religion. And next Sunday I shall direct your attention to the mischief which has been done by this un-Christian and irreligious vice.

To-day let us look for a few moments, broadly and generally, at the essential irreligiousness of bigotry. It is irreligious because it is based upon an unworthy conception of the Deity. It assumes that the favour of God is vouchsafed or denied to men according to the state of their opinions. Now this cannot be. It is simply impossible. For there is hardly anything more thoroughly independent of our own wills than the opinions or beliefs which at any given time we may happen to hold. It is only within very narrow limits that men are responsible for their beliefs. All who have received sufficient education to recognise the fact that opinions differ, are under a moral obligation to investigate those which they already hold, and to reject them if they prove unsatisfactory. They are under a moral obligation to examine carefully, so far as lies in their power, the opinions of those who differ from them, and to determine that their own creed shall be as comprehensive and as perfect as possible. But life is so short, and the calls upon our time so many, that we cannot learn everything. And the particular direction of our studies will have been determined for us by our inherited capacity and temperament, by the influence of relatives and friends and acquaintances, and many other accidental circumstances. Dean Stanley once acutely remarked, "How different would have been the fortunes of the Church of England if Newman could have read German!" A variety of circumstances had combined to direct Newman's attention to theology, in the narrow ecclesiastical sense of that word. He had become somehow or other possessed with the idea, that the writings of what are called *the Fathers* were scarcely inferior in value to the words of Holy Writ. And so he gave himself up for many years to the most minute and laborious study of their works, and saturated his spiritual nature with their commonplace and narrow-minded sentiments. The consequence was that he had neither time nor inclination for the study of philosophy, and "the grand development of human thought from Aristotle down to Hegel was a sealed book to him." To those who have become acquainted with it, "all sects and denominations shrink into vanity." But Newman was so busy with "the Fathers" that the world's greatest thinkers, as far as he was concerned, might as well never have lived. Their thoughts exerted no more perceptible influence upon him than upon an unborn babe. Had it been otherwise, he would have discovered the dignity—nay, the divinity—of human reason; he would have seen the ideas of the Deity gradually revealing themselves in the progressive development of the human mind; and neither he nor the thousands who have followed him would ever have joined the Church of Rome. Yet who will dare to blame him because his studies took the direction which they did? There are few men living with a keener intellect, there is no man living with a purer conscience, than John Henry Newman. But he is a remarkable and memorable illustration of the universal law, that our beliefs are mainly determined for us by circumstances over which we have no control.

Though slight differences in men's creeds may be due to voluntary effort on the one hand, or to wilful negligence on the other, the larger and more important varieties always result from external influences which it was quite impossible to alter or resist. We might all of us at this moment, for example, be Buddhists or Mohammedans, fire-worshippers or idolaters of the lowest and most degraded type, but for the accident of our birth; and unless external influences be brought to bear upon a man—especially the influences of education—he will never be able to improve his creed to any considerable extent. A human being whom evil destiny has placed in the wilds of Africa or in the slums of London, is not to be blamed for holding opinions different from yours or mine. He cannot help it. He does not desire to be elevated or improved; and even if he did, by no conceivable effort—while his surroundings remained the same—could he ever manage to acquire any of those purer and higher beliefs which others have received by inheritance without any effort at all.

The bigot's notion, then, that there is any saving merit in the opinions which he holds, is utterly without foundation. His opinions may be the very worst which, under the circumstances, it was possible for him to entertain. All that is good in them may have come to him without any exertion on his part: he may not have made the slightest attempt to get rid of what is bad; while those persons he looks down upon with contempt may have struggled unceasingly to seek and to find the truth. But to this the bigot would probably reply that his opinions are the best possible opinions, and that therefore they do not need any investigation. He supposes him-

Bigotry: its Irreligiousness. 241

self somehow or other to be endowed with all truth. What nonsense! How can he be sure that there have never existed opinions still better than his own, of which circumstances have kept him in ignorance? No one can be certain that his own opinions are the best, unless he has compared them with all other opinions held in all other ages and all other countries by all other men. To make such a comparison would require the greatest ability and the most ample leisure; nay, even with these advantages the task could never be completely and satisfactorily accomplished. And supposing that it could — supposing we were certain that nothing had escaped our observation—supposing we at last knew by actual comparison that our own opinions were really in every respect superior to all others which had been previously and elsewhere held, something would still be wanting to prove that they were the best possible opinions, namely, the demonstration that the human race had reached in *us* its highest conceivable development. But, so far from being able to prove this, we have no reason for thinking it true: we have every reason for knowing it to be false. Ever since the world began, there has been continual progress in the development of human ideas. And is that progress to cease, simply because we happen to have been born, and to have conferred upon some of these ideas the honour of our approval? To ask the question is to answer it. The thought is too ridiculous to be entertained for a single moment by any but those who are utterly and hopelessly mad. In a word, every one may be certain that he does not hold the best possible opinions; no one can be sure that he holds the best actual opinions; and circumstances compel the great majority of the human race to hold opinions that are erroneous and even degraded.

From all this it follows that the possession of a particular belief cannot be necessary for the enjoyment of the favour of God. If it were, what would become of those whose circumstances have rendered it inevitable that they should believe something else? Are they to perish through no fault of their own? Instead of being compensated for their earthly disadvantages, are they, on account of them, to be eternally damned? This is certainly not the teaching of the Bible, which declares that "God will have all men to be saved, and that His tender mercies are over all His works." Men are at last beginning to believe these declarations. They are at last beginning to perceive that God has not only revealed Himself with comparative fulness to a few, but that He is gradually revealing Himself with increasing clearness to all, in proportion as they are able to bear it. Those of you who have read the recently published Memoirs of Mark Pattison will remember the interesting account which he gives of his deliverance from the thraldom of sectarianism. He was brought up originally in the narrow faith and sympathies of Puritanism. But by-and-by he came to believe in the Church — first in the Anglican, and afterwards in the Catholic or universal Church, whose members, united by a common creed, were to be found in all parts of the world. This idea at first filled him with enthusiasm. But even in this broader notion he could not ultimately rest. "The idea of the Catholic Church," he says, "is only a mode of conceiving the dealings of Divine Providence with the whole race of mankind. But reflection on the history and condition of humanity, taken as a whole, gradually convinced me that this theory of the relation of all living beings to the Supreme Being was too narrow and inadequate. It makes an equal Providence—the Father of all—care only for a mere handful of the species, leaving the rest to the chances of eternal misery. If God interferes at all to procure the happiness of mankind, it must be on a far more comprehensive scale than by providing for them a Church of which the majority will never hear. It was on this line of thought that I passed out of the Catholic phase to that highest development, in which all religions appear in their historical light, as efforts of the human spirit to understand and to enter into communion with God." In other words, what is called the Church, however broadly that word may be interpreted, is but one of the means of communion between God and man.

This is the only view which is compatible with the goodness of God. If, as bigotry asserts, He withheld His favour from men on account of opinions which, owing to their surroundings, they had no alternative but to hold, He would be guilty of the grossest cruelty and injustice. The bigot is given to posing as a very religious man; but he is in reality the impersonation of irreligion. In the Life of Nathaniel Hawthorne it is related that his little daughter Una, who was fond of inventing and telling stories, one day told her brother about a very naughty child, who gradually became naughtier and naughtier, until at last, as the culmination of her wickedness, she struck God. Alas, how often God is struck! Is it not striking God to deny that His tender mercies are over all His works? Is it not striking God to say that He is more particular about orthodoxy than about goodness? Is it not striking God to think that He punishes us for what we cannot help? Is it not striking God to believe that He places men in darkness, and then damns them for having had no light? Is it not striking God to credit Him with characteristics unworthy of a devil? Bigotry, believe me, is only another name for blasphemy,—the most insidious, and yet the foulest, blasphemy.

Common Sins.

IX.

BIGOTRY: ITS MISCHIEVOUS EFFECTS.

"Our fathers worshipped in this mountain; and ye say, that in Jerusalem is the place where men ought to worship."—JOHN iv. 20.

BY bigotry is to be understood, as I have said, the worship of a creed. The bigoted man prides himself upon his opinions and beliefs, and upon the special forms and ceremonies of his worship. They are, he considers, quite perfect; and on account of them he fancies himself to be a special favourite with heaven. Those who hold different opinions or practise different ceremonies seem to him as good as lost. Now we have noticed the general prevalence of this state of mind. We have seen that it exists not only in the great Roman Catholic Church, but also in the smaller Churches of Protestantism, and that it is to be found even amongst the members of the most insignificant sect.

We have seen, further, that, though so common throughout Christendom, it is essentially un-Christian. It was strongly denounced by Christ. "The Father," He said, "seeketh spiritual worshippers. The hour cometh, when men shall neither in this mountain, nor yet in Jerusalem, worship the Father,"—that is, when they will no longer regard locality as essential to true worship. They will at last perceive the comparative worthlessness of what is outward in religion, and the paramount importance of what is inward. God regards neither the place nor the form of worship, but the heart and life of the worshipper.

We have seen, too, that bigotry, which is so essentially un-Christian, is equally incompatible with any real religion, inasmuch as it is based upon a blasphemous conception of the Deity. True religion consists in the worship, not of power, but of goodness. Now unless the Supreme Being deals equitably with His creatures, He cannot be good, He cannot deserve the name of God. And He would not be dealing equitably with them were His favour confined within the petty limits of any sect or Church. If His tender mercies are—as they should be—over all His works, He cannot, while revealing Himself completely to the few, hide Himself as completely from the many. He must reveal Himself to all, in proportion as they are able to bear it.

And He does. This is proved by the science of Comparative Religion — a study to which I would most earnestly commend your attention. The investigation of the various religions of the world has shown that there is a wonderful harmony underlying their diversity, and that each of them is an attempt to interpret a Revelation which is eternal and universal. Let us take an extreme example. You will find it in Max Müller's 'Lectures on the Science of Religion.' An old Samoyede woman, being asked by Castren whether she ever said her prayers, replied, " Every morning I step out of my tent, and bow before the sun, and say, 'When thou risest, I too rise from my bed.' And every evening I say, 'When thou sinkest down, I too sink down to rest.'" That was her prayer—perhaps the whole of her religious service. A poor prayer it may seem to us, but not to her; for it made her look twice at least every day away from earth and up to heaven; it implied that her life was bound up with a larger and higher life; it encircled the daily routine of her earthly existence with something of a divine halo. The Bible, then, reflection, and scientific investigation—all combine to show that the Spirit of God is universally present with men, reminding them of the infinite and eternal source from which their own being is derived. And the fact that some men have interpreted this universal revelation more fully and distinctly than others, is due for the most part to circumstances over which they have had no control, and for which, therefore, they cannot be held responsible.

The bigot, on the contrary, by his assumption that the Almighty is angry with men for holding opinions which their surroundings compelled them to hold, by his assumption that the Deity is specially mindful of a few members of the race, and more or less indifferent to the rest,— by these assumptions the bigot virtually attacks the character of God. In reality, he blasphemes.

It remains for me this morning to draw your attention to some of the mischievous consequences which result from this blasphemous state of mind.

In the first place, it leads to intellectual stagnation. The bigot believes that on all the most important subjects he knows the whole truth. If anything has escaped him, it can only be some trifle or other which is not worth considering. Although, as he fancies, the majority of his fellows know nothing about the Deity, he himself knows everything:—

> " He can God's thoughts and acts pourtray,
> In fair historical array,
> From Adam to the Judgment Day."

He, poor, finite, deluded creature, fancies that he has completely fathomed the Infinite. For him, therefore, progress in knowledge is impossible. He could not change any of his opinions, he could not even get an additional one, without spoiling that finished work of spiritual art which his creed appears to him to be. When the Psalmist thought of God, he said, " Such knowledge is too wonderful for me; it is high, I cannot attain unto it." But the bigot thinks he has attained it. " Except ye become as little children," said Christ, "ye cannot enter into the kingdom of heaven." But so far from having a childlike spirit, the bigot is certain that he already knows everything. Having once learnt his creed, he sees no occasion for using his mind any further; and he is glad to be relieved from so painful an exertion. Upon secular knowledge he looks down with disdain. Science he regards with suspicion. Everything essential to salvation is contained in his creed; and the whole duty of man, he thinks, consists in keeping that passport to heaven unchanged and intact. Though he may use the beautiful words of St Chrysostom, " Granting me in this world knowledge of Thy truth," what he really means is this—" Granting me in this world remembrance of my creed."

Secondly, bigotry deprives men of the necessary stimulus to right-doing. The bigot has taken upon himself to reverse the teaching of Christ. Our Lord laid special stress upon conduct. The bigot lays special stress upon creed. The result cannot but be disastrous. Since he believes that salvation depends upon the possession of those opinions which he himself actually holds, it is apt to become to him a matter of entire indifference whether his actions are right or wrong. There is a story told of a candidate for Scotch orders who, in answer to the question, " What is the value of good works?" replied that perhaps a man might not be much the worse for a few of them. This is scarcely a parody of the extreme bigot's doctrine. The poet Whittier speaks of

> "Antinomians free from law,
> Whose very sins were holy."

And even when the bigot is not quite indifferent to conduct, he is so busy thinking of the mote of heresy in his neighbour's eye, that he has little time for considering the beam of wickedness in his own eye. The superiority of his creed—if it be superior—carries with it a greater weight of responsibility; but he fancies, on the contrary, that it relieves him from responsibility altogether, that its excellence will compensate for any moral delinquency. The bigot's watchword is really this—"He can't go wrong whose creed is in the right;" and in such a maxim there is a potent stimulus to sin.

Thirdly, bigotry makes men either selfish or cruel—more frequently, I suppose, the former. Bigots imagine that God has treated them with greater favour than He has vouchsafed to the rest of mankind. They are fond of singing, in the words of an old hymn—

> "We are a garden walled around,
> Chosen and made peculiar ground."

With such a creed, we need not wonder at

their selfishness. We cannot expect a man to be better than his God. Why should he trouble himself about those whom he believes the Almighty ignores. He looks forward, as a rule, with perfect complacency to the future destruction of the race. So long as he is saved, he does not care what becomes of the rest. His so-called religion, instead of making him more human and sympathetic, really isolates him from the great majority of mankind. He cannot tolerate those whose creed differs from his own. He would not be happy in heaven if there were a chance of his being contradicted. Rather than have any one admitted who differs from him, he would prefer to spend his eternity alone. Indeed such a prospect would not be at all disagreeable; for he has always been accustomed to find complete satisfaction in himself.

Sometimes, however, the bigot, in spite of his demoralising creed, is unselfish enough to desire that others should be saved; and in that case he becomes a persecutor. Believing that every one will be lost who does not agree with him, he endeavours to bring about this agreement by inflicting on them suffering and torture, or by putting them to death as a warning to the heretics that survive. Bigots nowadays, being less numerous, have not the power which they once possessed, and consequently their persecutions have to be conducted on a smaller and less noticeable scale. But let us never forget what they did when they had the chance; and what many of them, if they could, would gladly do again. The number of their victims is almost incredible. In 1546 it was officially stated that in Holland and Friesland more than thirty thousand persons suffered death for being Anabaptists. In Spain, during Torquemada's ministry, the Inquisition punished upwards of one hundred and five thousand persons, of whom eighty-eight thousand were burned. In Andalusia alone, during a single year, the Inquisition put to death two thousand Jews, not to speak of seventeen thousand who underwent some other form of punishment. Moreover, as Buckle points out, the unknown victims of persecution must be far more numerous than the known. History gives no account of those who suffered only in mind. Many were so terrified at the thought of the thumbscrew or the rack, that they were driven to an outward abandonment of their real opinions, forced into an apostasy which their hearts abhorred, and made to

Bigotry: its Mischievous Effects. 255

pass the remainder of their life in the practice of a constant and humiliating hypocrisy. And if, further, we call to mind how the small but noble army of scientific martyrs had their lives made a burden to them by bigots; if we call to mind how invariably prophets and apostles, philosophers and reformers, have been execrated and hounded down by bigots; if we call to mind that Socrates was poisoned and that Christ was crucified by bigots,—we shall be convinced that there is no enormity of which they are not capable.

Fourthly, there is one more serious evil, connected with the vice we are discussing, to which I would draw your attention. Bigotry calls itself, and is constantly mistaken for, religion. The bigot is always loud in self-assertiveness. He vociferates to the world that he is very religious, and he is unfortunately too often believed. And what is the result? Every noble-minded, right-hearted man who has made this mistake and taken the bigot at his word, comes to loathe the very name of religion, and to look upon it as the direst evil with which our world is cursed. Nine-tenths of the abuse heaped upon religion by so-called infidels and atheists is in a sense perfectly legitimate; for what they are in reality abusing is, not religion in the proper sense of the term, but bigotry. When Lucretius says, "To so many evils has religion persuaded men," when he personifies Religion, and represents her as standing with horrid mien over the prostrate form of terrified Humanity,—he is thinking all the time of bigotry, which is the very antithesis of religion. Though Draper entitles his book, 'The Conflict between Science and Religion,' what he really describes is the conflict between science and bigotry; and with bigotry religion has absolutely nothing in common.

And the same remark applies to the objections brought against Christianity. In ninety - nine cases out of a hundred they have nothing whatever to do with the Christianity of Christ—though they apply with perfect accuracy to certain caricatures and perversions of Christianity, invented and kept alive by bigots.[1] Had Christ been a bigot, Christianity would be doomed. Sooner or later men would discover that it was a pestilent superstition, and would shake it off as an encumbrance and disgrace. This undoubtedly is the fate in store for the bigot's misrepresentation of the Gospel of Christ. But in the meantime incalculable mischief is effected by the common confusion between bigotry and religion. A great

[1] *E.g.*, Mr Cotter Morrison's 'Service of Man.'

number of persons are always the slaves of language: they are invariably taken in by words; they inevitably fancy that two things are the same, however much they may in reality differ, if only they are called by the same name. Such persons will always regard the bigot as a representative of religion, because he is pleased to call himself religious. And even men of culture, who by a little reading and reflection might discover that there was something in existence legitimately called religion, and differing from bigotry as much as light differs from darkness—even these men of culture are often so busy and preoccupied with other affairs, that they never perceive this simple and important distinction. When the bigot says, "I am a religious man, I am a Christian," they illogically, and yet not unnaturally, reply, "Then away with religion and Christianity!" So that bigotry—itself the worst form of irreligion—is responsible for that religious indifference which is so frequently to be found among those who are too wise and too good to be bigots.

From all this it follows that in the denunciation of bigotry it is impossible to be too severe. To condemn bigots is not bigotry. We have no right to tolerate intolerance. For bigotry there can be no excuse; and we should never, therefore, attempt to palliate it. Any mistake may be forgiven a man, except that of supposing himself incapable of mistake. Any heresy may be tolerated in a man, except the doctrine that the God whom he worships is unjust. A moment's reflection will suffice to show that worship ought not to be accorded to a Being who did wrong. A moment's reflection will suffice to show that it is impossible for a handful of the human race to be in possession of infinite truth. And those who persist in clinging to the mad and blasphemous delusion of the bigot must be denounced, and denounced, and denounced, till they be forced into reflection, till they give up their bigotry for very shame.

There will come a time, thank God, when bigotry shall be no more! The hour cometh, and now is, when men shall worship the Father, neither on this mountain nor yet in Jerusalem; when those who respect no opinions but their own shall have for ever passed away. O Bigotry, thou art doomed! Thou hast fortified thyself in thy narrow sphere with the bulwarks of anathemas and threatenings of hell. Thou hast imagined that thou couldst stop the development of human thought, and stem the tide of human progress. As its waves have been driven back now and again by the strength of thy bulwarks, thou hast laughed thy low, diabolical laugh, and hast imagined thyself perpetually, eternally victorious. But thou art greatly mistaken. Thou art doomed. The tide of human progress, lashed into fury by thy constant opposition, shall gather itself up in its giant strength for another, and this time a successful, effort, and once for all shall sweep thee from off the face of the earth, with all thy follies and superstitions, thine atrocities and thy crimes!

Our Right to Immortality.

I.

THE OBLIGATIONS OF THE DEITY.

"Abraham drew near, and said, Wilt Thou also destroy the righteous with the wicked? . . . That be far from Thee to do after this manner. . . . Shall not the Judge of all the earth do right?"—GENESIS xviii. 23-25.

ABRAHAM here assumes, you see, that the same principles of morality which apply to human beings apply equally to the divine. If God were to do certain things, they would be wrong, even though He did them. He has no more right, for example, according to Abraham, to slay the righteous with the wicked, than a human judge would have to condemn an innocent man to the gallows. Abraham's faith was such that he felt assured the Almighty would do nothing which an enlightened conscience must

The Obligations of the Deity. 261

condemn. This passage will serve us to-day as a suggestive motto.

We have been engaged now for two Sundays upon the subject of Immortality.[1] You remember, I tried to show you that a belief in immortality was the only basis—the only rational basis —for real religion. We saw that such a belief was necessary—in the first place, because the denial of immortality inevitably amounts to the denial of God. This world of ours bears unmistakable witness to a supremely powerful Being; but apart from the hypothesis of a future life, it gives no evidence of His benevolence or justice. On the contrary, the inequalities and miseries and unsatisfied longings of the race would suggest that He was cruel and capricious. If this life be our only life, the supreme Power in the universe is not good—that is, is not God. And we saw further, in the second place, that without a belief in immortality there could be no religion, because nothing can be more *depressing* than the thought that in a few short years— nay, at any moment—we may pass into nothingness; whereas the essential characteristic of religion, the characteristic which distinguishes it from superstition, is the fact that it is inspir-

[1] See my 'Basis of Religion.'

ing and stimulating, that it nerves us for the moral conflict of life.

After preaching these sermons I received the following interesting letter. The writer says: "I am an unwilling agnostic, conscious that my energies are sapped by lack of faith. Still I cannot see in this depression, nor in the inequality of human lives, any proof of the fact of immortality. Is it proved that we have any right to happiness? May not a higher morality than any we have yet attained enable us to ask for nothing for our individual selves? 'If God would give us the best and greatest gift—that which, above all others, we might long for and aspire after—it is this, that He might give us to be used and sacrificed for the best and greatest end.' May not the hope of immortality be only a moral luxury? There is an immortality the recognition of which is perhaps sufficient to stimulate the energies of purely moral people—namely, the fact that we have influence enough to set rolling good or evil through countless generations; that every action and thought is in this way immortal, and that in the *results* of our lives we may live for ever."

My correspondent, you will notice, admits that disbelief in a future life is essentially depressing, that it does sap the moral energies. But she says, and justly, that this depression is no proof of immortality. I did not, of course, offer it as such. What it does establish, however, is *one or other* of two alternatives, either immortality or atheism. Without believing in immortality it is impossible to believe in a Being properly called God. But my correspondent, as I gather, would not admit that I had proved even this. And many others in my congregation perhaps would agree with her. Therefore let us look once more at the matter from a somewhat different point of view to that which we formerly occupied. The subject is of the greatest importance especially in the present day.

Immortality is not only denied by materialists, who for the most part are destitute of any strong religious feelings, but it is sometimes doubted by persons in whom the religious sentiments are singularly strong—as, for example, by Amiel. It is doubted for one or more of the following reasons, all of which are expressed or implied in the letter I have just read: (I.) It is said, God is under no obligation to give us immortality. (II.) The question of His goodness is not affected by anything He may do or may not do. Our notions of right and wrong are inapplicable to the Deity. (III.) Our extinction may be necessary for the accomplishment of some great scheme which, though we cannot comprehend it, is really glorious and divine. Now let us examine these views.

I. "God is under no obligation to give us immortality;" or, as my correspondent puts it, "What right have we to happiness?" Now this is the expression of an opinion which, curiously enough, is often held in common by the most thoughtless and the most thoughtful persons. Those who hold it evidently assume that as regards God we can have no rights—that upon Him we have no legitimate claims. We are to call Him God, not because His acts are good, but simply and solely because He has made us. The fact of His having created us would entitle Him to act towards us in any way He might happen to please, without for a moment forfeiting His right to be called God. There is no reciprocity of obligation between us and Him. He has all the rights; we have all the duties. Though the creature is bound to act well by the Creator, the Creator is not bound to act well by the creature. Because He has created us, therefore He may do with us anything, or everything, or nothing.

The Obligations of the Deity.

Now let me venture to point out that this is neither the doctrine of the Bible nor of commonsense. The Bible speaks of the Creator as being the Father of His creatures; and manifestly, in the case of a father and his children the obligations are not all on one side—they are mutual. It is true that even this human relationship is often very much misunderstood. People sometimes exaggerate the duties of children, while they completely ignore the duties of parents. They speak as if all the obligations were on the children's side, as if the claims of the parents were everything, and the claims of the children nothing. But surely the obligations of the father to his child are as great and as serious —nay, far greater and far more serious—than those of the child to his father. The duties of a parent are not diminished by the fact of parentage: on the contrary, they are thereby increased. Is a father, forsooth, at liberty to neglect, to starve, to degrade, to torture a child, simply because it is his own? Why, it is just this—just the fact of the child's being his—which would render such conduct pre-eminently heinous. Since he is responsible for the child's existence, he is under the most solemn obligation to do everything he can to make that existence a success. And indeed he has no right to be a father at all, unless there is some reasonable prospect of his being able to provide satisfactorily for the comfort and wellbeing of his offspring. Many human beings have refused to marry, for fear they should bring into existence children who would be inevitably diseased, and whose lives would therefore be inevitably wretched. And do you think that an infinite and omnipotent Creator is under less obligation than a weak and finite man? On the contrary, the higher you rise in the scale of being, the more do you find that the sphere of obligation is enlarged. And therefore the obligations of the Deity must be no less infinite than His rights. Do you think that the Creator, if He were so disposed, would be justified in creating men for the express purpose of their being tortured? Do you think that He would be at liberty to create them with yearnings for happiness that could never be gratified, with a longing for perfection that would never be realised? Surely a being who could do so would not be God. To be a Creator is a proof of power; but, unless might is right, it is in itself no proof of goodness. Whether the Creator is, or is not, to be called good, will depend upon the manner in which He deals with His creatures. By the very fact of creation, He has laid Himself under an obligation to deal kindly and justly with the beings He has made. He is bound to respect the yearnings and hopes of which He Himself is the author. Our right to happiness, therefore, lies in the fact that we desire it. He who made us, and implanted this desire within us, must sooner or later fulfil it, or else He would forfeit His right to the title of God.

But (II.) it has been maintained by eminently thoughtful and eminently religious persons, that we cannot argue in this way from ourselves to God. Conduct which would be wrong for us, they say, may be right for Him. Our idea of goodness is not a standard which can be fittingly applied to the Deity. Actions which, judged by our moral principles, must be called wrong, might, if looked at from a higher point of view, prove to be the very best. The goodness of the Creator is one thing, the goodness of the creature another. The divine character is infinite, and therefore can never be comprehended by finite man. This is the view which was expounded at length by Dean Mansel in his Bampton Lectures on the "Limits of Religious Thought."

The answer to it seems to me very simple. The word infinite, when used as an adjective, does not change the nature of that to which it is applied, but merely expresses its quantity or intensity. For example, when we speak of infinite space, we do not mean to say that there are two kinds of space—one finite and the other infinite— but only that the *one* space exists everywhere, that there are no limits to its extension. Similarly, when we speak of the infinite goodness of God, we should not think of two different kinds of goodness, but only that the same quality, which is to be found in a measurable degree amongst ourselves, exists in an immeasurable degree in the Deity. It follows, therefore, that infinite space and infinite goodness are not things of which we are ignorant. So far as infinite space is space, we are acquainted with it, for it exists all around us. So far as infinite goodness is goodness, we know it, for it is to be found amongst many of our neighbours and acquaintances. It is only the infinity of space, the infinity of goodness—that is to say, their maximum of quantity or intensity—which it is beyond the reach of our faculties to grasp. This is most certainly the Scriptural view of the matter. The Bible delights in attributing to God the best human characteristics, and in representing them as differing from ours only in degree: as, for example, in the passage, "Can a woman forget her child? Yea, she may forget; yet will I not forget thee."

But at any rate, if you still think that the divine and human goodness must be totally different in kind as well as in degree, then I ask, why do you still persist in calling them by the same name? According to Dean Mansel, words like personality, love, justice, goodness, when applied to God, must be understood in a different sense from that which they bear in relation to man. In what sense they are applicable to God he does not explain. All he tells us is that they may mean exactly the opposite of what is generally understood by them. If so, we have arrived by another route at the Unknowable of Mr Herbert Spencer. Little as Mansel suspected it, his premises in the Bampton Lectures were precisely identical with the premises of Mr Spencer in 'The First Principles.' Their conclusions are different—because Mr Spencer's is logical, Dean Mansel's is not. They are quite agreed that the divine character must be totally different from ours. Yet Mansel would have us, after all intelligible meaning has been eliminated from the words, still speak of God as good and kind and just. Spencer, more wisely, advises us to confess our ignorance and say nothing.

The untenableness of Mansel's position was once and for ever shown by John Stuart Mill, in his examination of Sir William Hamilton's Philosophy. "I take my stand," says Mill, "upon the acknowledged principle of logic and morality, that when we mean different things we have no right to call them by the same name. Language has no meaning for the terms just, merciful, benevolent, good, save that in which we predicate them of our fellow-creatures; and unless that is what we intend to express by them, we have no business to employ them. If, in ascribing goodness to God, I do not mean the goodness of which I have some knowledge, but an incomprehensible attribute of an incomprehensible substance, which, for aught I know, may be a totally different quality from that which I love and venerate—and even must, if Mr Mansel is to be believed, be in some important particulars opposed to this—what do I mean by calling it goodness? and what reason have I for venerating it? If I know nothing about what the attribute is, I cannot tell that it is a proper object for veneration. To say that God's goodness may be different in kind from man's goodness—what is it but saying, with a slight change of phraseology, that God may possibly not be good? To assert in words what we do not think in meaning, is as suitable a definition as can be given of a moral falsehood. . . . Neither is this to set up my own limited intellect as a criterion of divine or of any other wisdom. If a person is wiser and better than myself, not in some unknown and unknowable meaning of the terms, but in their known human acceptation, I am ready to believe that what this person thinks may be true, and that what he does may be right, when, but for the opinion I have of him, I should think otherwise. But this is because I believe that he and I have at bottom the same standard of truth and rule of right, and that he probably understands better than I the facts of the particular case. If I thought it not improbable that his notion of right was my notion of wrong, I should not defer to his judgment. Similarly in regard to God, if I feel He is really good, in the ordinary meaning of that word though to an extraordinary degree, I can believe that His actions are right even when I do not understand them. But if, instead of the glad tidings that there exists a Being in whom all the excellences which the human mind can conceive exist in a degree inconceivable to us, I am informed that the world is ruled by a being whose attributes are infinite, but what they are we cannot learn, nor what are the principles of his government, except that the highest human morality which we are capable of conceiving does not sanction them,— convince me of it, and I will bear my fate as I may. But when I am told that I must believe this, and at the same time call this being by the names which express the highest human morality, I say in plain terms that I will not. Whatever power such a being may have over me, there is one thing which he shall not do—he shall not compel me to worship him. I will call no being good who is not what I mean when I apply that epithet to my fellow-creatures. And if such a being can sentence me to hell for not so calling him, to hell I will go."

Throughout this passage there breathes the true spirit of religion. For religion is only another name for the worship of goodness. The same sentiments were uttered long ago by the prophet Isaiah: " Woe unto them that put light for darkness, and darkness for light; woe unto them that call evil good, and good evil!" Religion does not consist in escaping hell, but in adoring supremely that which supremely deserves adoration. It is not religion, it is blasphemy, to assert that God is capable of conduct which in a man would be universally condemned. What would you say of a father who instilled into his child's heart desires which could not be realised, who trained him to expect what he would never receive, who gave him such false impressions as to his future prospects and position that when he awoke from his delusion he would be driven to despair? What would you say of such a father? Why, you would say he was a monster of iniquity, unworthy of the name of man, unworthy even of the name of brute. And yet it is a being like that whom some have not hesitated to call God!

By these remarks I hope I have partially justified what I said the other day, and what I now repeat: God and immortality stand or fall together. If death made an end of us for ever, humanity would be a contemptible failure, and its creator would not deserve the name of God. "If we are to have a religion, it is necessary for us to believe that the Power which checks and thwarts us intends to give us in the end not less than we had hoped for, but rather infinitely more."[1] Is it giving us infinitely more, when we have such a passionate longing for immortality, to answer it by annihilation? Is it giving us infinitely more,

[1] These are the words of the author of 'Natural Religion.'

when we have yearned and struggled for perfection, to cut us off before it can possibly be achieved? Is it giving us infinitely more to turn to destruction the whole human race, when so many of them have never tasted the cup of happiness, when so many of them could not but be vile?

Our Right to Immortality.

II.

THE HONOUR OF THE DEITY.

"Abraham drew near, and said, Wilt Thou also destroy the righteous with the wicked? . . . That be far from Thee to do after this manner. . . . Shall not the Judge of all the earth do right?"—GENESIS xviii. 23-25.

YOU will often hear these words misquoted. They are frequently used apart from the context, to show that God is at liberty to do anything, and that the fact of His doing it would make it right. Whereas Abraham's meaning was exactly the opposite. He intended to say that God was only at liberty to do those things which were in themselves right. For example, to "slay the righteous with the wicked" would be wrong, and therefore God ought not to do it. "That be far from Thee to slay the righteous with the wicked; for shall not the Judge of all the earth do right?" If right conduct be expected from weak, finite, erring men, *a fortiori* must it be expected from the infinite Creator, the Judge of all the earth.

We saw last Sunday that our claim to immortality has been denied on three grounds, two of which we then examined. It is said, in the first place, that God is under no obligations of any kind, and therefore under no obligation to give us immortality. We saw, however, that the Creator is bound to promote the wellbeing of His creatures, no less than a human father is bound to promote the wellbeing of his children. The fact of creation, indeed, carries with it an infinite burden of responsibility. The desires which our Maker has implanted in us He must sooner or later fulfil, or He would forfeit His right to the title of God. And I pointed out further, in the second place, how it is often said that we cannot argue from ourselves to God, that our standard of right and wrong is inapplicable to Him, and that therefore the question of His goodness is not affected by anything He may do or leave undone. But we saw that this position was also untenable. If our notions of morality are altogether inapplicable to the Deity, if what would be wrong in us may be right in Him, and *vice versa*, it is manifestly absurd to call Him good or just or kind. These words mean nothing unless they mean qualities which are to be found in human beings; and if the divine attributes are different from the human, not only in degree but in kind, we have no business to call them by the same names. So that it is impossible logically to believe that God is good, and at the same time to believe that He is capable of conduct which an enlightened human conscience would condemn.

This morning I pass on to consider the third ground on which our right to immortality has been denied. It is said that our extinction may be necessary for the accomplishment of some great scheme, some higher end than could be served by our survival—an end which, though we cannot understand it, is nevertheless glorious and divine. For the attainment of such an end, it is said, we ought to be willing sacrifices.

Now I assert there can be no such end. This assertion, it may be objected, is one which a finite mind is not at liberty to make, for it implies omniscience, and is quite incapable of justification. But, if you think for a moment, you will see that it does not imply omniscience, and that it is not incapable of justification. There is a good deal of nonsense, it seems to me, often talked about the limitation of our faculties. It is sometimes said, for example, that to an infinite intellect everything would appear quite different to what we, in our finitude, can imagine. But there are many things which a finite mind can know with practically infinite certainty; we could not be more sure of them even if we were ourselves infinite. It does not require omniscience to feel sure that twice two make four. I am aware it was maintained by J. S. Mill that to omniscience they might make something else. But in this he has had very few supporters. And oddly enough, in the eloquent passage I read you last Sunday from his criticism upon Mansel's Bampton Lectures, he himself denies this doctrine of the complete relativity of truth. He there maintains, you remember, that truth—so far as it is apprehended at all—must appear one and the same both to a finite and to an infinite intelligence. He asserts that the principles of morality apply to God as well as to man, and that therefore the finite is perfectly capable of judging whether or not the Infinite should be called good. "I will call no being good," he says, "who is not what I mean when I apply that epithet to my fellow-creatures. When we mean different things, we have no right to call them by the same name." If, therefore, we believe that God is good, we must also believe that His conduct can never be such as our consciences would condemn.

Now just as we are capable of perceiving that there cannot be two kinds of goodness essentially different from one another, so we are capable of perceiving that there can be no higher end than immortality. Let us see.

That higher end certainly cannot be the glory of God. Those who think so must have a strange idea of glory. The glory of the Creator is inevitably bound up with the glory of His creatures. If they are failures, He has failed. If this world be a system complete in itself, if this life is not to be followed by another, if hopes are born only to be blighted, yearnings roused only to be crushed, beings created only to be destroyed,— then the Author of nature is either very wicked or very weak. If He had skill, He had not love; if He had love, He had not skill. Either He does not desire the wellbeing of His creatures, or He could not accomplish it. A being like that is of course no object for worship. He deserves only pity or execration—pity if such a world is the best He could make, execration if it is not. If our most passionate desires are doomed to everlasting disappointment, if our noblest aspirations are to remain for ever unfulfilled, if after thinking ourselves endowed with the power of an endless life we are to die out like the flame of a candle,—then so long as any remembrance of us lingers in the universe, we shall be nothing but a reproach to our Maker, bearing witness to the fact that, whatever He may be, He is no God. Our extinction redound to the glory of God! Why, what would prove impotence in a creature cannot prove power in a Creator; what would bring contempt upon the finite, cannot bring honour to the Infinite; what in us would be disgrace, cannot in Him be glory. If there be no immortality, the Creator will be involved in eternal shame. Our extinction redound to the glory of God! To say so is to maintain that the crowning achievement of the Deity is to have created an infinite number of abortions!

So the "higher end" attainable through our extinction cannot be the glory of God. And it is equally easy to see that it cannot be the welfare of others. For what are these others, whose welfare must be purchased at such a cost, whose happiness involves our everlasting destruction? They are but finite creatures like ourselves. And surely we have as much right to the satisfaction of *our* wants and hopes as they can possibly have to the satisfaction of *theirs*. The most sensitive minds have always shrunk from the thought that any sentient creature, however low in the scale of being, should be absolutely and eternally sacrificed for another's sake. You remember Tennyson's words:—

> " Oh, yet we trust that somehow good
> Will be the final goal of ill.
>
> . . . . . .
>
> That nothing walks with aimless feet,
>   That not one life shall be destroyed
>   Or cast as rubbish to the void,
> When God hath made the pile complete;
>
> That not a worm is cloven in vain,
>   That not a moth with vain desire
>   Is shrivelled in a fruitless fire,
> Or but subserves another's gain."

On this ground even sober-minded and orthodox men like Bishop Butler have not hesitated to maintain that immortality is perhaps in store for the whole sentient creation. But be that as it may, it is a recognised principle, as regards human beings at any rate, that no one has a right to happiness which can only be procured through the complete ruin of another. To take away the life of a fellow-creature merely to please one's self is commonly called murder. It is quite true that in social and in family life sacrifices are required from the individual for the sake of others ; but the individual receives compensation, because similar sacrifices are required from others for his sake. The sacrifices are only justifiable, from a moral point of view, when they are reciprocal. For example, a poor man cannot educate half-a-dozen children so well as he could educate one; but he is not for that reason at liberty to drown five of them, in order that he may give this superior education to the survivor. The attainment of the highest conceivable education, if it involved such sacrifices, would be after all nothing more than the attainment of the lowest conceivable end. And similarly, even supposing that the happiness of certain individuals in the future might be enhanced by our annihilation—I don't see why it should be; on the contrary, unless they were irretrievably degraded, the thought of what had been done to secure their happiness would for ever prevent them from being happy —but supposing, for the sake of argument, that through ignorance, or for some other reason, they were actually happier than, but for our annihilation, they could have been, this would be a happiness to which they had no right. In other words, it would not be a high but a low end—an absolutely immoral end—which would be gained by our extinction.

It may be said—indeed it often has been said by mystics, as I am reminded in a letter received this week—that the loss of our individuality would really be a gain, "because it is self which keeps us from God, and therefore we can be united to Him only by the destruction or absorption of self. It is our spiritual ambition to have no will but His. Certain saints have, or think they have, so completely subdued their wills to God's, that they have ceased to exist—they have died to themselves. Is not this the logical result of faith in His will? Is it not proved hereby that annihilation is in accordance with spiritual progress?"

This is at first sight a plausible argument; but it derives its plausibility from an ambiguous use of terms. When we say it is self which keeps us from God, we are really thinking of the lower desires and affections in our nature, which we feel to be out of harmony with other affections that we are accustomed to regard as higher. But just because this want of harmony is experienced, it follows that the higher affections belong to us as much as the lower, and have therefore at least as good a right to the title of self. Now self, in this sense, does not keep us from God; on the contrary, among the higher desires, is one which prompts us directly to seek for Him. The antagonism to be overcome, therefore, is not between self and God, but between the lower and the higher self. It is only the lower self that we require to lose. And, indeed, not even this is to be altogether lost. It needs but to be *harmonised* with that higher self which is already in sympathy with God.

The loss of individuality would be, as is admitted, the loss of consciousness. And to lose consciousness is to lose, among other things, the consciousness of God, and therefore to be separated from Him. In one sense, it is true, whatever happened we should be united to Him, by reason of His omnipresence, just as the material world is united. But the highest form of union is communion; and that, without consciousness, is impossible. It is not consciousness which keeps us from God, but only the predominance in consciousness of feelings and emotions with which the presence of God is incompatible. When the higher desires begin to predominate, then consciousness brings us into personal communion with God. Similarly, if we are told to "have no

The Honour of the Deity. 285

will but God's," we must remember that this is a metaphorical and rhetorical expression. It does not mean—at least it need not mean—that we are to will nothing, but that we are to will the same things as God wills. It may be said of matter that it has no will but God's, because it has no will at all. And if the same can ever be said of us in the same sense, we shall have descended to the level of the material world. Our having no will but God's is an honour to us and a glory to Him, only if we have a will of our own, and yet use it in harmony with His. Do you think, supposing death put an end to men for ever, that two friends who had been closely united in life, would be still more closely united in the unconsciousness of the tomb? Did their sense of personal identity keep them apart? On the contrary, it was that which pre-eminently bound them together. For each of them, in being conscious of his own individuality, became aware of the fact that it was only completed by the individuality of the other.

The loss of self therefore, using self in the sense of individuality, would be an unmitigated curse. To pass from communion with God into mere union, from voluntary co-operation with His will into the involuntary submission of unconsciousness, from personality into a state undistinguishable from matter,—this of a truth is to attain, not the highest end, but the very lowest.

There is one other point I should like to mention before I conclude. Immortality—that is, the preservation of the individual—may be considered the highest possible end, for a reason which even physical science to some extent justifies. The reason is this: the development and the preservation of the individual would seem to be the end which has all along been aimed at in the process of evolution. According to Herbert Spencer, evolution means a change from homogeneity to heterogeneity; and the highest form of heterogeneity is what we call individuality. As Miss Cobbe says—" The advance through inorganic, vegetative, animated and self-conscious existence, and again from the lowest savage to the loftiest philosopher, is all in the direction of a more and more perfect, complete and definite personality. The severance of the ego from the not-ego, for example, may indeed be held in one sense to be the supreme result of all the machinery of the physical life; and the whole history of thought tends to show that the better recognition of the distinction has been at the root of the superiority of the Western over the Eastern and classic nations. To suppose that there is a height in the range of being, whereto having attained, this slowly evolved personality suddenly collapses like a volcanic island, and subsides into the ocean of impersonal being, is to suppose that the whole scheme of things is self-stultifying, a great much ado about nothing, the building up of a tower which should reach to heaven, but which, like a child's house of cards, as soon as it is finished will be again swept flat." From the point of view of evolution, therefore, it follows that any end attainable through our extinction would be not high but low—so ridiculously low as to make the process which led to it appear utterly beneath contempt. If the destruction of personality be the final end of evolution, then the history of the universe is but a gigantic farce. We have a right to immortality which there are no reasonable grounds for disputing. Unless there be injustice and irrationality at the heart of things, it cannot be denied us. In the name of all that is high and noble, I *demand* eternal life.[1]

[1] See also my 'Agnosticism,' Part II.

The Practical Nature of Christianity.

"A new commandment I give unto you, That ye love one another." —John xiii. 34.
" This is my commandment, That ye love one another." —John xv. 12.
" These things I command you, That ye love one another."—John xv. 17.
" By this shall all men know that ye are my disciples, if ye have love one to another."—John xiii. 35.
" When the Son of man shall come in His glory: . . . before Him shall be gathered all nations, and He shall separate them one from another. . . . Then shall the King say unto them on His right hand, Come: . . . for I was an hungered, I was thirsty, I was a stranger, naked, sick, in prison, and ye ministered unto me. Then shall He say also to them on the left hand, Depart: . . . for I was an hungered, I was thirsty, I was a stranger, naked, sick, in prison, and ye ministered not unto me. Inasmuch as ye did it not unto one of the least of these my brethren, ye did it not unto me."—Matt. xxv. 31-45.

WE are in a sense too familiar with the Bible. No doubt the fact that its words have fallen upon our ears from our earliest childhood, has gathered around them a number of associations which are of almost priceless value. But on the other hand, the very same repetition which tends to produce and increase these associations, tends at the same time to obscure the full and exact meaning of the words themselves. The New Testament abounds in expressions which would startle us if we were to hear them now for the first time. We have, however, become so accustomed to the sound of them, that they produce upon us little or no effect. How many of us, I wonder, have felt the full force of the passages which I have selected for my text? No one can clearly appreciate their significance, without being struck by the appalling contrast between the Christianity of Christ and the Christianity of Christendom.

There can be no doubt that Jesus enunciated the new commandment as a summary of the whole of His teaching. It occurs in the farewell address that He delivered to His disciples at the close of the Last Supper. In the course of that address the commandment is three times repeated. Their obedience to it, he assures them, will afford an unerring criterion of their discipleship. "*By this* shall all men know that ye are my disciples, if ye have love one to another." And further, as we learn from the record of St Matthew, Christ also asserted that when men pass into the unseen world they will be acquitted or condemned according as they have, or have not, obeyed this same law of Love. "*Come: for* I was in need, and ye ministered unto me. *Depart: for* I was in need, and ye ministered not unto me." The one all-comprehensive question in the day of judgment will be—if we are to accept the teaching of Christ— has a man been actuated by the spirit of love, or has he not?

Now, do you suppose it would be possible, by studying the average Christianity of Christendom, to discover that Christ had taught anything of the kind? A person brought up in ignorance of the words of Christ should be able to reproduce the spirit of the most important of them, and to construct His teaching in its most fundamental aspects, by an examination of the lives and conduct of those who call themselves Christians. Admitting the ideality of Christ's Gospel, admitting that He set up a standard which in this life it is impossible for any man completely to reach, still the lives of those who call themselves after His name should give *some clue* to the general scope and tenor of the doctrines which He taught. But can we say that, as a rule, this conformity does actually exist between the precepts of Christ and the practices of His disciples. Is the life of the average Christian manifestly, unmistakably governed by the new commandment? Suppose we put an ecclesiastical history into the hands of some one who had never read the Bible, and asked him to try and discover from it the gist of Christ's teaching, what do you think would be his opinion? He would find that century after century many of the leading members of the Christian Church consecrated almost the whole of their enthusiasm to the definition of metaphysical terms, and the formulating of theological creeds, and that they anathematised, excommunicated, and persecuted—often to death—those who used other terms or understood them in a different sense. And so he would be forced to the conclusion that Christ's purpose must have been to found a new system of metaphysics, and that He differed from other metaphysicians only in having declared eternal salvation to depend upon the acceptance of a correct terminology. Or suppose, again, that we asked the same person ignorant of the Bible, to examine the lives and conduct of those who now call themselves Christians, and to try and discover in this way what it was upon which Christ had laid supreme stress, would he, think you, get much nearer to the

292 *Practical Nature of Christianity.*

mark? He might find out that they had been baptised in infancy, that they had learnt the Catechism as children, that they were accustomed on certain days to come to church, to sing hymns, to say prayers, to receive the Communion. And since, in thousands and tens of thousands of cases, it is *only* by such practices that those who profess Christianity differ perceptibly from those who do not, he would very probably come to the conclusion that it must have been Christ's chief intention to found a new system of ceremonial observance.[1]

Moreover—and this is stranger still—not only would it frequently be impossible for any one unacquainted with the teaching of Christ to discover it from the conduct of His professed disciples, but many of those disciples themselves, who have read and re-read the New Testament till they almost know it by heart, are nevertheless absolutely ignorant of the actual nature of Christianity, and have not in the faintest degree conceived what it is that Christ requires of them. Many persons consider themselves Christians because they have, as they think, an orthodox creed, or because they conform to certain observances which go under the general name of

[1] See also a sermon on misdirected enthusiasm in my 'Defects of Modern Christianity.'

worship. They really imagine that by holding certain opinions and performing certain ceremonies they are working out the salvation of Christ. This is what they understand by the Gospel, and every other representation of it they unhesitatingly denounce. It is an appalling fact that a sermon which aimed at stimulating men to the performance of moral duties, or to the cultivation of a kindly spirit, would be characterised by numbers of professing Christians as not a Gospel sermon. And even those who do recognise the importance of conduct, who, from a sense of gratitude or affection, do really try to be like their Master, are often nevertheless inclined to look upon duty and salvation as essentially distinct. But Christ's salvation, as He understood it, was a salvation from sin. In other words, according to Christ, duty and salvation are identical.

Nothing could possibly be further from the truth than the common notion that Christ's purpose was to save men from the punishment which they deserve, to enable the Almighty hereafter to treat the wicked as if they had been good, and to take them to heaven when they ought by rights to have been in hell. Such a theory is no less immoral than absurd. To shield men from the punishment they deserve is not only unjust, it is cruel; for the suffering of punishment is needed to cure them of their sin. *Punishment is an essential part of salvation.* Without it no one would ever be saved at all. But we may go farther and say, not only would it be cruel to ward off from a man the punishment he deserves, it would be impossible. Even supposing the external consequences of sin were miraculously averted from the wrong-doer, there would still remain something from which Omnipotence itself could not save him. There is a harvest of *character* that follows from human actions; and this is at once the most important, the most certain, and the most unavoidable form of retribution. Wrong-doing is not conduct which God has chosen capriciously to forbid and to punish, but conduct which, in the very nature of things, must inevitably be productive of misery and degradation. So long as the cause continues in operation, the effect must of necessity follow. Heaven and hell are not spheres to which men are tyrannically consigned, or from which they can be tyrannically removed. The place a man goes to in the future, as in the present, is emphatically *his own* place—the place for which by his conduct he has prepared himself. You remember Satan's words in 'Paradise Lost'—

"Which way I fly is hell. Myself am hell."

Practical Nature of Christianity. 295

The worst of all tortures for a bad man is to be brought into the society of the good. To one who hated righteousness, heaven would be a more frightful place than hell. How could he bear, in the tattered and filthy rags of his uncleanness, to come near to those who had washed their robes and made them white in the blood of the Lamb? If the worm that dieth not and the flame that is not quenched, if the pangs of conscience and remorse would plague him in hell, when surrounded by those who were as bad or worse than himself, think you not that they would plague him with an infinitely sharper sting in heaven, where he would be confronted by the spirits of the just made perfect? To take any one who was unfitted for it into the highest heaven, would be in reality to thrust him lower than the lowest hell. Sin carries its own hell along with it; and therefore the man who refuses to be saved from sin cannot conceivably be saved from punishment—no, not even by God Himself.

Now all sin is ultimately resolvable into selfishness. From an undue love of self, from an excessive desire for self-gratification, springs every form of wrong-doing. Murder, theft, slander, for example, and all other crimes, result from the neglect of the rights of others. And in addition to the *positive* injuries which selfishness may lead men to inflict upon us, the mere *negative* absence of interest in our welfare is not without its bad effects. We sometimes meet with men who never commit any punishable crime, but who are to the last degree cold, callous, hardhearted, and selfish. We are quite sure they would not rob or murder us, but we are equally sure they would not move their little finger to do us any good—they would not raise their hand to save us from destruction. Now such men do incalculable mischief. They injure the moral nature of their neighbours, whose affections are dwarfed, or it may be destroyed, by their inhumanity, just as fruit is blighted by the frost. They do all that in them lies to make other men into moral pigmies like themselves. And since the selfish man *is* a moral pigmy, it follows that he has not only, by his selfishness, had a bad influence upon others, but that he has also thereby injured himself. True manhood is only attained by him who has learnt to live in the lives of his fellow-men. That which pre-eminently distinguishes a human being from a brute is the latent capacity to identify the lives of others with his own. The isolated individual, confined to the narrow sphere of his own private desires and pleasures, is not, properly speaking, to be called a man. The meagre, paltry life of such an one is more fitly described as death. So long as we remain shut up within ourselves, we are, in the emphatic language of the Bible, lost. We cannot realise ourselves within ourselves; we cannot come to perfection by ourselves. It is the very purpose of our existence that the petty life which pertains to us as units should be expanded and developed, so as to embrace the wider, richer, diviner life of the family, the community, the race.

When this development is taking place within us, we are being saved. Christ saw, more clearly than any of the world's teachers before or since, that the eradication of selfishness, if it could be accomplished, would be at once the destruction of evil and the perfecting of humanity. Christ felt this so keenly, and dwelt upon it so frequently, that it was possible for Him to *sum up* the whole of His teaching in the one great commandment which bids us love one another. Selfishness is only to be eradicated by love. The spirit of love, therefore, is absolutely essential to salvation; and he who feels himself devoid of it may know for certain that he is not being saved. Salvation consists in being rescued, not from hell, but from the conduct which leads to hell. It is, of course, possible to be as selfish in seeking heaven as in trying to make a fortune upon earth. We may endeavour to get there simply because we believe it to be a comfortable and desirable place; we may take pleasure in the thought that it will be restricted to a small number of persons; or at any rate, we may feel perfectly indifferent as to what becomes of the rest. Now, to seek heaven in this way is, according to Christ, to fit oneself for hell. A man cannot avail himself of Christ's salvation in selfish isolation from his fellows; for the very essence of that salvation is unselfishness. To think of nothing but saving one's own soul is the surest way to lose it. We can only—at least so Christ most plainly teaches —we can only work out our own salvation by learning to be kind. Christianity is unselfishness, or it is nothing.

But, it may be asked, if Christianity be merely unselfishness, why did Christ insist so strongly upon faith? Did not He who laid down the new commandment also say, " God so loved the world, that He gave His only begotten Son, that whosoever believeth in Him might not perish, but have everlasting life"? Yes, He did; and the explanation is very simple. Christ laid stress upon faith just because He laid still greater stress upon love and its consequent unselfishness. Faith is the means, unselfishness is the end. And for the complete accomplishment of the end no other means will suffice. It is this demand for faith which renders Christ's religion so pre-eminently reasonable. By this demand it may be best distinguished from other systems, such as Buddhism and Positivism, which also insist upon the importance of kindliness and love. The founder of Buddhism, five hundred years before Christ, had given utterance to the golden rule, and had set so splendid an example of a self-sacrificing life that it has never been surpassed, save by Him whom we call Lord. The founder of Positivism insisted, and his followers still continue to insist, with the greatest earnestness and eloquence, upon the duty of letting our affections go forth unreservedly and enthusiastically towards all who bear, or ever shall bear, the form of man. But though these systems agree with Christianity in the inculcation of unselfishness, they differ from Christianity inasmuch as they rest upon no rational foundation. Christianity alone provides, in the doctrine of eternal life, a reasonable basis for unselfishness. It must be admitted that occasionally individuals have succeeded in manifesting goodness and self-sacrifice without any belief in immortality. But they have done so only by a noble inconsistency. What is the use of character to a being whose ultimate end is extinction or unconsciousness? And why should he concern himself about his fellows? If he thinks that they may at any moment be turned into clay, how can he feel for them reverence or love? Belief in eternal life is the only true foundation for morality and religion. Nothing will help a man so clearly to recognise the extreme importance of character, and to take so keen an interest in the welfare of his fellows, as the conviction that there is latent within himself and them "the power of an endless life." And this stimulus is experienced by the man who has faith in Christ. But faith means still more. Christ said that it consisted in "eating the flesh and drinking the blood of the Son of Man." No words could express a closer or more absolute union. They imply the absorption not only of the beliefs, but also of the feelings and emotions and aims of the Redeemer. They imply that the nature of the Master will "pass into and become" the nature of the disciple. When this transformation is effected in us — and not till then — we shall take an enthusiastic interest in the welfare of every member of the human

Practical Nature of Christianity. 301

race, we shall love others as Christ has loved us.

This was the aim of the Redeemer. And who, I ask, can compare with it the conduct of Christians without being startled by the contrast? startled not so much because they fall short of the standard—that was to be expected—but because in so many instances they have another standard altogether. Some have set up the standard of creed. The one thing needful, they fancy, is to be orthodox. And being sure that their own opinions are correct, they consider themselves at liberty to hate, to vilify, to persecute, perhaps even to exterminate, those whose opinions are different from their own. They will fight over the definition of the very Prince of Peace! Others have erected the standard of ritual. So long as they perform certain ceremonies, they feel quite sure of heaven. They will go to an early celebration, and afterwards make themselves troublesome and disagreeable at home. Nothing would induce them to use a needle and thread on Sunday, but they will spend almost the entire day in endeavouring to ruin a neighbour's reputation. They bow profoundly at the name of Jesus; but as for His new commandment, He might as well never have uttered it at all for any perceptible influence which it exerts over their lives. It is constantly said that those who profess Christianity are not better than other men, but, on the contrary, rather worse—narrower in their sympathies, harsher in their judgments, more petty in their aims, more grossly selfish in their conduct,—a peculiar people indeed, but only in the sense of being peculiarly unpleasant. The accusation is often but too just. And it is easy to see the incalculable mischief which must have been done to the cause of Christianity by the illegitimate assumption of the name of Christian. Christianity has been but little injured by open, honest opposition. But those who think they are Christians, when they are nothing of the kind—the false professors of Christianity—have very nearly been its ruin. Their whole lives are in flagrant contradiction to the fundamental principles of Christianity. But having chosen to call themselves after His name, they have made His religion appear contemptible and vile. "They have crucified the Son of God afresh and put Him to an open shame."

"Face loved of little children long ago,
   Head hated of the priests and rulers then,
Say, was not this thy Passion, to foreknow
   In Thy death's hour the deeds of Christian men?"

Do not, I beseech you, judge Christianity by

Practical Nature of Christianity. 303

the worst of those who call themselves Christians. Do not even judge it by the best. Look at it as it was taught by Christ. Without it humanity can never be made perfect. Unselfishness is essential to the complete development both of the individual and of the race. And by far the best stimulus to unselfishness is the inspiring influence of Jesus. The misrepresentations and superstitions which have obscured and disfigured His Gospel are bound sooner or later, like all evil things, to be exposed and destroyed. Then Christianity will enter on a career of rapid and triumphant progress — progress that will never cease until there is a new earth wherein dwelleth righteousness, until the new Jerusalem has descended out of heaven from God.[1]

[1] In regard to the progress of Christianity, see also the concluding discourse in my 'Origin of Evil, and other Sermons.'

Antagonism between Dogma and Philosophy.

PAPER READ BEFORE THE JUNIOR CLERGY SOCIETY,
ON FEBRUARY 9, 1886.

BY Dogma, I understand a creed which claims to be final and all-comprehensive. By philosophy, I understand the progressive explanation of things.

"That is dogma," says Mr Garbett, p. 18, in his Bampton Lectures on Dogmatic Faith, "and that alone, upon which has been set the seal of the Divine infallibility." This is precisely what I do *not* mean by dogma. With the fact or the nature of the inspiration of the Scriptures I am not at all at present concerned. What I have to say against dogma is as valid on the view of plenary inspiration, as it would be if there were no such thing as inspiration at all. Dogma is not the Scriptures, but an interpretation of the Scriptures; and no interpretation can claim for itself the infallibility belonging to that which is interpreted.

The highest degree of fallibility in dogma is perfectly compatible with the highest degree of infallibility in the Scriptures. Mr Garbett farther on, p. 20, alters his definition of dogma, as of course it was necessary for him to do, if his treatise were to be at all applicable to the subject he had in hand. He says: " I employ the word dogma for a revealed truth [that is the same use of it as before], AND for ecclesiastical formulas so far, and so far only, as they truly express the mind of God. It is a condition arising from the delivery of the faith into the charge of the saints, that the formulating of its truths, for convenience and instruction and defence, is necessarily a human work. Nor will any one deny the abstract possibility of human error in the process." So that dogmas in this second sense—in the sense, namely, of ecclesiastical formulas—are not dogmas in the first sense; they are not things "on which has been set the seal of the Divine infallibility;" they are things in regard to which we must admit "the abstract possibility of human error." On p. 17 he says: " Dogma is only another word for a positive truth, positively asserted, in contrast to an opinion, conjecture, or speculation. It is a proposition regarded as so certainly true as to be presented for acceptance, but not for discussion." But on p. 19 he admits that "positiveness of statement is incongruous with what is human;" and therefore, inasmuch as the formulating of Christian truth is, according to Mr Garbett's own confession, a human work involving abstract possibility of error, positiveness of statement is inadmissible in the case of formulæ.

Mr Garbett's confusion between revealed truth and its interpretation is very common, but most unfortunate. There are no two things which should be more carefully distinguished; otherwise authority may be claimed for both which belongs only to one, or be denied to both when it should only be denied to one. The absurdity of classing the two things together should be apparent on the hastiest glance at ecclesiastical history, for a considerable portion of that history is taken up with an account of the controversies and wranglings that arose from time to time in regard to the interpretative formulæ. If there were *one* dogmatic system, the whole of which the believers in dogma had always embraced, and none of which they had ever disputed, we could understand its being put on the same level as revealed truth and

Dogma and Philosophy. 307

considered infallible. It would have in its favour, if not the *consensus gentium,* yet the *consensus ecclesiæ.* But there is no such system. Dogma, which is supposed to be indisputably certain, has always been the battle-ground of the fiercest and most protracted disputes. Even the Popes, from the very chair of St Peter, have given forth contradictory utterances. The truth is one and the same, but there are endless differences in the interpretation of it. The Bible is "the book where each his dogma seeks and each his dogma finds." These diversified, and often contradictory, interpretations cannot possibly express the mind of God, in the same way and with the same authority as the one unchanging truth which they are supposed to interpret. We have Homoousianism and Homoiousianism, Arianism and Athanasianism, the expiatory and revelatory theories of the Atonement, the Romish, Lutheran, and Zwinglian view of the Eucharist, eternal punishment, annihilation, and universalism, and a hundred other incompatible doctrines,—all professing to be the correct interpretation of Bible truth. Since, then, revealed truth is one and unchangeable, and the formulæ many and variable, why in the name of common sense should we class the two things together?

The distinction between the Scriptures and

their interpretation is clearly recognised by our Church in the XXIst Article: " General councils when they be gathered together (forasmuch as they be an assembly of men, whereof all be not governed with the Spirit and Word of God) may err, and sometimes have erred, even in things pertaining unto God. Wherefore things ordained by them as necessary to salvation have neither strength nor authority, unless it may be declared that they be taken out of Holy Scriptures."

By dogma then, in this paper, I shall understand an interpretation of the Bible, or a humanly devised formula, not the Bible itself.

There is another distinction of very great importance—viz., the distinction between a creed and a dogma. Every dogma is a creed; but the converse is not true—every creed is not a dogma. A dogma is a creed which claims for itself an infallibility that must never be doubted, an authority that must never be gainsaid, a completeness and perfection that can never be surpassed. The sceptic flippantly despises creeds; the dogmatist slavishly cringes before them; the philosopher takes the *via media*—

> " Not clinging to some ancient saw,
> Not mastered by some modern term,
> Not swift, nor slow to change, but firm "—

firm in his allegiance to the truth—so firm, that when he really finds a belief to be erroneous he will venture to discard it, no matter whose belief it may have been. A creed is a means to progress; a dogma is a barrier against progress. Dogmas, therefore, are most injurious; creeds most useful. Creeds are needed in every sphere of investigation. G. H. Lewes tells us, in his 'Seaside Studies,' that for years very little progress was made in zoology, because the workers in that department of science had no definite creed to guide them. There is no antagonism between philosophy and creeds; on the contrary, creeds are the handmaids of philosophy. A creed means, etymologically and really, that which is believed. It is a register of results in the search for truth. It is a landmark showing the point which has been reached in the march of human thought—a march which never can have an end. A creed consists of the opinions arrived at in a certain age, by certain men, on certain subjects, which they have transmitted (or ought to have transmitted) for the guidance, and not for the extinction, of future thought and investigation. It is a starting-point, not a goal. Just as an invading army (to use an illustration of Hamilton's) makes good each position gained by planting a citadel, in order that they may be better able to set forth again to larger and more certain conquests; so it is necessary that creeds should be constructed, in order that men may be better prepared for making further progress into the still outstanding, still unexplored realms of truth. This is clearly recognised in the daily service of our Church, which is brought to a close with the prayer of St Chrysostom. For the words, "granting us in this world knowledge of Thy truth," dogmatists ought to substitute, "granting us in this world remembrance of our creed." A creed becomes a dogma, and in becoming a dogma becomes a curse, when it sets itself up as an infallible, perfect, and ultimate exposition of truth. Let me then ask you to bear in mind that what I now say has not the slightest reference to *creeds*, which are aids to progressive reflection and investigation. I am speaking exclusively against *dogmas*, which are confessedly incompatible with progress.

Aristotle defines Philosophy as "the art of doubting well." Dogma may be defined as the art of believing ill. Dogma believes, or tries to believe, it knows all the truth, in order that it may thereby avoid the trouble of seeking any. Philosophy doubts whether it knows any, in order that it may seek all. To philosophise, or to doubt well, is to doubt, not as the Pyrrhonist, but as the Cartesian. Descartes tells us, in his tract on his Method: "As I made it my business in each matter to reflect particularly upon what might fairly be doubted and prove a source of error, I gradually rooted out from my mind all the errors which had hitherto crept into it; not that in this I imitated the sceptics, who doubt only that they may doubt, and seek nothing beyond uncertainty itself; for, on the contrary, my design was simply to find ground of assurance, and cast aside the loose earth and sand, that I might reach the rock or the clay." Philosophy is the attempt progressively to explain the words nature, man, and God. Philosophy says with the Apostle Paul, "Prove all things." *Impavidi progrediamur* is, or should be, the watchword of philosophers. Philosophy perceives that Truth is high as heaven, deep as hell, broad as the universe, infinite as God, everlasting as eternity.[1] Philosophy is painfully conscious that there is

> "A deep below the deep,
> And a height beyond the height:
> Our hearing is not hearing,
> And our seeing is not sight."

What would you think of an athlete who was

[1] See also three sermons on the connection between reason and faith in my 'Defects of Modern Christianity.'

going to run a race, and who became so enamoured of the arrangements at the first end of the course, that while others were pressing on towards the goal, he contented himself with going round and round the starting-post? No less absurd is the man who thinks that, as soon as he can repeat his creed like a parrot, he has mastered truth. It is an old remark, but one as true as it is old, that truth cannot be symbolised by a circle, but rather by an infinite line. The men who think they have given the ultimate explanation of universal mystery, or of any part of it, must be either madmen or fools. In the nature of things a finite mind can never do more than approximate to a knowledge of the infinite; but, generation after generation, we ought to be getting nearer to that full and adequate knowledge which can never be actually attained. There will never come a time when we shall not be able to say—

"Yet I doubt not through the ages one unceasing purpose runs,
And the thoughts of men are broadened with the progress of
    the suns."

But dogma has never understood this, and will never understand it.[1] "We are the people, and

[1] The spirit of the dogmatists is amusingly illustrated in Hodge's 'Systematic Theology,' where the author gives the

Dogma and Philosophy. 313

wisdom will die with us," say the dogmatists. "The whole of the human race, save the small minority holding our opinions, were altogether and damnably in the wrong; we, an infinitesimal minority, are altogether right."[1]

Dogma was once coextensive with universal knowledge. It forbade original thought and research, not only in theology, but even in the physical sciences. Even now the worst of the dogmatists watch over the investigations of the physicists with the angriest jealousy. I remember a year or two ago at Cambridge, when a University preacher suggested in the course of his sermon that *if* the theory of evolution should ever be established the Christian religion would

various views that have been held about the various doctrines, ending up always with what he calls the right view, which is a pleasing synonym for the less harmonious expression—Hodge's view.

[1] The smallness of the minority, so far from causing uneasiness to the dogmatists, is often a source of self-congratulation. There is a story told of a man who was engaged in writing a book about sects. He was informed that in the extreme north of Scotland there was a small denomination which was quickly dying out. He went up in search of it; and when he came to the village, he was directed to the house of the leading member. The great man was not at home, but our investigator entered into conversation with the great man's wife. He said to her he had been informed that their numbers were small. "''Deed ay, sir," said the woman, "there's jist mysel' an' Jock, an' I'm na sae very sure o' Jock."

not be thereby invalidated, two or three old dons got up and walked out of the church. Dogma had said that God made the world in one way, and *the mere supposition* that He *could* have made it in another these old gentlemen regarded as the most unpardonable heresy.

Most of the dogmatists, however, have now relinquished their claim to superintend the natural sciences. They resisted as long as they could; but they found at last that they were playing a losing game, and that their position was becoming constantly more and more ignominious. Some of them are now bold enough to say they never attacked scientific truths. Cardinal Cullen, five or six years ago, declared that the Church did not really oppose the doctrine of Galileo, but only *seemed* to oppose it. The wiser portion of the dogmatists, or, more accurately speaking, the less foolish portion, have been led, by a painful and inglorious experience, to hand over natural philosophy almost entirely to the mercy of scientific specialists. They have now intrenched themselves in the citadel of theology. This is their *dernier ressort*, and they know it.

Let us ask, Have the dogmatists any more right in theology than they have anywhere else? Why should not theology, like other sciences, be content to be progressive? Why should it set itself up as the *ne plus ultra* of the knowledge of God? Theology is confessedly a human work, and can have therefore no claim to infallibility. The Regius Professor of Divinity in the University of Oxford drew attention some time ago to the danger of theology becoming stagnant, and warned theologians against resting content with the mere reproduction of the past.[1] But dogmatists think that theology should be stagnant, and they regard the attempt to get beyond our ancestors as a sort of juvenile impertinence. It is a very common, but a very false, argument from analogy, that our ancestors must have known more than we can know, because they were born before us. The reason why a father is wiser than his child (if he be wiser) is not, of course, that he was born first, but that he has lived longer, and therefore had more experience. When a child has grown up, he may be, and should be, wiser than his father; for he has had the benefit of his father's experience, and he has

---

[1] The theologian who is not a dogmatist, but a philosopher, will say with the poet:—

> "Our little systems have their day,
> They have their day and cease to be;
> They are but broken lights of Thee,
> And thou, O Lord, art *more* than they."

had his own experience besides. As Bacon long ago pointed out, if he who has had most experience be rightly regarded as the father of him who has had least, then *we* are the fathers and grandfathers of our ancestors; for they had their experience, but not ours; we have had the benefit of both. All honour to them for the truths which they discovered! All shame to us if we do not discover more!

To do the theologians justice, they are not alone in their dogmatism. The "eternal popery of the human heart" has been exemplified even by philosophy itself—at least by something that was falsely called philosophy. Of all kinds of dogma, that of would-be philosophers is the worst and most unjustifiable. They, at any rate, should have known better. Philosophy professes to be the very antithesis to dogma. A dogmatist can no more be a philosopher, in the proper acceptation of the term, than a dumb man can give lessons in elocution. In so far as philosophy has become dogmatic, it has been false to itself—it has ceased to be philosophy.

Look at Aristotelianism during the middle ages—when the logic, and the physics, and the metaphysics of Aristotle had been exalted into dogmas. The gospel of that period was the anagram which had been made out of the name of the Stagirite: *Aristoteles iste sol erat.* Human ambition rose no higher than to shine with a light borrowed from this "sol." Hardly any one dreamed of thinking for himself. The circle of human knowledge was made to coincide with the discoveries of Aristotle. There is a story told of a certain monk who had detected some spots on the sun, and who rushed to his father superior to tell him of the phenomenon. The reply of his superior (so called) must, I should fancy, have made a cynic of that monk for the rest of his life. "My son," said the holy and silly father, "I have read through Aristotle many times, and I find no mention of any such thing; therefore rest assured either your glass or your vision is defective." Another of these reverend fathers refused to look through a telescope, for fear he should see something which had never been observed by Aristotle. A certain professor of philosophy in Padua came to Galileo, and requested that he would explain to him the meaning of the word parallax, which he said he wished to refute, having heard that it was opposed to Aristotle's doctrine touching the relative situation of the earth. As late as 1624 the Parliament of Paris issued a decree banishing all who publicly maintained theses against Aristotle. In 1629 it was decreed that to contradict the principles of Aristotle was to contradict the Church; and we know what that meant in those days. When Ramus solicited the permission of Beza to teach in Geneva, he was told "the Genevese have decreed once for all that, neither in logic nor in any other branch of knowledge, will they depart from the principles of Aristotle." Gentlemen, I believe that had not a few giant souls burst the chains with which the disciples of Aristotle had loaded mankind, things would soon have come to such a pass that the whole of human life would have been regulated according to what was, or was not, contained in that philosopher's writings; that all opinions (however unimportant in themselves) would have been considered heretical and therefore indictable, that all actions (however trifling) would have been accounted criminal and therefore punishable, unless something could be found in Aristotle to justify them: so that at last a man would have stood a good chance of being expatriated for an inadvertent gape, or hanged for an untimely laugh, unless he could have proved by quotations from Aristotle the legitimacy of those relaxations. In fact the Stagirite, poor man, through no fault

Dogma and Philosophy. 319

of his own, but through the folly of his disciples in converting him into a dogma, was very nearly becoming the father of a universal reign of humbug.

Look again at Positivism, or rather Comteism. What brilliant originality and intellectual stimulus there was in Comte's earlier writings! But the later development of his system became (and justly) a laughing-stock to his enemies and a mournful sorrow to his friends. Why? Just because the later development was dogmatic. It was to be decided by the priests of Positivism what theories the common people were to believe, and what subjects the men of science were to investigate. The High Priest of Humanity proposed to saddle the world, to quote Professor Huxley's expression, with a sort of Roman Catholicism *minus* Christianity.

The radical defect of Hegelianism, too, seems to me to lie in its professed comprehensiveness and finality. I believe there is more to be learned from Hegel than from any preceding philosopher; I believe that Hegel is to be the philosopher of the future; but his system, *as a system*, seems to me to carry on the face of it its own condemnation, because it claims to be a complete explanation of the universe.

And as to theological dogma, history teems with instances of the enervating and demoralising effects which it has exercised, not only upon the ignoble and ignorant, but even upon the wisest and noblest of men. I may mention an instance or two taken almost at random. The work of Copernicus, at which he had laboured thirty years in the quiet leisure of his prebendal stall, was published after his death, and edited by Professor Ossiander, who, in the customary preface which he added, represented the whole doctrine as a hypothesis—in spite of the scientific form in which Copernicus had left it, and the superfluity of proof with which he had supported it.

Descartes, through fear of the clergy, recalled his completely finished work and submitted it to a thorough revision. Against his better convictions, he withdrew from it his theory of the revolution of the earth.

Fear of the Church, increased by so many a stake and *auto da fe*, led to a good deal of unphilosophical—not to say dishonest—"hedging." An effort after liberty of thought was made in the middle ages by the suggestion of twofold truth, philosophical and theological, which may exist side by side in spite of their entire contradiction. In this way thinkers managed to keep on good terms with dogma. *E.g.*, Occam practically threw the whole of theology overboard by declaring its doctrines incapable of proof; but theoretically he saved it by an appeal to faith— and saved himself along with it. A teacher at Paris, Jean de Brescans, excused himself in 1247 for his "errors," by observing that he had maintained the heretical doctrines only as philosophically, and not as theologically, true. Descartes introduced his account of the development of the world from small particles with the observation, that of course God had created the world at one time, but that it was very interesting to see how the world might have developed itself, although we knew it had not really done so.

The introduction of the improved Gregorian Kalendar was opposed by the Protestant clergy, merely because this correction had proceeded from the Catholic Church. The Senate of Tübingen justified their opposition by the irrational reason that Christ cannot be at one with Antichrist.

Kepler was warned by the Consistory in Stuttgart that he must subdue his too speculative spirit, and govern himself in all things according

x

to the Word of God, and leave the Church of the Lord Christ untroubled by his unnecessary subtleties, scruples and glosses.

Under the influence of dogma, Malebranche professed to believe in an objective existence of matter, which was quite incompatible with the rest of his philosophical principles; because if he had not done so, the doctrine of transubstantiation would have fallen to the ground. Under the influence of dogma, Bacon and Pascal said, in almost the same words, the more absurd and incredible [*i.e., unbelievable*] any divine mystery is, the greater honour we do God in *believing* it.

Under the influence of dogma, Hobbes—whose theory was near to open atheism, who in an atheistic State would have had any citizen hanged if he taught the existence of a God, who explains the difference between religion and superstition in this way, " Fear of power invisible feigned by the mind or imagined by tales, publicly allowed, is religion; not allowed, is superstition,"—under the influence of dogma, Hobbes uttered the following pious cant: " Seeing our faith that the Scriptures are the Word of God, began from the confidence and trust we repose in the Church, there can be no doubt but that their interpretation of the same Scriptures, where any doubt or controversy shall arise, is *safer* for any man to trust to than his own reasoning or spirit — *i.e.*, than his own opinion."

Under the influence of dogma, Galileo recanted. The *holy* Inquisition—as it called itself, with an unconscious irony which its bitterest enemies could not have surpassed,—the holy Inquisition threatened and terrified the venerable sage until they forced him into perjury. Clothed in the sackcloth of a repentant criminal, Galileo fell on his knees before the assembled cardinals, and invoked the Divine aid in abjuring the doctrine of the earth's motion and vowing never again to teach it. " In surveying the melancholy picture," says Sir David Brewster, " it is difficult to decide whether religion or philosophy was most degraded. While we witness the presumptuous priest pronouncing infallible the decrees of his own erring judgment, we see the high-minded philosopher abjuring the eternal and immutable truths which he himself had the glory of establishing."

Dogma perpetrates its iniquities in the name of religion: we cannot wonder, therefore, that by Lucretius, Swinburne and others, the two should be invariably confounded. You remember how Lucretius speaks of the hideous face of religion (i. 61); you remember, too, his often-quoted line—" To so many evils has religion persuaded man." These and all other maledictions that have been—or can ever be—uttered, are *less than the due* of dogma.

Thousands and tens of thousands of martyrs have proved their devotion to truth by the eloquent testimony of anguish. Because they refused to be false to their convictions, they were "stoned, were sawn asunder, were tempted, were slain with the sword; they were tortured, not accepting deliverance, that they might obtain a better resurrection; they had trial of cruel mockings and scourgings, yea, moreover, of bonds and imprisonment; they wandered about in sheepskins and goatskins, dwelt in deserts and in mountains, and in dens and caves of the earth, being destitute, afflicted, tormented." There has been no prophet, nor apostle, nor philosopher, nor reformer whom dogma has not execrated—against whom it has not howled out the accusation, which the Ephesians brought against St Paul, that the world was being turned by him upside down. The very truisms of one age were often regarded in the preceding generation as impious blasphemies, justly punished by fines and imprisonment, by torture and death :—

> "For all the past of time reveals
> A bridal dawn of thunder-peals,
> Whenever thought hath wedded fact."

Let me call to your minds one or two familiar illustrations. Anaxagoras, after the early Greek philosophers had long groped in vain for a First Cause, which they fancied was to be found in the principles of water, air, or fire,—Anaxagoras saw and said that the origin of all things must ultimately be traced to Intelligence. This his countrymen could not tolerate; it was too novel, too absurd. Private judgment must be punished, they said, when it wandered so far from the truth. He was banished from Greece, and had a narrow escape of death. Socrates, who was one of the first to perceive that morality must be something deeper, something altogether different, from expediency,—Socrates, whose conceptions of Deity were too lofty to tally with the childish orthodoxy of his contemporaries,—Socrates, who was brave enough to express the memorable utterance, " I will venture to be true to my conviction, though all the world oppose it,"—Socrates, the purest, the wisest, the noblest of men, was accused, forsooth, of being an atheist and of corrupting the young, and was despatched with a cup of hemlock. Giordano Bruno, one of the subtlest thinkers of the middle ages, suggested the hypothesis that our earth was not the only abode of life in the universe. For this he was arrested and burnt at the stake,—according to the words of the writ, "for the maintenance and welfare of the Holy Church, and the rights and liberties of the same." Dogma branded Spinosa with the name of atheist: whereas the real fault of his system is, that he completely loses his own personality in the Divine; as Hegel put it, "There is too much of God in Spinosa." Dogma embittered the lives of Frederick Maurice and Frederick Robertson, because they were too pure to acquiesce in all the meannesses and superstitions then current in the Church. But the crowning iniquity of dogma is this—it crucified Jesus of Nazareth, because His life was too sublime, too divine, to tally with orthodox Pharisaism.

Well then, gentlemen, I maintain that philosophy and dogma are as opposite as light and darkness; *are*, in fact, light and darkness. One can only exist by the displacement of the other. In proportion as a man is under the influence of dogma, so far will he be destitute of the philosophical spirit; in proportion as a man is a philosopher, so far will he be opposed to dogma. The conflict between dogma and philosophy—between the art of doubting well and the art of believing ill—is a hand-to-hand, life-and-death struggle. Sometimes in the past the one has been victorious, and sometimes the other. Sooner or later one will be destroyed; and I think the signs of the times warrant me in saying that that one will *not* be philosophy.[1]

[1] As will be seen from a reference to my volume on 'Inspiration,' I do not believe in the infallibility of the Bible. But I have argued here *ad hominem*, and shown that dogma is, and must be, fallible, even though we assume the plenary inspiration of the Scriptures.

THE END.

PRINTED BY WILLIAM BLACKWOOD AND SONS.

WORKS BY PROFESSOR MOMERIE.

I.

PERSONALITY;

THE BEGINNING AND END OF METAPHYSICS,

AND A NECESSARY ASSUMPTION IN ALL POSITIVE PHILOSOPHY.

Fourth Edition, revised. Crown 8vo, 3s.

"This is a little book, but it contains more sound philosophy than many pretentious treatises....... In an admirably lucid way the author scatters to the winds the baseless assumptions of the sense philosophy."—*British Quarterly Review.*

"It is not often that we have to complain of the brevity of a sermon or of a treatise on philosophy; but in the case of a little book of the latter kind, recently published anonymously, we have found the arguments so cogent, the style so clear, and the matter at issue so important, that we heartily wish that the writer had allowed himself room for the fuller treatment of his subject....... We confidently refer our readers to this well-reasoned volume."—*Modern Review.*

"Professor Momerie's remarks on the doctrines of the defenders of empiricism present a close, and thoroughly scientific, examination of the views these thinkers put forth as to the nature of sensation, perception, and cognition....... The arguments are throughout conducted with marked logical power, and the conclusions are very important in relation to the present aspect of philosophical thought in England."—*Scotsman.*

"The work under our notice will well repay the careful reading of those who wish to have at their command plain answers to modern positivism."—*Ecclesiastical Gazette.*

"His discussion of these questions stamps Dr Momerie as an acute metaphysician, a philosophical scholar, and a powerful dialectician."—*Glasgow Herald.*

"When published anonymously received a very hearty welcome by all who were interested in the advent of a new writer of great power, of happy diction, and of independent thinking."—*Montrose Standard.*

WILLIAM BLACKWOOD & SONS, EDINBURGH AND LONDON.

And all Booksellers.

II.

THE ORIGIN OF EVIL;

AND OTHER SERMONS.

Sixth Edition. Crown 8vo, 5s.

"Professor Momerie has done well to publish his sermons; they are good reading....... A real contribution to the side of common-sense religion."—*Saturday Review.*

"We decidedly recommend them to persons perplexed by the speculations of modern science."—*Spectator.*

"This is a remarkable volume of sermons. Though it consists of only about 300 pages, it contains an amount of thought and learning which might have been expanded into a bulky folio."—*Glasgow Mail.*

"These sermons are some of the very best produced in this country within the last hundred years."—*Inquirer.*

"The author is an original thinker, whose sympathies are very wide."—*Guardian.*

"Those who preach may learn much from their perusal."—*Christian World.*

"Out of the common run, they give one a refreshing sense of novelty and power."—*Glasgow Herald.*

"Die Vorträge zeigen allenthalben eine schöne Harmonie zwischen Schriftwahrheit und Lebenswahrheit."—*Deutsches Litteraturblatt.*

"Der Verfasser behandelt in diesen Vorträgen wichtige Fragen aus dem Gebiet des christlichen Lebens. Wir heben besonders die über das Leiden hervor, in denen der Verfasser tiefe beherzigenswerthe Gedanken ausspricht. Wir nehmen keinen Anstand, diese Vorträge zum Besten zu rechnen, was über diesen Gegenstand gesagt worden."—*Christliches Bücherschatz.*

"The author of the 'Origin of Evil' will go sadly astray if he does not make his mark on the age."—*London Figaro.*

"We should almost like to have heard these sermons preached. We are willing to read them carefully, and recommend them to others for like reading, even though, in almost every instance, we dissent from the author's pleading."—*National Reformer.*

"These sermons are everything that sermons ought *not* to be."—*English Independent.*

WILLIAM BLACKWOOD & SONS, EDINBURGH AND LONDON.

And all Booksellers.

III.

DEFECTS OF MODERN CHRISTIANITY;
AND OTHER SERMONS.

Fourth Edition. Crown 8vo, 5s.

"Throughout Mr Momerie's attractive little volume the morning air of the new world breathes through the dry leaves of the old theology."—*Westminster Review.*

"There is an intellectuality, spirituality, and a simplicity in Mr Momerie's sermons, that should make them models for young preachers."—*Christian Union.*

"Professor Momerie, by his former books, has already laid the foundation of a reputation as a philosophical thinker and an able expositor of religious subjects. The present volume is marked by equal ability, intellectual force, independent and original thinking, and will confirm the favourable opinion which he has already produced.......Whatever views readers may detect as different from their own, they will not fail to admire the author's powerful enforcement of the practical side of Christianity.......There follows, as the second part of the volume, nine lectures on the Book of Job; and we have not read before, within the same compass, a more masterly and interesting exposition of that great poem.......There are also three admirable sermons on 'The Connection between Reason and Faith,' which will repay repeated reading.......The volume deserves to be widely read; and whether readers agree or not in all respects with the author, they will not rise from the perusal without feeling that Christianity is something grander than they have ordinarily realised it to be, and that the Christian life is the bravest and most beautiful life possible."—*Aberdeen Journal.*

"Very fresh and striking."—*Globe.*

"Although he is a polished and accomplished scholar, he simply defies the conventionalities of churches and schools."—*Literary World.*

WILLIAM BLACKWOOD & SONS, EDINBURGH AND LONDON.

And all Booksellers.

IV.

THE BASIS OF RELIGION;

BEING AN EXAMINATION OF 'NATURAL RELIGION.'

Third Edition. Crown 8vo, 2s. 6d.

"As a controversialist, Professor Momerie is no less candid than he is remorselessly severe."—*Scotsman.*

"As a revelation of the pretentiousness of that philosophy [Positivism], Dr Momerie's powerful essay is very valuable."—*Fifeshire Journal.*

"The result of profound study and earnest thought......This attempt to sketch out a basis for rational theology is fitted to the needs of the times. ......Professor Momerie has won for himself a name as one of the most powerful and original thinkers of the day."—*Globe.*

"Professor Momerie has wide views of men and things, resembling in this quality the author of 'Ecce Homo' himself, and he has attacked from the Cambridge University pulpit the book 'Natural Religion,' accusing it of considerable vagueness of conception and of considerable misconception of critical points of its own argument. The present book presents the substance of these sermons in the form of a brief essay.......We would recommend our readers to see for themselves how those confusions of thought, by which the school of writers—of whom the author of 'Natural Religion' is an eminent representative—seek to save religion when supernaturalism has disappeared, are exposed. We are certain they will be charmed with the accurate philosophical thinking of Professor Momerie, with his unpretentious display of keen logical reasoning, conveyed in lucid and forcible language which arrays and adorns it like a well-fitting garment."—*Eskdale Advertiser.*

"Greater force is given to this essay, since the author is himself an advanced thinker."—*Christian Union.*

WILLIAM BLACKWOOD & SONS, EDINBURGH AND LONDON.

And all Booksellers.

V.

AGNOSTICISM.

Third Edition. Crown 8vo, 5s.

"To readers who do not demand that 'the scheme of salvation in its fulness' should be enunciated in every sermon, this volume, which is happily free from rhetoric, and for the most part from any ostentation of the reading which it indicates, will be interesting from its acuteness, learning, and insight."—*Saturday Review.*

"This is a really good book. It is profound in thought, large and comprehensive in view, liberal in spirit, and delightfully clear and simple in style. We wish that theologians and philosophers in general would write in Professor Momerie's manner.......Following the chapters on Agnosticism, there are ten other chapters on the book of Ecclesiastes. They form an admirable and scholarly analysis of that strange and melancholy book."—*The Inquirer.*

"We are thankful for so masterly, so comprehensive, and so complete a vindication of the principles of Christian Theism, with its powerful refutation of the main positions of Agnosticism. The book meets a real and widespread need, in a style as trenchant and effective as it is popular."—*Freeman.*

"Dr Momerie's breadth of intellect and sympathy, his clear thinking and well-chastened style, as well as his deep religiousness, which will, no doubt, after a time assume a more positively evangelical form, eminently adapt him to be a teacher to his generation. He has freed himself, by we know not what process, from many of the prejudices of the older schools ; but he can search into the very soul of unbelieving sophistry, and the spirit of his exhortation is always ennobling and heavenward."—*Methodist Times.*

"It is long since we have met with a volume of sermons which will so well repay a careful study."—*Ecclesiastical Gazette.*

"The work of a majestic intellect."—*Fifeshire Journal.*

WILLIAM BLACKWOOD & SONS, EDINBURGH AND LONDON.

And all Booksellers.

VI.

PREACHING AND HEARING;

AND OTHER SERMONS.

Third Edition. Crown 8vo, 5s.

"The author, himself one of the most eloquent preachers of the day, is eminently qualified to do justice to his subject. He has brought to it an experience and scholarly proficiency which few men could have done."—*Christian Union.*

"For such preaching as this, and for all the ample learning and wise thought by which it is fortified, the Church of God has every reason to be thankful."—*Literary World.*

"Marked by all the force, acuteness, and eloquence which we have learnt to expect from him, and in addition by a knowledge of men and manners not generally associated with philosophical research......His literary style is another proof, if proof were needed, of the vast resources of the simple Anglo-Saxon."—*Fifeshire Journal.*

"His sermons are unlike any sermons we can call to mind."—*Guardian.*

"If such sermons were often to be heard from the pulpit, preachers would not have to complain of empty pews or inattentive listeners."—*Rock.*

"Their delivery was quite startling."—*Swansea Journal.*

"Those who would know what pulpit boldness in the present day really means should make these sermons their study."—*Christian World.*

"The present volume is more directly popular in style, and amply maintains the reputation of the writer."—*Inquirer.*

WILLIAM BLACKWOOD & SONS, EDINBURGH AND LONDON.

And all Booksellers.

VII.

BELIEF IN GOD.

Second Edition.   Crown 8vo, 3s.

"One of the most brilliant arguments for the Divine existence."—*Christian World.*

"In some respects Professor Momerie is the ablest preacher of his day. ......He is ever endeavouring to present recondite problems in the simplest, clearest language, and in this he is eminently successful....... It is not too abstruse even for mere smatterers in philosophical discussion. Considering its scope, it is indeed astonishingly lucid."—*Dundee Advertiser.*

"No preacher need be ashamed to face the most scientific sceptic with this little book in his hand."—*Literary World.*

"From the time that Professor Momerie published anonymously the volume on 'The Origin of Evil,' his writings have been devoured with exceptional keenness by intelligent readers. Many were the conjectures as to who the author of that work was, but it was universally allowed that the anonymous writer was destined to leave his mark upon the mind of the country: he was a daring and fresh thinker, and was possessed of rare unravelling power. This little volume bears the impress of his majestic intellect....... It is a model of lucid style, clear and consecutive reasoning, fairness to an honourable opponent, and humility in victory."—*Perthshire Advertiser.*

"'Belief in God' was originally written for the 'Helps to Belief' Series, but the editor, thinking it too abstruse, recommended considerable alterations. We are devoutly thankful the gifted Professor refused to mutilate his work, and withdrew it from the series."—*Nonconformist.*

"His criticism of Herbert Spencer's theory of the Unknowable is very acute."—*Glasgow Herald.*

"It is spread out into only eighty pages, but those eighty pages contain more material for thought than many another volume or series of volumes contain in eight hundred."—*Inquirer.*

WILLIAM BLACKWOOD & SONS, EDINBURGH AND LONDON.

And all Booksellers.

VIII.

INSPIRATION;
AND OTHER SERMONS.

Second Edition.   Crown 8vo, 5s.

"Canon Liddon, preaching last Sunday afternoon in St Paul's Cathedral, declared that it would be difficult to maintain the authority of Christ as a teacher of religious truth if the Book of Daniel were written in the second, and not in the sixth century B.C. Statements of this kind are as deplorable as they are unwarranted.......A happier and a wiser method of dealing with the relations of science and criticism to the Scriptures has been adopted by Professor Momerie in his new volume."—*Christian World.*

"The gifted Professor has broken at many points with rigid orthodoxy. He is a Broad Churchman of the Broad Churchmen. But his very breadth and catholicity of view, the unswerving steadfastness of his search after truth, and his gift of powerful expression, make him an ally whom even the narrowest sticklers for the faith without change cannot be blind enough to throw over."—*Fifeshire Journal.*

"The sermons on 'Pessimism' constitute a treatise in themselves."—*Irish Ecclesiastical Gazette.*

"The abilities of Dr Momerie, and his services with respect to those questions in which the spheres of religion and philosophy touch, are well known; and there is much in the present volume that will repay attentive perusal. The treatment of pessimism leaves nothing to be desired."—*Saturday Review.*

"Professor Momerie's latest volume fully bears out his reputation for originality, vigour, and lucidity."—*John Bull.*

"A unique contribution to the literature of the day."—*Lady's Pictorial.*

"Here is a bold note, boldly struck; it is only one of many in the book that deserve the attention of opponents as well as friends, and that only a brave man dared touch."—*Scottish Leader.*

"In the course of this remarkable book he passes in review many of the doctrinal questions which are now agitating the Church, and gives a rational explanation of some of the difficulties that perplex both young and old students of theology."—*Dundee Advertiser.*

"Professor Momerie has approached his work with a mental penetration and spiritual devotion worthy of so distinguished a Biblical scholar. The initial chapter, which discusses 'The Evolution of the Bible,' is a masterly exposition. There is a freshness and potency in the author's thought and reasoning that both charm and convince."—*Christian Union.*

WILLIAM BLACKWOOD & SONS, EDINBURGH AND LONDON.

And all Booksellers.

IX.

CHURCH AND CREED.

Second Edition. Crown 8vo, 4s. 6d.

"I cannot say that I am in the habit of reading many sermons. But I did read 'Church and Creed,' and I can recommend them to all those desirous of allying religion with common-sense."—*Truth.*

"Short, pithy, brilliant discourses."—*The World.*

"Persons who still retain the old-fashioned notion that an ordained clergyman holds, in some sense, a brief for the defence, will be bewildered by this wholesale tearing to pieces of dogmas and creeds; and many more, while admiring much in the sermons themselves, will probably take exception, not so much to what is said as to where it is said. 'Church and Creed,' however, is a remarkable book, and a sign of the times which will be noted with different feelings by various classes of thinkers."—*Life.*

"Original, fearless, reverent criticism."—*Yorkshire Post.*

"Simple yet masterly."—*Lincolnshire Free Press.*

"The discourses, one and all, in the volume before us are indeed works of art."—*Glasgow Herald.*

"His lessons on self-sacrifice are well worth careful attention."—*Ecclesiastical Gazette.*

"Dr Momerie is a law unto himself, and is a great illustration of the freedom of thought allowed in the English pulpit. Take for example the sermon in the present volume, entitled 'The Gods of the Bible,' and see what a new face it puts upon our cherished notions of a uniform deistic belief. The whole of the present volume overflows with similar dry, fearless, decisive, almost caustic enunciations that cut athwart hereditary faiths, and it requires a strong mind to follow the preacher as he advances from one startling proposition to another."—*Irish Ecclesiastical Gazette.*

"It is this cheerful and healthful view of life, combined with a hatred of all bigotry and narrowness, that makes Professor Momerie's sermons the inspiration that crowded congregations find them. The man who can persuade people in these pessimistic days that God meant them to laugh and enjoy the life He has given them, and yet be in the truest sense of the word religious, is doing a service to the age which it greatly needs."—*Literary World.*

"It is to be earnestly hoped that the great Head of the Church will raise up an Athanasius in our midst to combat and refute the errors with which it abounds."—*Newbery House Magazine.*

WILLIAM BLACKWOOD & SONS, EDINBURGH AND LONDON.

And all Booksellers.

CATALOGUE

OF

MESSRS BLACKWOOD & SONS' PUBLICATIONS.

PHILOSOPHICAL CLASSICS FOR ENGLISH READERS.
EDITED BY WILLIAM KNIGHT, LL.D.,
Professor of Moral Philosophy in the University of St Andrews.

In crown 8vo Volumes, with Portraits, price 3s. 6d.

Now ready—

DESCARTES, by Professor Mahaffy, Dublin.—BUTLER, by Rev. W. Lucas Collins, M.A.—BERKELEY, by Professor Campbell Fraser, Edinburgh.—FICHTE, by Professor Adamson, Owens College, Manchester.—KANT, by Professor Wallace, Oxford.—HAMILTON, by Professor Veitch, Glasgow.—HEGEL, by Professor Edward Caird, Glasgow.—LEIBNIZ, by J. Theodore Merz.—VICO, by Professor Flint, Edinburgh—HOBBES, by Professor Croom Robertson, London.—HUME, by the Editor.—SPINOZA, by the Very Rev. Principal Caird, Glasgow.—BACON: Part I. The Life by Professor Nichol, Glasgow.—BACON: Part II. Philosophy, by the same Author.—LOCKE, by Professor Campbell Fraser, Edinburgh.

In preparation.
MILL, by the Right Hon. A. J. Balfour.

FOREIGN CLASSICS FOR ENGLISH READERS.
EDITED BY MRS OLIPHANT.

In crown 8vo, 2s. 6d.

Contents of the Series.

DANTE, by the Editor.—VOLTAIRE, by General Sir E. B. Hamley, K.C.B.—PASCAL, by Principal Tulloch.—PETRARCH, by Henry Reeve, C.B.—GOETHE, By A. Hayward, Q.C.—MOLIÈRE, by the Editor and F. Tarver, M.A.—MONTAIGNE, by Rev. W. L. Collins, M.A.—RABELAIS, by Walter Besant, M.A.—CALDERON, by E. J. Hasell.—SAINT SIMON, by Clifton W. Collins, M.A.—CERVANTES, by the Editor.—CORNEILLE AND RACINE, by Henry M. Trollope.—MADAME DE SÉVIGNÉ, by Miss Thackeray.—LA FONTAINE, AND OTHER FRENCH FABULISTS, by Rev. W. Lucas Collins, M.A.—SCHILLER, by James Sime, M.A., Author of 'Lessing, his Life and Writings.'—TASSO, by E. J. Hasell.—ROUSSEAU, by Henry Grey Graham.—ALFRED DE MUSSET, by C. F. Oliphant.

In preparation.
LEOPARDI. By the Editor.

Now COMPLETE.
ANCIENT CLASSICS FOR ENGLISH READERS.
EDITED BY THE REV. W. LUCAS COLLINS, M.A.

Complete in 28 Vols. crown 8vo, cloth, price 2s. 6d. each. And may also be had in 14 Volumes, strongly and neatly bound, with calf or vellum back, £3, 10s.

Contents of the Series.

HOMER: THE ILIAD, by the Editor.—HOMER: THE ODYSSEY, by the Editor.—HERODOTUS, by George C. Swayne, M.A.—XENOPHON, by Sir Alexander Grant, Bart., LL.D.—EURIPIDES, by W. B. Donne.—ARISTOPHANES, by the Editor.—PLATO, by Clifton W. Collins, M.A.—LUCIAN, by the Editor.—ÆSCHYLUS, by the Right Rev. the Bishop of Colombo.—SOPHOCLES, by Clifton W. Collins, M.A.—HESIOD AND THEOGNIS, by the Rev. J. Davies, M.A.—GREEK ANTHOLOGY, by Lord Neaves.—VIRGIL, by the Editor.—HORACE, by Sir Theodore Martin, K.C.B.—JUVENAL, by Edward Walford, M.A. — PLAUTUS AND TERENCE, by the Editor.—THE COMMENTARIES OF CÆSAR, by Anthony Trollope.—TACITUS, by W. B. Donne.—CICERO, by the Editor.—PLINY'S LETTERS, by the Rev. Alfred Church, M.A., and the Rev. W. J. Brodribb, M.A.—LIVY, by the Editor.—OVID, by the Rev. A. Church, M.A.—CATULLUS, TIBULLUS, AND PROPERTIUS, by the Rev. Jas. Davies, M.A.—DEMOSTHENES, by the Rev. W. J. Brodribb, M.A.—ARISTOTLE, by Sir Alexander Grant, Bart., LL.D.—THUCYDIDES, by the Editor.—LUCRETIUS, by W. H. Mallock, M.A.—PINDAR, by the Rev. F. D. Morice, M.A.

Saturday Review.—"It is difficult to estimate too highly the value of such a series as this in giving 'English readers' an insight, exact as far as it goes, into those olden times which are so remote, and yet to many of us so close."

CATALOGUE

OF

MESSRS BLACKWOOD & SONS'
PUBLICATIONS.

ALISON. History of Europe. By Sir ARCHIBALD ALISON, Bart., D.C.L.
1. From the Commencement of the French Revolution to the Battle of Waterloo.
   LIBRARY EDITION, 14 vols., with Portraits. Demy 8vo, £10, 10s.
   ANOTHER EDITION, in 20 vols. crown 8vo, £6.
   PEOPLE'S EDITION, 13 vols. crown 8vo, £2, 11s.
2. Continuation to the Accession of Louis Napoleon.
   LIBRARY EDITION, 8 vols. 8vo, £6, 7s. 6d.
   PEOPLE'S EDITION, 8 vols. crown 8vo, 34s.
3. Epitome of Alison's History of Europe. Twenty-ninth Thousand, 7s. 6d.
4. Atlas to Alison's History of Europe. By A. Keith Johnston.
   LIBRARY EDITION, demy 4to, £3, 3s.
   PEOPLE'S EDITION, 31s. 6d.

―――― Life of John Duke of Marlborough. With some Account of his Contemporaries, and of the War of the Succession. Third Edition. 2 vols. 8vo. Portraits and Maps, 30s.

―――― Essays : Historical, Political, and Miscellaneous. 3 vols. demy 8vo, 45s.

ACTA SANCTORUM HIBERNIÆ ; Ex Codice Salmanticensi. Nunc primum integre edita opera CAROLI DE SMEDT et JOSEPHI DE BACKER, e Soc. Jesu, Hagiographorum Bollandianorum ; Auctore et Sumptus Largiente JOANNE PATRICIO MARCHIONE BOTHAE. In One handsome 4to Volume, bound in half roxburghe, £2, 2s. ; in paper wrapper, 31s. 6d.

AIRD. Poetical Works of Thomas Aird. Fifth Edition, with Memoir of the Author by the Rev. JARDINE WALLACE, and Portrait. Crown 8vo, 7s. 6d.

ALLARDYCE. The City of Sunshine. By ALEXANDER ALLARDYCE. Three vols. post 8vo, £1, 5s. 6d.

―――― Memoir of the Honourable George Keith Elphinstone, K.B., Viscount Keith of Stonehaven, Marischal, Admiral of the Red. 8vo, with Portrait, Illustrations, and Maps, 21s.

ALMOND. Sermons by a Lay Head-master. By HELY HUTCHINSON ALMOND, M.A. Oxon., Head-master of Loretto School. Crown 8vo, 5s.

ANCIENT CLASSICS FOR ENGLISH READERS. Edited by Rev. W. LUCAS COLLINS, M.A. Price 2s. 6d. each. *For list of Vols., see page 2.*

AYTOUN. Lays of the Scottish Cavaliers, and other Poems. By W. EDMONDSTOUNE AYTOUN, D.C.L, Professor of Rhetoric and Belles-Lettres in the University of Edinburgh. New Edition. Fcap. 8vo, 3s. 6d.
Another Edition, being the Thirtieth. Fcap. 8vo, cloth extra, 7s. 6d.
Cheap Edition. Fcap. 8vo. Illustrated Cover. Price 1s. Cloth, 1s. 3d.

―――― An Illustrated Edition of the Lays of the Scottish Cavaliers. From designs by Sir NOEL PATON. Small 4to, in gilt cloth, 21s.

―――― Bothwell : a Poem. Third Edition. Fcap. 7s. 6d.

―――― Poems and Ballads of Goethe. Translated by Professor AYTOUN and Sir THEODORE MARTIN, K.C.B. Third Edition. Fcap., 6s.

AYTOUN. Bon Gaultier's Book of Ballads. By the SAME. Fifteenth
Edition. With Illustrations by Doyle, Leech, and Crowquill. Fcap. 8vo, 5s.
—— The Ballads of Scotland. Edited by Professor AYTOUN.
Fourth Edition. 2 vols. fcap. 8vo, 12s.
—— Memoir of William E. Aytoun, D.C.L. By Sir THEODORE
MARTIN, K.C.B. With Portrait. Post 8vo, 12s.
BACH. On Musical Education and Vocal Culture. By ALBERT
B. BACH. Fourth Edition. 8vo, 7s. 6d.
—— The Principles of Singing. A Practical Guide for Vocalists
and Teachers. With Course of Vocal Exercises. Crown 8vo, 6s.
—— The Art of Singing. With Musical Exercises for Young
People. Crown 8vo, 3s.
—— The Art Ballad : Loewe and Schubert. With Music Illus-
trations. With a Portrait of LOEWE. Third Edition. Small 4to. 5s.
BALLADS AND POEMS. By MEMBERS OF THE GLASGOW
BALLAD CLUB. Crown 8vo, 7s. 6d
BANNATYNE. Handbook of Republican Institutions in the
United States of America. Based upon Federal and State Laws, and other
reliable sources of information. By DUGALD J. BANNATYNE, Scotch Solicitor,
New York ; Member of the Faculty of Procurators, Glasgow. Cr. 8vo, 7s. 6d.
BELLAIRS. The Transvaal War, 1880-81. Edited by Lady BEL-
LAIRS. With a Frontispiece and Map. 8vo, 15s.
—— Gossips with Girls and Maidens, Betrothed and Free.
New Edition. Crown 8vo, 3s. 6d. Cloth, extra gilt edges, 5s.
BESANT. The Revolt of Man. By WALTER BESANT, M.A.
Ninth Edition. Crown 8vo, 3s. 6d.
—— Readings in Rabelais. Crown 8vo, 7s. 6d.
BEVERIDGE. Culross and Tulliallan; or Perthshire on Forth. Its
History and Antiquities. With Elucidations of Scottish Life and Character
from the Burgh and Kirk-Session Records of that District. By DAVID
BEVERIDGE. 2 vols. 8vo, with Illustrations, 42s.
—— Between the Ochils and the Forth ; or, From Stirling
Bridge to Aberdour. Crown 8vo, 6s.
BLACK. Heligoland and the Islands of the North Sea. By
WILLIAM GEORGE BLACK. Crown 8vo, 4s.
BLACKIE. Lays and Legends of Ancient Greece. By JOHN
STUART BLACKIE, Emeritus Professor of Greek in the University of Edin-
burgh. Second Edition. Fcap. 8vo. 5s.
—— The Wisdom of Goethe. Fcap. 8vo. Cloth, extra gilt, 6s.
—— Scottish Song : Its Wealth, Wisdom, and Social Signifi-
cance. Crown 8vo. With Music. 7s. 6d.
—— A Song of Heroes. Crown 8vo, 6s.
BLACKWOOD'S MAGAZINE, from Commencement in 1817 to
December 1891. Nos. 1 to 914, forming 150 Volumes.
—— Index to Blackwood's Magazine. Vols. 1 to 50. 8vo, 15s.
BLACKWOOD. Tales from Blackwood. Price One Shilling each,
in Paper Cover. Sold separately at all Railway Bookstalls.
They may also be had bound in cloth, 18s., and in half calf, richly gilt, 30s.
Or 12 volumes in 6, roxburghe, 21s., and half red morocco, 28s.
—— Tales from Blackwood. New Series. Complete in Twenty-
four Shilling Parts. Handsomely bound in 12 vols., cloth, 30s. In leather
back, roxburghe style, 37s. 6d. In half calf, gilt, 52s. 6d. In half morocco, 55s.
—— Tales from Blackwood. Third Series. Complete in 6
vols. Handsomely bound in cloth, 15s. ; or in 12 vols. 18s. The 6 vols. bound
in roxburghe, 21s. Half calf, 25s. Half morocco, 28s. Also in 12 parts, price
1s. each.
—— Travel, Adventure, and Sport. From ' Blackwood's
Magazine.' Uniform with ' Tales from Blackwood.' In Twelve Parts, each
price 1s. Or handsomely bound in 6 vols., 15s. Half calf, 25s.

BLACKWOOD. New Uniform Series of Three-and-Sixpenny Novels
(Copyright). Crown 8vo, cloth. Now ready:—
BEGGAR MY NEIGHBOUR. By E. D. Gerard.
THE WATERS OF HERCULES. By the Same.
SONS AND DAUGHTERS. By Mrs Oliphant.
FAIR TO SEE. By L. W. M. Lockhart.
THE REVOLT OF MAN. By Walter Besant.
MINE IS THINE. By L. W. M. Lockhart.
ALTIORA PETO. By Laurence Oliphant.
DOUBLES AND QUITS. By L. W. M. Lockhart.
LADY BABY. By D. Gerard.
HURRISH. By the Hon. Emily Lawless.
THE BLACKSMITH OF VOE. By Paul Cushing.
THE DILEMMA. By the Author of 'The Battle of Dorking.'
MY TRIVIAL LIFE AND MISFORTUNE. By A Plain Woman.
PICCADILLY. By Laurence Oliphant. With Illustrations.

Others in preparation.

——— Standard Novels. Uniform in size and legibly Printed.
Each Novel complete in one volume.
FLORIN SERIES, Illustrated Boards. Or in New Cloth Binding, 2s. 6d.
TOM CRINGLE'S LOG. By Michael Scott.
THE CRUISE OF THE MIDGE. By the Same.
CYRIL THORNTON. By Captain Hamilton.
ANNALS OF THE PARISH. By John Galt.
THE PROVOST, &c. By John Galt.
SIR ANDREW WYLIE. By John Galt.
THE ENTAIL. By John Galt.
MISS MOLLY. By Beatrice May Butt.
REGINALD DALTON. By J. G. Lockhart.
PEN OWEN. By Dean Hook.
ADAM BLAIR. By J. G. Lockhart.
LADY LEE'S WIDOWHOOD. By General Sir E. B. Hamley.
SALEM CHAPEL. By Mrs Oliphant.
THE PERPETUAL CURATE. By Mrs Oliphant.
MISS MARJORIBANKS. By Mrs Oliphant.
JOHN: A Love Story. By Mrs Oliphant.

SHILLING SERIES, Illustrated Cover. Or in New Cloth Binding, 1s. 6d.
THE RECTOR, and THE DOCTOR'S FAMILY. By Mrs Oliphant.
THE LIFE OF MANSIE WAUCH. By D. M. Moir.
PENINSULAR SCENES AND SKETCHES. By F. Hardman.
SIR FRIZZLE PUMPKIN, NIGHTS AT MESS, &c.
THE SUBALTERN.
LIFE IN THE FAR WEST. By G. F. Ruxton.
VALERIUS: A Roman Story. By J. G. Lockhart.

BLACKMORE. The Maid of Sker. By R. D. BLACKMORE, Author of 'Lorna Doone,' &c. New Edition. Crown 8vo, 6s.

BLAIR. History of the Catholic Church of Scotland. From the Introduction of Christianity to the Present Day. By ALPHONS BELLESHEIM, D.D., Canon of Aix-la-Chapelle. Translated, with Notes and Additions, by D. OSWALD HUNTER BLAIR, O.S.B., Monk of Fort Augustus. Complete in 4 vols. demy 8vo, with Maps. Price 12s. 6d. each.

BOSCOBEL TRACTS. Relating to the Escape of Charles the Second after the Battle of Worcester, and his subsequent Adventures. Edited by J. HUGHES, ESQ., A.M. A New Edition, with additional Notes and Illustrations, including Communications from the Rev. R. H. BARHAM, Author of the 'Ingoldsby Legends.' 8vo, with Engravings, 16s.

BROUGHAM. Memoirs of the Life and Times of Henry Lord Brougham. Written by HIMSELF. 3 vols. 8vo, £2, 8s. The Volumes are sold separately, price 16s. each.

BROWN. The Forester: A Practical Treatise on the Planting, Rearing, and General Management of Forest-trees. By JAMES BROWN, LL.D., Inspector of and Reporter on Woods and Forests. Fifth Edition, revised and enlarged. Royal 8vo, with Engravings, 36s.

BROWN. The Ethics of George Eliot's Works. By JOHN CROMBIE BROWN. Fourth Edition. Crown 8vo, 2s. 6d.

BROWN. A Manual of Botany, Anatomical and Physiological. For the Use of Students. By ROBERT BROWN, M.A., Ph.D. Crown 8vo, with numerous Illustrations, 12s. 6d.

BRUCE. In Clover and Heather. Poems by WALLACE BRUCE. New and Enlarged Edition. Crown 8vo, 4s. 6d.
A limited number of Copies of the First Edition, on large hand-made paper, 12s. 6d.

BRYDALL. Art in Scotland; its Origin and Progress. By ROBERT BRYDALL, Master of St George's Art School of Glasgow. 8vo, 12s. 6d.

BUCHAN. Introductory Text-Book of Meteorology. By ALEXANDER BUCHAN, M.A., F.R.S.E., Secretary of the Scottish Meteorological Society, &c. Crown 8vo, with 8 Coloured Charts and Engravings, 4s. 6d.

6 LIST OF BOOKS PUBLISHED BY

BUCHANAN. The Shirè Highlands (East Central Africa). By JOHN BUCHANAN, Planter at Zomba. Crown 8vo, 5s.

BURBIDGE. Domestic Floriculture, Window Gardening, and Floral Decorations. Being practical directions for the Propagation, Culture, and Arrangement of Plants and Flowers as Domestic Ornaments. By F. W. BURBIDGE. Second Edition. Crown 8vo, with numerous Illustrations, 7s. 6d.

—— Cultivated Plants: Their Propagation and Improvement. Including Natural and Artificial Hybridisation, Raising from Seed, Cuttings, and Layers, Grafting and Budding, as applied to the Families and Genera in Cultivation. Crown 8vo, with numerous Illustrations, 12s. 6d.

BURTON. The History of Scotland: From Agricola's Invasion to the Extinction of the last Jacobite Insurrection. By JOHN HILL BURTON, D.C.L., Historiographer-Royal for Scotland. New and Enlarged Edition. 8 vols., and Index. Crown 8vo, £3, 3s.

—— History of the British Empire during the Reign of Queen Anne. In 3 vols. 8vo. 36s.

—— The Scot Abroad. Third Edition. Crown 8vo, 10s. 6d.

—— The Book-Hunter. New Edition. With Portrait. Crown 8vo, 7s. 6d.

BUTE. The Roman Breviary: Reformed by Order of the Holy Œcumenical Council of Trent; Published by Order of Pope St Pius V.; and Revised by Clement VIII. and Urban VIII.; together with the Offices since granted. Translated out of Latin into English by JOHN, Marquess of Bute, K.T. In 2 vols, crown 8vo. cloth boards, edges uncut. £2, 2s.

—— The Altus of St Columba. With a Prose Paraphrase and Notes. In paper cover, 2s. 6d.

BUTLER. Pompeii: Descriptive and Picturesque. By W. BUTLER. Post 8vo, 5s.

BUTT. Miss Molly. By BEATRICE MAY BUTT. Cheap Edition, 2s.

—— Eugenie. Crown 8vo, 6s. 6d.

—— Elizabeth, and Other Sketches. Crown 8vo, 6s.

—— Novels. New and Uniform Edition. Crown 8vo, each 2s. 6d. Delicia. *Now ready.*

CAIRD. Sermons. By JOHN CAIRD, D.D., Principal of the University of Glasgow. Sixteenth Thousand. Fcap. 8vo, 5s.

—— Religion in Common Life. A Sermon preached in Crathie Church, October 14, 1855, before Her Majesty the Queen and Prince Albert. Published by Her Majesty's Command. Cheap Edition, 3d.

CAMPBELL. Critical Studies in St Luke's Gospel: Its Demonology and Ebionitism. By COLIN CAMPBELL, B.D., Minister of the Parish of Dundee, formerly Scholar and Fellow of Glasgow University. Author of the 'Three First Gospels in Greek, arranged in parallel columns. Post 8vo, 7s. 6d.

CAMPBELL. Sermons Preached before the Queen at Balmoral. By the Rev. A. A. CAMPBELL, Minister of Crathie. Published by Command of Her Majesty. Crown 8vo, 4s. 6d.

CAMPBELL. Records of Argyll. Legends, Traditions, and Recollections of Argyllshire Highlanders, collected chiefly from the Gaelic. With Notes on the Antiquity of the Dress, Clan Colours or Tartans of the Highlanders. By LORD ARCHIBALD CAMPBELL. Illustrated with Nineteen full-page Etchings. 4to, printed on hand-made paper, £3, 3s.

CANTON. A Lost Epic, and other Poems. By WILLIAM CANTON. Crown 8vo, 5s.

CARRICK. Koumiss; or, Fermented Mare's Milk: and its Uses in the Treatment and Cure of Pulmonary Consumption, and other Wasting Diseases. With an Appendix on the best Methods of Fermenting Cow's Milk. By GEORGE L. CARRICK, M.D., L.R.C.S.E. and L.R.C.P.E., Physician to the British Embassy, St Petersburg, &c. Crown 8vo, 10s. 6d.

CARSTAIRS. British Work in India. By R. CARSTAIRS. Cr. 8vo, 6s.

WILLIAM BLACKWOOD AND SONS. 7

CAUVIN. A Treasury of the English and German Languages.
Compiled from the best Authors and Lexicographers in both Languages.
By JOSEPH CAUVIN, LL.D. and Ph.D., of the University of Göttingen, &c.
Crown 8vo, 7s. 6d.

CAVE-BROWN. Lambeth Palace and its Associations. By J.
CAVE-BROWN, M.A., Vicar of Detling, Kent, and for many years Curate of Lambeth Parish Church. With an Introduction by the Archbishop of Canterbury.
Second Edition, containing an additional Chapter on Medieval Life in the Old Palaces. 8vo, with Illustrations, 21s.

CHARTERIS. Canonicity; or, Early Testimonies to the Existence and Use of the Books of the New Testament. Based on Kirchhoffer's 'Quellensammlung.' Edited by A. H. CHARTERIS, D.D., Professor of Biblical Criticism in the University of Edinburgh. 8vo, 18s.

CHRISTISON. Life of Sir Robert Christison, Bart., M.D., D.C.L. Oxon., Professor of Medical Jurisprudence in the University of Edinburgh. Edited by his Sons. In two vols. 8vo. Vol. I.—Autobiography. 16s. Vol. II.—Memoirs. 16s.

CHURCH SERVICE SOCIETY. A Book of Common Order : Being Forms of Worship issued by the Church Service Society. Sixth Edition. Crown, 8vo, 6s. Also in 2 vols, crown 8vo, 6s. 6d.

CLELAND. Too Apt a Pupil. By ROBERT CLELAND. Author of 'Barbara Allan, the Provost's Daughter.' Crown 8vo, 6s.

CLOUSTON. Popular Tales and Fictions: their Migrations and Transformations. By W. A. CLOUSTON, Editor of 'Arabian Poetry for English Readers,' &c. 2 vols. post 8vo, roxburghe binding, 25s.

COBBAN. Master of his Fate. By J. MACLAREN COBBAN, Author of 'The Cure of Souls,' 'Tinted Vapours,' &c. New and Cheaper Edition. Crown 8vo, paper cover, 1s. Cloth, bevelled boards, 3s. 6d.

COCHRAN. A Handy Text-Book of Military Law. Compiled chiefly to assist Officers preparing for Examination ; also for all Officers of the Regular and Auxiliary Forces. Comprising also a Synopsis of part of the Army Act. By Major F. COCHRAN, Hampshire Regiment Garrison Instructor, North British District. Crown 8vo, 7s. 6d.

COLQUHOUN. The Moor and the Loch. Containing Minute Instructions in all Highland Sports, with Wanderings over Crag and Corrie, Flood and Fell. By JOHN COLQUHOUN. Seventh Edition. With Illustrations. 8vo, 21s.

COTTERILL. Suggested Reforms in Public Schools. By C. C. COTTERILL, M.A. Crown 8vo, 3s. 6d.

CRANSTOUN. The Elegies of Albius Tibullus. Translated into English Verse, with Life of the Poet, and Illustrative Notes. By JAMES CRANSTOUN, LL.D., Author of a Translation of 'Catullus.' Crown 8vo, 6s. 6d.

—— The Elegies of Sextus Propertius. Translated into English Verse, with Life of the Poet, and Illustrative Notes. Crown 8vo, 7s. 6d.

CRAWFORD. Saracinesca. By F. MARION CRAWFORD, Author of 'Mr Isaacs,' 'Dr Claudius,' 'Zoroaster,' &c. &c. Fifth Ed. Crown 8vo, 6s.

CRAWFORD. The Doctrine of Holy Scripture respecting the Atonement. By the late THOMAS J. CRAWFORD, D.D., Professor of Divinity in the University of Edinburgh. Fifth Edition. 8vo, 12s.

—— The Fatherhood of God, Considered in its General and Special Aspects. Third Edition, Revised and Enlarged. 8vo, 9s.

—— The Preaching of the Cross, and other Sermons. 8vo, 7s. 6d.

—— The Mysteries of Christianity. Crown 8vo, 7s. 6d.

CRAWFORD. An Atonement of East London, and other Poems. By HOWARD CRAWFORD, M.A. Crown 8vo, 5s.

CUSHING. The Blacksmith of Voe. By PAUL CUSHING, Author of 'The Bull i' th' Thorn.' Cheap Edition. Crown 8vo, 3s. 6d.

—— Cut with his own Diamond. A Novel. 3 vols. cr. 8vo, 25s. 6d.

DAVIES. Norfolk Broads and Rivers; or, The Waterways, Lagoons, and Decoys of East Anglia. By G. CHRISTOPHER DAVIES. Illustrated with Seven full-page Plates. New and Cheaper Edition. Crown 8vo, 6s.

—— Our Home in Aveyron. Sketches of Peasant Life in Aveyron and the Lot. By G. CHRISTOPHER DAVIES and Mrs BROUGHALL. Illustrated with full-page Illustrations. 8vo, 15s. Cheap Edition, 7s. 6d.

DAYNE. In the Name of the Tzar. A Novel. By J. BELFORD DAYNE. Crown 8vo, 6s.

—— Tribute to Satan. A Novel. Crown 8vo, 2s. 6d.

DE LA WARR. An Eastern Cruise in the 'Edeline.' By the Countess DE LA WARR. In Illustrated Cover. 2s.

DESCARTES. The Method, Meditations, and Principles of Philosophy of Descartes. Translated from the Original French and Latin. With a New Introductory Essay, Historical and Critical, on the Cartesian Philosophy. By Professor VEITCH, LL.D., Glasgow University. Ninth Edition. 6s. 6d.

DICKSON. Gleanings from Japan. By W. G. DICKSON, Author of 'Japan: Being a Sketch of its History, Government, and Officers of the Empire.' With Illustrations. 8vo, 16s.

DOGS, OUR DOMESTICATED: Their Treatment in reference to Food, Diseases, Habits, Punishment, Accomplishments. By 'MAGENTA.' Crown 8vo, 2s. 6d.

DOMESTIC EXPERIMENT, A. By the Author of 'Ideala: A Study from Life.' Crown 8vo, 6s.

DR HERMIONE. By the Author of 'Lady Bluebeard,' 'Zit and Xoe.' Crown 8vo, 6s.

DU CANE. The Odyssey of Homer, Books I.-XII. Translated into English Verse. By Sir CHARLES DU CANE, K.C.M.G. 8vo, 10s. 6d.

DUDGEON. History of the Edinburgh or Queen's Regiment Light Infantry Militia, now 3rd Battalion The Royal Scots; with an Account of the Origin and Progress of the Militia, and a Brief Sketch of the old Royal Scots. By Major R. C. DUDGEON, Adjutant 3rd Battalion The Royal Scots. Post 8vo, with Illustrations, 10s. 6d.

DUNCAN. Manual of the General Acts of Parliament relating to the Salmon Fisheries of Scotland from 1828 to 1882. By J. BARKER DUNCAN. Crown 8vo, 5s.

DUNSMORE. Manual of the Law of Scotland as to the Relations between Agricultural Tenants and their Landlords, Servants, Merchants, and Bowers. By W. DUNSMORE. 8vo, 7s. 6d.

DUPRÉ. Thoughts on Art, and Autobiographical Memoirs of Giovanni Duprè. Translated from the Italian by E. M. PERUZZI, with the permission of the Author. New Edition. With an Introduction by W. W. STORY. Crown 8vo, 10s. 6d.

ELIOT. George Eliot's Life, Related in her Letters and Journals. Arranged and Edited by her husband, J. W. CROSS. With Portrait and other Illustrations. Third Edition. 3 vols. post 8vo, 42s.

—— George Eliot's Life. (Cabinet Edition.) With Portrait and other Illustrations. 3 vols. crown 8vo, 15s.

—— George Eliot's Life. With Portrait and other Illustrations. New Edition, in one volume. Crown 8vo, 7s. 6d.

—— Works of George Eliot (Cabinet Edition). Handsomely printed in a new type, 21 volumes, crown 8vo, price £5, 5s. The Volumes are also sold separately, price 5s. each, viz.:—
Romola. 2 vols.—Silas Marner, The Lifted Veil, Brother Jacob. 1 vol.—Adam Bede. 2 vols.—Scenes of Clerical Life. 2 vols.—The Mill on the Floss. 2 vols.—Felix Holt. 2 vols.—Middlemarch. 3 vols.—Daniel Deronda. 3 vols.—The Spanish Gypsy. 1 vol.—Jubal, and other Poems, Old and New. 1 vol.—Theophrastus Such. 1 vol.—Essays. 1 vol.

—— Novels by GEORGE ELIOT. Cheap Edition. Adam Bede. Illustrated. 3s. 6d., cloth.—The Mill on the Floss. Illustrated. 3s. 6d., cloth.—Scenes of Clerical Life. Illustrated. 3s., cloth.—Silas Marner: the Weaver of Raveloe. Illustrated. 2s. 6d., cloth.—Felix Holt, the Radical. Illustrated. 3s. 6d., cloth.—Romola. With Vignette. 3s. 6d., cloth.

ELIOT. Middlemarch. Crown 8vo, 7s. 6d.
—— Daniel Deronda. Crown 8vo, 7s. 6d.
—— Essays. New Edition. Crown 8vo, 5s.
—— Impressions of Theophrastus Such. New Ed. Cr. 8vo, 5s.
—— The Spanish Gypsy. New Edition. Crown 8vo, 5s.
—— The Legend of Jubal, and other Poems, Old and New. New Edition. Crown 8vo, 5s.
—— Wise, Witty, and Tender Sayings, in Prose and Verse. Selected from the Works of GEORGE ELIOT. Eighth Edition. Fcap. 8vo, 6s.
—— The George Eliot Birthday Book. Printed on fine paper, with red border, and handsomely bound in cloth, gilt. Fcap. 8vo, cloth, 3s. 6d. And in French morocco or Russia, 5s.
ESSAYS ON SOCIAL SUBJECTS. Originally published in the 'Saturday Review.' New Ed. First & Second Series. 2 vols. cr. 8vo, 6s. each.
EWALD. The Crown and its Advisers ; or, Queen, Ministers, Lords and Commons. By ALEXANDER CHARLES EWALD, F.S.A. Crown 8vo, 5s.
FAITHS OF THE WORLD, The. A Concise History of the Great Religious Systems of the World. By various Authors. Crown 8vo, 5s.
FARRER. A Tour in Greece in 1880. By RICHARD RIDLEY FARRER. With Twenty-seven full-page Illustrations by LORD WINDSOR. Royal 8vo, with a Map, 21s.
FERRIER. Philosophical Works of the late James F. Ferrier, B.A. Oxon., Professor of Moral Philosophy and Political Economy, St Andrews. New Edition. Edited by Sir ALEX. GRANT, Bart., D.C.L., and Professor LUSHINGTON. 3 vols. crown 8vo, 34s. 6d.
—— Institutes of Metaphysic. Third Edition. 10s. 6d.
—— Lectures on the Early Greek Philosophy. 3d Ed. 10s. 6d.
—— Philosophical Remains, including the Lectures on Early Greek Philosophy. 2 vols., 24s.
FITZROY. Dogma and the Church of England. By A. I. FITZROY. Post 8vo, 7s. 6d.
FLINT. The Philosophy of History in Europe. By ROBERT FLINT, D.D., LL.D., Professor of Divinity, University of Edinburgh. 2 vols. 8vo. [New Edition in preparation.
—— Theism. Being the Baird Lecture for 1876. Seventh Edition. Crown 8vo, 7s. 6d.
—— Anti-Theistic Theories. Being the Baird Lecture for 1877. Fourth Edition. Crown 8vo, 10s. 6d.
—— Agnosticism. Being the Croall Lectures for 1887-88.
[In the press.
FORBES. Insulinde: Experiences of a Naturalist's Wife in the Eastern Archipelago. By Mrs H. O. FORBES. Crown 8vo, with a Map. 4s. 6d.
FOREIGN CLASSICS FOR ENGLISH READERS. Edited by Mrs OLIPHANT. Price 2s. 6d. For List of Volumes published, see page 2.
FOSTER. The Fallen City, and Other Poems. By WILL FOSTER. In 1 vol. Crown 8vo. [Immediately.
FULLARTON. Merlin: A Dramatic Poem. By RALPH MACLEOD FULLARTON. Crown 8vo, 5s.
GALT. Novels by JOHN GALT. Fcap. 8vo, boards, 2s.; cloth, 2s. 6d. Annals of the Parish.—The Provost.—Sir Andrew Wylie.—The Entail.
GENERAL ASSEMBLY OF THE CHURCH OF SCOTLAND.
—— Prayers for Social and Family Worship. Prepared by a Special Committee of the General Assembly of the Church of Scotland. Entirely New Edition, Revised and Enlarged. Fcap. 8vo, red edges, 2s.
—— Prayers for Family Worship. A Selection from the complete book. Fcap. 8vo, red edges, price 1s.

GENERAL ASSEMBLY OF THE CHURCH OF SCOTLAND.
—— Scottish Hymnal, with Appendix Incorporated. Published for Use in Churches by Authority of the General Assembly. 1. Large type, cloth, red edges, 2s. 6d.; French morocco, 4s. 2. Bourgeois type, limp cloth, 1s.; French morocco, 2s. 3. Nonpareil type, cloth, red edges, 6d.; French morocco, 1s. 4d. 4. Paper covers, 3d. 5. Sunday-School Edition, paper covers, 1d. No. 1, bound with the Psalms and Paraphrases, French morocco, 8s. No. 2, bound with the Psalms and Paraphrases, cloth, 2s.; French morocco, 3s.

GERARD. Reata: What's in a Name. By E. D. GERARD. New Edition. Crown 8vo, 6s.
—— Beggar my Neighbour. Cheap Edition. Crown 8vo, 3s. 6d.
—— The Waters of Hercules. Cheap Edition. Crown 8vo, 3s. 6d.

GERARD. The Land beyond the Forest. Facts, Figures, and Fancies from Transylvania. By E. GERARD. In Two Volumes. With Maps and Illustrations. 25s.
—— Bis: Some Tales Retold. Crown 8vo, 6s.
—— A Secret Mission. 2 vols. crown 8vo, 17s.

GERARD. Lady Baby. By DOROTHEA GERARD, Author of 'Orthodox.' Cheap Edition. Crown 8vo, 3s. 6d.
—— Recha. Second Edition. Crown 8vo, 6s.

GERARD. Stonyhurst Latin Grammar. By Rev. JOHN GERARD. Fcap. 8vo, 3s.

GILL. Free Trade: an Inquiry into the Nature of its Operation. By RICHARD GILL. Crown 8vo, 7s. 6d.
—— Free Trade under Protection. Crown 8vo, 7s. 6d.

GOETHE'S FAUST. Translated into English Verse by Sir THEODORE MARTIN, K.C.B. Part I. Second Edition, post 8vo, 6s. Ninth Edition, fcap., 3s. 6d. Part II. Second Edition, revised. Fcap. 8vo, 6s.

GOETHE. Poems and Ballads of Goethe. Translated by Professor AYTOUN and Sir THEODORE MARTIN, K.C.B. Third Edition, fcap. 8vo, 6s.

GOODALL. Juxta Crucem. Studies of the Love that is over us. By the late Rev. CHARLES GOODALL, B.D., Minister of Barr. With a Memoir by Rev. Dr Strong, Glasgow, and Portrait. Crown 8vo, 6s.

GORDON CUMMING. Two Happy Years in Ceylon. By C. F. GORDON CUMMING. With 15 full-page Illustrations and a Map. 2 vols. 8vo, 30s.
—— At Home in Fiji. Fourth Edition, post 8vo. With Illustrations and Map. 7s. 6d.
—— A Lady's Cruise in a French Man-of-War. New and Cheaper Edition. 8vo. With Illustrations and Map. 12s. 6d.
—— Fire-Fountains. The Kingdom of Hawaii: Its Volcanoes, and the History of its Missions. With Map and Illustrations. 2 vols. 8vo, 25s.
—— Wanderings in China. New and Cheaper Edition. 8vo, with Illustrations. 10s.
—— Granite Crags: The Yō-semité Region of California. Illustrated with 8 Engravings. New and Cheaper Edition. 8vo, 8s. 6d

GRAHAM. The Life and Work of Syed Ahmed Khan, C.S.I. By Lieut.-Colonel G. F. I. GRAHAM, B.S.C. 8vo, 14s.

GRAHAM. Manual of the Elections (Scot.) (Corrupt and Illegal Practices) Act, 1890. With Analysis, Relative Act of Sederunt, Appendix containing the Corrupt Practices Acts of 1883 and 1885, and Copious Index. By J. EDWARD GRAHAM, Advocate. 8vo, 4s. 6d.

GRANT. Bush-Life in Queensland. By A. C. GRANT. New Edition. Crown 8vo, 6s.

GRIFFITHS. Locked Up. By Major ARTHUR GRIFFITHS, Author of 'The Wrong Road,' 'Chronicles of Newgate,' &c. With Illustrations by C. J. STANILAND, R.I. Crown 8vo, 2s. 6d.

GUTHRIE-SMITH. Crispus: A Drama. By H. GUTHRIE-SMITH. In one volume. Fcap. 4to, 5s.

HAINES. Unless! A Romance. By RANDOLPH HAINES. Crown
8vo, 6s.
HALDANE. Subtropical Cultivations and Climates. A Handy
Book for Planters, Colonists, and Settlers. By R. C. HALDANE. Post 8vo, 9s.
HALLETT. A Thousand Miles on an Elephant in the Shan States.
By HOLT S. HALLETT, M. Inst. C.E., F.R.G.S., M.R.A.S., Hon. Member Manchester and Tyneside Geographical Societies. 8vo, with Maps and numerous Illustrations, 21s.
HAMERTON. Wenderholme : A Story of Lancashire and Yorkshire Life. By PHILIP GILBERT HAMERTON, Author of 'A Painter's Camp.' A New Edition. Crown 8vo, 6s.
HAMILTON. Lectures on Metaphysics. By Sir WILLIAM HAMILTON, Bart., Professor of Logic and Metaphysics in the University of Edinburgh. Edited by the Rev. H. L. MANSEL, B.D., LL.D., Dean of St Paul's ; and JOHN VEITCH, M.A., LL.D., Professor of Logic and Rhetoric, Glasgow. Seventh Edition. 2 vols. 8vo, 24s.
―――― Lectures on Logic. Edited by the SAME. Third Edition.
2 vols., 24s.
―――― Discussions on Philosophy and Literature, Education and
University Reform. Third Edition, 8vo, 21s.
―――― Memoir of Sir William Hamilton, Bart., Professor of Logic
and Metaphysics in the University of Edinburgh. By Professor VEITCH, of the University of Glasgow. 8vo, with Portrait, 18s.
―――― Sir William Hamilton : The Man and his Philosophy.
Two Lectures delivered before the Edinburgh Philosophical Institution, January and February 1883. By the SAME. Crown 8vo, 2s.
HAMLEY. The Operations of War Explained and Illustrated. By
General Sir EDWARD BRUCE HAMLEY, K.C.B., K.C.M.G., M.P. Fifth Edition, revised throughout. 4to, with numerous Illustrations, 30s.
―――― National Defence ; Articles and Speeches. Post 8vo, 6s.
―――― Shakespeare's Funeral, and other Papers. Post 8vo, 7s. 6d.
―――― Thomas Carlyle : An Essay. Second Ed. Cr. 8vo, 2s. 6d.
―――― On Outposts. Second Edition. 8vo, 2s.
―――― Wellington's Career ; A Military and Political Summary.
Crown 8vo, 2s.
―――― Lady Lee's Widowhood. Crown 8vo, 2s. 6d.
―――― Our Poor Relations. A Philozoic Essay. With Illustrations, chiefly by Ernest Griset. Crown 8vo, cloth gilt, 3s. 6d.
HAMLEY. Guilty, or Not Guilty? A Tale. By Major-General
W. G. HAMLEY, late of the Royal Engineers. New Edition. Crown 8vo, 3s. 6d.
HARRISON. The Scot in Ulster. The Story of the Scottish
Settlement in Ulster. By JOHN HARRISON, Author of ' Oure Tounis Colledge.' Crown 8vo, 2s. 6d.
HASELL. Bible Partings. By E. J. HASELL. Crown 8vo, 6s.
―――― Short Family Prayers. Cloth, 1s.
HAY. The Works of the Right Rev. Dr George Hay, Bishop of
Edinburgh. Edited under the Supervision of the Right Rev. Bishop STRAIN. With Memoir and Portrait of the Author. 5 vols. crown 8vo, bound in extra cloth, £1, 1s. The following Volumes may be had separately—viz.:
The Devout Christian Instructed in the Law of Christ from the Written Word. 2 vols., 8s.—The Pious Christian Instructed in the Nature and Practice of the Principal Exercises of Piety. 1 vol., 3s.
HEATLEY. The Horse-Owner's Safeguard. A Handy Medical
Guide for every Man who owns a Horse. By G. S. HEATLEY, M.R.C.V.S. Crown 8vo, 5s.
―――― The Stock-Owner's Guide. A Handy Medical Treatise for
every Man who owns an Ox or a Cow. Crown 8vo, 4s. 6d.
HEDDERWICK. Lays of Middle Age ; and other Poems. By
JAMES HEDDERWICK, LL.D. Price 3s. 6d.

HEDDERWICK. Backward Glances; or, Some Personal Recollections. With a Portrait. Post 8vo, 7s. 6d.
HEMANS. The Poetical Works of Mrs Hemans. Copyright Editions.—Royal 8vo, 5s.—The Same, with Engravings, cloth, gilt edges, 7s. 6d. —Six Vols. in Three, fcap., 12s. 6d.
SELECT POEMS OF MRS HEMANS. Fcap., cloth, gilt edges, 3s.
HERKLESS. Cardinal Beaton Priest and Politician. By JOHN HERKLESS, Minister of Tannadice. With a Portrait. Post 8vo, 7s. 6d.
HOME PRAYERS. By Ministers of the Church of Scotland and Members of the Church Service Society. Second Edition. Fcap. 8vo, 3s.
HOMER. The Odyssey. Translated into English Verse in the Spenserian Stanza. By PHILIP STANHOPE WORSLEY. Third Edition, 2 vols. fcap., 12s.
——— The Iliad. Translated by P. S. WORSLEY and Professor CONINGTON. 2 vols. crown 8vo, 21s.
HUTCHINSON. Hints on the Game of Golf. By HORACE G. HUTCHINSON. Sixth Edition, Enlarged. Fcap. 8vo, cloth, 1s.
IDDESLEIGH. Lectures and Essays. By the late EARL OF IDDESLEIGH, G.C.B., D.C.L., &c. 8vo, 16s.
——— Life, Letters, and Diaries of Sir Stafford Northcote, First Earl of Iddesleigh. By ANDREW LANG. With Three Portraits and a View of Pynes. Third Edition. 2 vols. Post 8vo, 31s. 6d.
POPULAR EDITION. In one volume. With two Engravings. Post 8vo, 7s. 6d.
INDEX GEOGRAPHICUS : Being a List, alphabetically arranged, of the Principal Places on the Globe, with the Countries and Subdivisions of the Countries in which they are situated, and their Latitudes and Longitudes. Imperial 8vo, pp. 676, 21s.
JEAN JAMBON. Our Trip to Blunderland ; or, Grand Excursion to Blundertown and Back. By JEAN JAMBON. With Sixty Illustrations designed by CHARLES DOYLE, engraved by DALZIEL. Fourth Thousand. Cloth, gilt edges, 6s. 6d. Cheap Edition, cloth, 3s. 6d. Boards, 2s. 6d.
JENNINGS. Mr Gladstone : A Study. By LOUIS J. JENNINGS, M.P., Author of 'Republican Government in the United States,' 'The Croker Memoirs,' &c. Popular Edition. Crown 8vo, 1s.
JERNINGHAM. Reminiscences of an Attaché. By HUBERT E. H. JERNINGHAM. Second Edition. Crown 8vo, 5s.
——— Diane de Breteuille. A Love Story. Crown 8vo, 2s. 6d.
JOHNSTON. The Chemistry of Common Life. By Professor J. F. W. JOHNSTON. New Edition, Revised, and brought down to date. By ARTHUR HERBERT CHURCH, M.A. Oxon.; Author of 'Food: its Sources, Constituents, and Uses,' &c. With Maps and 102 Engravings. Cr. 8vo, 7s. 6d.
——— Elements of Agricultural Chemistry and Geology. Revised, and brought down to date. By Sir CHARLES A. CAMERON, M.D., F.R.C.S.I., &c. Sixteenth Edition. Fcap. 8vo, 6s. 6d.
——— Catechism of Agricultural Chemistry and Geology. New Edition, revised and enlarged, by Sir C. A. CAMERON. Eighty-sixth Thousand, with numerous Illustrations, 1s.
JOHNSTON. Patrick Hamilton : a Tragedy of the Reformation in Scotland, 1528. By T. P. JOHNSTON. Crown 8vo, with Two Etchings. 5s.
KER. Short Studies on St Paul's Letter to the Philippians. By Rev. WILLIAM LEE KER, Minister of Kilwinning. Crown 8vo, 5s.
KING. The Metamorphoses of Ovid. Translated in English Blank Verse. By HENRY KING, M.A., Fellow of Wadham College, Oxford, and of the Inner Temple, Barrister-at-Law. Crown 8vo, 10s. 6d.
KINGLAKE. History of the Invasion of the Crimea. By A. W. KINGLAKE. Cabinet Edition, revised. With an Index to the Complete Work. Illustrated with Maps and Plans. Complete in 9 Vols., crown 8vo, at 6s. each.

WILLIAM BLACKWOOD AND SONS. 13

KINGLAKE. History of the Invasion of the Crimea. Demy 8vo.
Vol. VI. Winter Troubles. With a Map, 16s. Vols. VII. and VIII. From the Morrow of Inkerman to the Death of Lord Raglan. With an Index to the Whole Work. With Maps and Plans. 28s.
——— Eothen. A New Edition, uniform with the Cabinet Edition of the 'History of the Invasion of the Crimea,' price 6s.

KNEIPP. My Water-Cure. As Tested through more than Thirty Years, and Described for the Healing of Diseases and the Preservation of Health. By SEBASTIAN KNEIPP, Parish Priest of Wörishofen (Bavaria). With a Portrait and other Illustrations. Only Authorised English Translation. Translated from the Thirtieth German Edition by A. de F. Crown 8vo, 5s.

KNOLLYS. The Elements of Field-Artillery. Designed for the Use of Infantry and Cavalry Officers. By HENRY KNOLLYS, Captain Royal Artillery; Author of 'From Sedan to Saarbrück,' Editor of 'Incidents in the Sepoy War,' &c. With Engravings. Crown 8vo, 7s. 6d.

LAMINGTON. In the Days of the Dandies. By the late Lord LAMINGTON. Crown 8vo. Illustrated cover, 1s.; cloth, 1s. 6d.

LAWLESS. Hurrish : a Study. By the Hon. EMILY LAWLESS, Author of 'A Chelsea Householder,' &c. Fourth Edition, crown 8vo, 3s. 6d.

LAWSON. Spain of To-day : A Descriptive, Industrial, and Financial Survey of the Peninsula, with a full account of the Rio Tinto Mines. By W. R. LAWSON. Crown 8vo, 3s 6d.

LEES. A Handbook of the Sheriff and Justice of Peace Small Debt Courts. 8vo, 7s. 6d.

LIGHTFOOT. Studies in Philosophy. By the Rev. J. LIGHTFOOT, M.A., D.Sc., Vicar of Cross Stone, Todmorden. Crown 8vo, 4s. 6d.

LOCKHART. Novels by LAURENCE W. M. LOCKHART. See Blackwoods' New Series of Three-and-Sixpenny Novels on page 5.

LORIMER. The Institutes of Law : A Treatise of the Principles of Jurisprudence as determined by Nature. By the late JAMES LORIMER, Professor of Public Law and of the Law of Nature and Nations in the University of Edinburgh. New Edition, revised and much enlarged. 8vo, 18s.
——— The Institutes of the Law of Nations. A Treatise of the Jural Relation of Separate Political Communities. In 2 vols. 8vo. Volume I., price 16s. Volume II., price 20s.

LOVE. Scottish Church Music. Its Composers and Sources. With Musical Illustrations. By JAMES LOVE. In 1 vol. post 8vo, 7s. 6d.

M'COMBIE. Cattle and Cattle-Breeders. By WILLIAM M'COMBIE, Tillyfour. New Edition, enlarged, with Memoir of the Author. By JAMES MACDONALD, of the 'Farming World.' Crown 8vo, 3s. 6d.

MACRAE. A Handbook of Deer-Stalking. By ALEXANDER MACRAE, late Forester to Lord Henry Bentinck. With Introduction by HORATIO ROSS, Esq. Fcap. 8vo, with two Photographs from Life. 3s. 6d.

M'CRIE. Works of the Rev. Thomas M'Crie, D.D. Uniform Edition. Four vols. crown 8vo, 24s.
——— Life of John Knox. Containing Illustrations of the History of the Reformation in Scotland. Crown 8vo. 6s. Another Edition, 3s. 6d.
——— Life of Andrew Melville. Containing Illustrations of the Ecclesiastical and Literary History of Scotland in the Sixteenth and Seventeenth Centuries. Crown 8vo, 6s.
——— History of the Progress and Suppression of the Reformation in Italy in the Sixteenth Century. Crown 8vo, 4s.
——— History of the Progress and Suppression of the Reformation in Spain in the Sixteenth Century. Crown 8vo, 3s. 6d.
——— Lectures on the Book of Esther. Fcap. 8vo, 5s.

MACDONALD. A Manual of the Criminal Law (Scotland) Procedure Act, 1887. By NORMAN DORAN MACDONALD. Revised by the LORD JUSTICE-CLERK. 8vo, cloth, 10s. 6d.

MACGREGOR. Life and Opinions of Major-General Sir Charles
Macgregor, K.C.B., C.S.I., C.I.E, Quartermaster-General of India. From
his Letters and Diaries. Edited by LADY MACGREGOR. With Portraits and
Maps to illustrate Campaigns in which he was engaged. 2 vols. 8vo, 35s.

M'INTOSH. The Book of the Garden. By CHARLES M'INTOSH,
formerly Curator of the Royal Gardens of his Majesty the King of the Belgians,
and lately of those of his Grace the Duke of Buccleuch, K.G., at Dalkeith Palace. 2 vols. royal 8vo, with 1350 Engravings. £4, 7s. 6d. Vol. I. On the
Formation of Gardens and Construction of Garden Edifices. £2, 10s.
Vol. II. Practical Gardening. £1, 17s. 6d.

MACINTYRE. Hindu-Koh: Wanderings and Wild Sports on and
beyond the Himalayas. By Major-General DONALD MACINTYRE, V.C., late
Prince of Wales' Own Goorkhas, F.R.G.S. *Dedicated to H.R.H. The Prince of
Wales.* New and Cheaper Edition, revised, with numerous Illustrations,
post 8vo, 7s. 6d.

MACKAY. A Sketch of the History of Fife and Kinross. A
Study of Scottish History and Character. By Æ. J. G. MACKAY, Sheriff of
these Counties. Crown 8vo, 6s.

MACKAY. A Manual of Modern Geography; Mathematical, Physical, and Political. By the Rev. ALEXANDER MACKAY, LL.D., F.R.G.S. 11th
Thousand, revised to the present time. Crown 8vo, pp. 688. 7s. 6d.

—— Elements of Modern Geography. 53d Thousand, revised to the present time. Crown 8vo, pp. 300, 3s.

—— The Intermediate Geography. Intended as an Intermediate
Book between the Author's 'Outlines of Geography' and 'Elements of Geography.' Fifteenth Edition, revised. Crown 8vo, pp. 238, 2s.

—— Outlines of Modern Geography. 188th Thousand, revised
to the present time. 18mo, pp. 118, 1s.

—— First Steps in Geography. 105th Thousand. 18mo, pp.
56. Sewed, 4d.; cloth, 6d.

—— Elements of Physiography and Physical Geography.
With Express Reference to the Instructions issued by the Science and Art
Department. 30th Thousand, revised. Crown 8vo, 1s. 6d.

—— Facts and Dates; or, the Leading Events in Sacred and
Profane History, and the Principal Facts in the various Physical Sciences.
For Schools and Private Reference. New Edition. Crown 8vo, 3s. 6d.

MACKAY. An Old Scots Brigade. Being the History of Mackay's
Regiment, now incorporated with the Royal Scots. With an Appendix containing many Original Documents connected with the History of the Regiment. By JOHN MACKAY (late) OF HERRIESDALE. Crown 8vo, 5s.

MACKENZIE. Studies in Roman Law. With Comparative Views
of the Laws of France, England, and Scotland. By LORD MACKENZIE, one of
the Judges of the Court of Session in Scotland. Sixth Edition, Edited by
JOHN KIRKPATRICK, Esq., M.A., LL.B., Advocate, Professor of History in
the University of Edinburgh. 8vo, 12s.

M'KERLIE. Galloway: Ancient and Modern. An Account of the
Historic Celtic District. By P. H. M'KERLIE, F.S.A. Scot., F.R.G.S., &c.
Author of 'Lands and their Owners in Galloway.' Crown 8vo, 7s. 6d.

M'PHERSON. Summer Sundays in a Strathmore Parish. By J.
GORDON M'PHERSON, Ph.D., F.R.S.E., Minister of Ruthven. Crown 8vo, 5s.

—— Golf and Golfers. Past and Present. With an Introduction by
the Right Hon. A. J. BALFOUR, and a Portrait of the Author. Fcap. 8vo, 1s. 6d.

MAIN. Three Hundred English Sonnets. Chosen and Edited by
DAVID M. MAIN. Fcap. 8vo, 6s.

MAIR. A Digest of Laws and Decisions, Ecclesiastical and Civil,
relating to the Constitution, Practice, and Affairs of the Church of Scotland.
With Notes and Forms of Procedure. By the Rev. WILLIAM MAIR, D.D.,
Minister of the Parish of Earlston. Crown 8vo. With Supplements, 8s.

MARMORNE. The Story is told by ADOLPHUS SEGRAVE, the
youngest of three Brothers. Third Edition. Crown 8vo, 6s.

MARSHALL. French Home Life. By FREDERIC MARSHALL,
Author of 'Claire Brandon.' Second Edition. 5s.

MARSHALL. It Happened Yesterday. A Novel. Crown 8vo, 6s.
MARSHMAN. History of India. From the Earliest Period to the
Close of the India Company's Government; with an Epitome of Subsequent
Events. By JOHN CLARK MARSHMAN, C.S.I. Abridged from the Author's
larger work. Second Edition, revised. Crown 8vo, with Map, 6s. 6d.
MARTIN. Goethe's Faust. Part I. Translated by Sir THEODORE
MARTIN, K.C.B. Second Ed., crown 8vo, 6s. Ninth Ed., fcap. 8vo, 3s. 6d.
—— Goethe's Faust. Part II. Translated into English Verse.
Second Edition, revised. Fcap. 8vo, 6s.
—— The Works of Horace. Translated into English Verse,
with Life and Notes. 2 vols. New Edition, crown 8vo, 21s.
—— Poems and Ballads of Heinrich Heine. Done into English Verse. Second Edition. Printed on *papier vergé*, crown 8vo, 8s.
—— The Song of the Bell, and other Translations from Schiller,
Goethe, Uhland, and Others. Crown 8vo, 7s. 6d.
—— Catullus. With Life and Notes. Second Ed., post 8vo, 7s. 6d.
—— Aladdin : A Dramatic Poem. By ADAM OEHLENSCHLAEGER. Fcap. 8vo, 5s.
—— Correggio : A Tragedy. By OEHLENSCHLAEGER. With
Notes. Fcap. 8vo, 3s.
—— King Rene's Daughter : A Danish Lyrical Drama. By
HENRIK HERTZ. Second Edition, fcap., 2s. 6d.
MARTIN. On some of Shakespeare's Female Characters. In a
Series of Letters. By HELENA FAUCIT, LADY MARTIN. Dedicated by permission to Her Most Gracious Majesty the Queen. New Edition, enlarged.
8vo, with Portrait by Lane, 7s. 6d.
MATHESON. Can the Old Faith Live with the New? or the
Problem of Evolution and Revelation. By the Rev. GEORGE MATHESON, D.D.
Third Edition. Crown 8vo, 7s. 6d.
—— The Psalmist and the Scientist; or, Modern Value of the
Religious Sentiment. New and Cheaper Edition. Crown 8vo, 5s.
—— Spiritual Development of St Paul. Crown 8vo, 5s.
—— Sacred Songs. New and Cheaper Edition. Cr. 8vo, 2s. 6d.
MAURICE. The Balance of Military Power in Europe. An
Examination of the War Resources of Great Britain and the Continental States.
By Colonel MAURICE, R.A., Professor of Military Art and History at the Royal
Staff College. Crown 8vo, with a Map. 6s.
MEREDYTH. The Brief for the Government, 1886-92. A Handbook for Conservative and Unionist Writers, Speakers, &c. Second Edition.
By W. H. MEREDYTH. Crown 8vo, 2s. 6d.
MICHEL. A Critical Inquiry into the Scottish Language. With
the view of Illustrating the Rise and Progress of Civilisation in Scotland. By
FRANCISQUE-MICHEL, F.S.A. Lond. and Scot., Correspondant de l'Institut de
France, &c. 4to, printed on hand-made paper, and bound in Roxburghe, 66s.
MICHIE. The Larch : Being a Practical Treatise on its Culture
and General Management. By CHRISTOPHER Y. MICHIE, Forester, Cullen House.
Crown 8vo, with Illustrations. New and Cheaper Edition, enlarged, 5s.
—— The Practice of Forestry. Cr. 8vo, with Illustrations. 6s.
MIDDLETON. The Story of Alastair Bhan Comyn ; or, The
Tragedy of Dunphail. A Tale of Tradition and Romance. By the Lady
MIDDLETON. Square 8vo 10s. Cheaper Edition, 5s.
MILLER. Landscape Geology. A Plea for the Study of Geology by
Landscape Painters. By HUGH MILLER, of H.M. Geological Survey. Cr.8vo, 3s.
MILNE. The Problem of the Churchless and Poor in our Large
Towns. With special reference to the Home Mission Work of the Church of
Scotland. By the Rev. ROBT. MILNE, M.A., D.D., Ardler. New and Cheaper
Edition. Crown 8vo, 1s.

MILNE-HOME. Mamma's Black Nurse Stories. West Indian Folk-lore. By MARY PAMELA MILNE-HOME. With six full-page tinted Illustrations. Small 4to, 5s.

MINTO. A Manual of English Prose Literature, Biographical and Critical: designed mainly to show Characteristics of Style. By W. MINTO, M.A., Professor of Logic in the University of Aberdeen. Third Edition, revised. Crown 8vo, 7s. 6d.

—— Characteristics of English Poets, from Chaucer to Shirley. New Edition, revised. Crown 8vo, 7s. 6d.

MOIR. Life of Mansie Wauch, Tailor in Dalkeith. By D. M. MOIR. With 8 Illustrations on Steel, by the late GEORGE CRUIKSHANK. Crown 8vo, 3s. 6d. Another Edition, fcap. 8vo, 1s. 6d.

MOMERIE. Defects of Modern Christianity, and other Sermons. By ALFRED WILLIAMS MOMERIE, M.A., D.Sc., LL.D. 4th Edition. Cr. 8vo, 5s.

—— The Basis of Religion. Being an Examination of Natural Religion. Third Edition. Crown 8vo, 2s. 6d.

—— The Origin of Evil, and other Sermons. Seventh Edition, enlarged. Crown 8vo, 5s.

—— Personality. The Beginning and End of Metaphysics, and a Necessary Assumption in all Positive Philosophy. Fourth Ed. Cr. 8vo, 3s.

—— Agnosticism. Third Edition, Revised. Crown 8vo, 5s.

—— Preaching and Hearing; and other Sermons. Third Edition, Enlarged. Crown 8vo, 5s.

—— Belief in God. Third Edition. Crown 8vo, 3s.

—— Inspiration; and other Sermons. Second Ed. Cr. 8vo, 5s.

—— Church and Creed. Second Edition. Crown 8vo, 4s. 6d.

MONTAGUE. Campaigning in South Africa. Reminiscences of an Officer in 1879. By Captain W. E. MONTAGUE, 94th Regiment, Author of 'Claude Meadowleigh,' &c. 8vo, 10s. 6d.

MONTALEMBERT. Memoir of Count de Montalembert. A Chapter of Recent French History. By Mrs OLIPHANT, Author of the 'Life of Edward Irving,' &c. 2 vols. crown 8vo, £1, 4s.

MORISON. Sordello. An Outline Analysis of Mr Browning's Poem. By JEANIE MORISON, Author of 'The Purpose of the Ages,' 'Ane Booke of Ballades,' &c. Crown 8vo, 3s.

—— Selections from Poems. Crown 8vo, 4s. 6d.

—— There as Here. Crown 8vo, 3s.

** A limited impression on handmade paper, bound in vellum, 7s. 6d.

MUNRO. On Valuation of Property. By WILLIAM MUNRO, M.A., Her Majesty's Assessor of Railways and Canals for Scotland. Second Edition. Revised and enlarged. 8vo, 3s. 6d.

MURDOCH. Manual of the Law of Insolvency and Bankruptcy: Comprehending a Summary of the Law of Insolvency, Notour Bankruptcy, Composition-contracts, Trust-deeds, Cessios, and Sequestrations; and the Winding-up of Joint-Stock Companies in Scotland; with Annotations on the various Insolvency and Bankruptcy Statutes; and with Forms of Procedure applicable to these Subjects. By JAMES MURDOCH, Member of the Faculty of Procurators in Glasgow. Fifth Edition, Revised and Enlarged, 8vo, £1, 10s.

MY TRIVIAL LIFE AND MISFORTUNE: A Gossip with no Plot in Particular. By A PLAIN WOMAN. Cheap Ed., crown 8vo, 3s. 6d.

By the SAME AUTHOR.

POOR NELLIE. New Edition. Crown 8vo, 6s.

NAPIER. The Construction of the Wonderful Canon of Logarithms (Mirifici Logarithmorum Canonis Constructio). By JOHN NAPIER of Merchiston. Translated for the first time, with Notes, and a Catalogue of Napier's Works, by WILLIAM RAE MACDONALD. Small 4to, 15s. *A few large paper copies may be had, printed on Whatman paper, price 30s.*

NEAVES. Songs and Verses, Social and Scientific. By an Old Contributor to 'Maga.' By the Hon. Lord NEAVES. Fifth Ed., fcap. 8vo, 4s.
——— The Greek Anthology. Being Vol. XX. of 'Ancient Classics for English Readers.' Crown 8vo, 2s. 6d.
NICHOLSON. A Manual of Zoology, for the Use of Students. With a General Introduction on the Principles of Zoology. By HENRY ALLEYNE NICHOLSON, M.D., D.Sc., F.L.S., F.G.S., Regius Professor of Natural History in the University of Aberdeen. Seventh Edition, rewritten and enlarged. Post 8vo, pp. 956, with 555 Engravings on Wood, 18s.
——— Text-Book of Zoology, for the Use of Schools. Fourth Edition, enlarged. Crown 8vo, with 188 Engravings on Wood, 7s. 6d.
——— Introductory Text-Book of Zoology, for the Use of Junior Classes. Sixth Edition, revised and enlarged, with 166 Engravings, 3s.
——— Outlines of Natural History, for Beginners; being Descriptions of a Progressive Series of Zoological Types. Third Edition, with Engravings, 1s. 6d.
——— A Manual of Palæontology, for the Use of Students. With a General Introduction on the Principles of Palæontology. By Professor H. ALLEYNE NICHOLSON and RICHARD LYDEKKER, B.A. Third Edition. Rewritten and greatly enlarged. 2 vols. 8vo, with Engravings, £3, 3s.
——— The Ancient Life-History of the Earth. An Outline of the Principles and Leading Facts of Palæontological Science. Crown 8vo, with 276 Engravings, 10s. 6d.
——— On the "Tabulate Corals" of the Palæozoic Period, with Critical Descriptions of Illustrative Species. Illustrated with 15 Lithograph Plates and numerous Engravings. Super-royal 8vo, 21s.
——— Synopsis of the Classification of the Animal Kingdom. 8vo, with 106 Illustrations, 6s.
——— On the Structure and Affinities of the Genus Monticulipora and its Sub-Genera, with Critical Descriptions of Illustrative Species. Illustrated with numerous Engravings on wood and lithographed Plates. Super-royal 8vo, 18s.
NICHOLSON. Communion with Heaven, and other Sermons. By the late MAXWELL NICHOLSON, D.D., Minister of St Stephen's, Edinburgh. Crown 8vo, 5s. 6d.
——— Rest in Jesus. Sixth Edition. Fcap. 8vo, 4s. 6d.
NICHOLSON. A Treatise on Money, and Essays on Present Monetary Problems. By JOSEPH SHIELD NICHOLSON, M.A., D.Sc., Professor of Commercial and Political Economy and Mercantile Law in the University of Edinburgh. 8vo, 10s. 6d.
——— Thoth. A Romance. Third Edition. Crown 8vo, 4s. 6d.
——— A Dreamer of Dreams. A Modern Romance. Second Edition. Crown 8vo, 6s.
NICOLSON AND MURE. A Handbook to the Local Government (Scotland) Act, 1889. With Introduction, Explanatory Notes, and Index. By J. BADENACH NICOLSON, Advocate, Counsel to the Scotch Education Department, and W. J. MURE, Advocate, Legal Secretary to the Lord Advocate for Scotland. Ninth Reprint. 8vo, 5s.
OLIPHANT. Masollam: a Problem of the Period. A Novel. By LAURENCE OLIPHANT. 3 vols. post 8vo, 25s. 6d
——— Scientific Religion; or, Higher Possibilities of Life and Practice through the Operation of Natural Forces. Second Edition. 8vo, 16s.
——— Altiora Peto. By LAURENCE OLIPHANT. Cheap Edition. Crown 8vo, boards, 2s. 6d.; cloth, 3s. 6d. Illustrated Edition. Crown 8vo, cloth, 6s.
——— Piccadilly: A Fragment of Contemporary Biography. With Illustrations by Richard Doyle. New Edition, 3s. 6d. Cheap Edition, boards, 2s. 6d.
——— Traits and Travesties; Social and Political. Post 8vo, 10s. 6d.

OLIPHANT. The Land of Gilead. With Excursions in the
Lebanon. With Illustrations and Maps. Demy 8vo, 21s.
―――― Haifa : Life in Modern Palestine. 2d Edition. 8vo, 7s. 6d.
―――― Episodes in a Life of Adventure ; or, Moss from a Rolling
Rolling Stone. Fifth Edition. Post 8vo, 6s.
―――― Memoir of the Life of Laurence Oliphant, and of Alice
Oliphant, his Wife. By Mrs M. O. W. OLIPHANT. Seventh Edition. In 2 vols.
post 8vo, with Portraits. 21s.
OLIPHANT. Katie Stewart. By Mrs OLIPHANT. 2s. 6d.
―――― The Duke's Daughter, and The Fugitives. A Novel. 3 vols.
crown 8vo, 25s. 6d.
―――― Two Stories of the Seen and the Unseen. The Open Door
—Old Lady Mary. Paper Covers, 1s.
―――― Sons and Daughters. Crown 8vo, 3s. 6d.
OLIPHANT. Notes of a Pilgrimage to Jerusalem and the Holy
Land. By F. R. OLIPHANT. Crown 8vo, 3s. 6d.
ON SURREY HILLS. By "A SON OF THE MARSHES." Cr. 8vo, 6s.
OSBORN. Narratives of Voyage and Adventure. By Admiral
SHERARD OSBORN, C.B. 3 vols. crown 8vo, 12s.
OSSIAN. The Poems of Ossian in the Original Gaelic. With a
Literal Translation into English, and a Dissertation on the Authenticity of the
Poems. By the Rev. ARCHIBALD CLERK. 2 vols. imperial 8vo, £1, 11s. 6d.
OSWALD. By Fell and Fjord ; or, Scenes and Studies in Iceland.
By E. J. OSWALD. Post 8vo, with Illustrations. 7s. 6d.
OWEN. Annals of a Fishing Village. Drawn from the Notes of
"A Son of the Marshes." Edited by J. A. OWEN. Crown 8vo, with Illustrations, 7s. 6d.
PAGE. Introductory Text-Book of Geology. By DAVID PAGE,
LL.D., Professor of Geology in the Durham University of Physical Science
Newcastle, and Professor LAPWORTH of Mason Science College, Birmingham.
With Engravings and Glossarial Index. Twelfth Edition. Revised and Enlarged. 3s. 6d.
―――― Advanced Text-Book of Geology, Descriptive and Industrial. With Engravings, and Glossary of Scientific Terms. Sixth Edition, revised and enlarged, 7s. 6d.
―――― Introductory Text-Book of Physical Geography. With
Sketch-Maps and Illustrations. Edited by CHARLES LAPWORTH, LL.D., F.G.S.,
&c., Professor of Geology and Mineralogy in the Mason Science College, Birmingham. 12th Edition. 2s. 6d.
―――― Advanced Text-Book of Physical Geography. Third
Edition, Revised and Enlarged by Prof. LAPWORTH. With Engravings. 5s.
PATON. Spindrift. By Sir J. NOEL PATON. Fcap., cloth, 5s.
―――― Poems by a Painter. Fcap., cloth, 5s.
PATON. Body and Soul. A Romance in Transcendental Pathology. By FREDERICK NOEL PATON. Third Edition. Crown 8vo, 1s.
PATTERSON. Essays in History and Art. By R. HOGARTH
PATTERSON. 8vo, 12s.
―――― The New Golden Age, and Influence of the Precious
Metals upon the World. 2 vols. 8vo, 31s. 6d.
PAUL. History of the Royal Company of Archers, the Queen's
Body-Guard for Scotland. By JAMES BALFOUR PAUL, Advocate of the Scottish
Bar. Crown 4to, with Portraits and other Illustrations. £2, 2s.
PEILE. Lawn Tennis as a Game of Skill. With latest revised
Laws as played by the Best Clubs. By Captain S. C. F. PEILE, B.S.C. Cheaper
Edition, fcap. cloth, 1s.
PETTIGREW. The Handy Book of Bees, and their Profitable
Management. By A. PETTIGREW. Fifth Edition, Enlarged, with Engravings. Crown 8vo, 3s. 6d.

PHILOSOPHICAL CLASSICS FOR ENGLISH READERS.
Edited by WILLIAM KNIGHT, LL.D., Professor of Moral Philosophy, University of St Andrews. In crown 8vo volumes, with portraits, price 3s. 6d.
[*For list of Volumes published, see page* 2.

PHILIP. The Function of Labour in the Production of Wealth.
By ALEXANDER PHILIP, LL.B., Edinburgh. Crown 8vo, 3s. 6d.

POLLOK. The Course of Time : A Poem. By ROBERT POLLOK,
A.M. Small fcap. 8vo, cloth gilt, 2s. 6d. Cottage Edition, 32mo, 8d. The Same, cloth, gilt edges, 1s. 6d. Another Edition, with Illustrations by Birket Foster and others, fcap., cloth, 3s. 6d., or with edges gilt, 4s.

PORT ROYAL LOGIC. Translated from the French ; with Introduction, Notes, and Appendix. By THOMAS SPENCER BAYNES, LL.D., Professor in the University of St Andrews. Tenth Edition, 12mo, 4s.

POTTS AND DARNELL. Aditus Faciliores : An easy Latin Construing Book, with Complete Vocabulary. By the late A. W. POTTS, M.A., LL.D., and the Rev. C. DARNELL, M.A., Head-Master of Cargilfield Preparatory School, Edinburgh. Tenth Edition, fcap. 8vo, 3s. 6d.

——— Aditus Faciliores Graeci. An easy Greek Construing Book, with Complete Vocabulary. Fourth Edition, fcap. 8vo, 3s.

POTTS. School Sermons. By the late ALEXANDER WM. POTTS, LL.D., First Head-Master of Fettes College. With a Memoir and Portrait. Crown 8vo, 7s. 6d.

PRINGLE. The Live-Stock of the Farm. By ROBERT O. PRINGLE.
Third Edition. Revised and Edited by JAMES MACDONALD. Cr. 8vo, 7s. 6d.

PUBLIC GENERAL STATUTES AFFECTING SCOTLAND
from 1707 to 1847, with Chronological Table and Index. 3 vols. large 8vo, £3, 3s.

PUBLIC GENERAL STATUTES AFFECTING SCOTLAND, COLLECTION OF. Published Annually with General Index.

RADICAL CURE FOR IRELAND, The. A Letter to the People
of England and Scotland concerning a new Plantation. With 2 Maps. 8vo, 7s. 6d.

RAMSAY. Rough Recollections of Military Service and Society.
By Lieut.-Col. BALCARRES D. WARDLAW RAMSAY. Two vols. post 8vo, 21s.

RAMSAY. Scotland and Scotsmen in the Eighteenth Century.
Edited from the MSS. of JOHN RAMSAY, Esq. of Ochtertyre, by ALEXANDER ALLARDYCE, Author of 'Memoir of Admiral Lord Keith, K.B.,' &c. 2 vols. 8vo, 31s. 6d.

RANKIN. A Handbook of the Church of Scotland. By JAMES
RANKIN, D.D., Minister of Muthill; Author of 'Character Studies in the Old Testament,' &c. An entirely New and much Enlarged Edition. Crown 8vo, with 2 Maps, 7s. 6d.

——— The Creed in Scotland. An Exposition of the Apostles'
Creed. With Extracts from Archbishop Hamilton's Catechism of 1552, John Calvin's Catechism of 1556, and a Catena of Ancient Latin and other Hymns. Post 8vo, 7s. 6d.

——— First Communion Lessons. Twenty-third Edition. Paper
Cover, 2d.

RECORDS OF THE TERCENTENARY FESTIVAL OF THE UNIVERSITY OF EDINBURGH. Celebrated in April 1884. Published under the Sanction of the Senatus Academicus. Large 4to, £2, 12s. 6d.

ROBERTSON. Early Religion of Israel. Being the Baird Lecture for 1888-89. By JAMES ROBERTSON, D.D., Professor of Oriental Languages in the University of Glasgow. In one Vol. crown 8vo. [*Immediately.*

ROBERTSON. Orellana, and other Poems. By J. LOGIE ROBERTSON, M.A. Fcap. 8vo. Printed on hand-made paper. 6s.

ROBERTSON. Our Holiday Among the Hills. By JAMES and
JANET LOGIE ROBERTSON. Fcap. 8vo, 3s. 6d.

ROSCOE. Rambles with a Fishing-rod. By E. S. ROSCOE. Crown
8vo, 4s. 6d.

ROSS. Old Scottish Regimental Colours. By ANDREW ROSS,
S.S.C., Hon. Secretary Old Scottish Regimental Colours Committee. Dedicated by Special Permission to Her Majesty the Queen. Folio. £2, 12s. 6d.

RUSSELL. The Haigs of Bemersyde. A Family History. By JOHN RUSSELL. Large 8vo, with Illustrations. 21s.

RUSSELL. Fragments from Many Tables. Being the Recollections of some Wise and Witty Men and Women. By GEO. RUSSELL. Cr. 8vo, 4s. 6d.

RUTLAND. Notes of an Irish Tour in 1846. By the DUKE OF RUTLAND, G.C.B. (Lord JOHN MANNERS). New Edition. Crown 8vo, 2s. 6d.

—— Correspondence between the Right Honble. William Pitt and Charles Duke of Rutland, Lord Lieutenant of Ireland, 1781-1787. With Introductory Note by John Duke of Rutland. 8vo, 7s. 6d.

RUTLAND. Gems of German Poetry. Translated by the DUCHESS OF RUTLAND (Lady JOHN MANNERS). [*New Edition in preparation.*

—— Impressions of Bad-Homburg. Comprising a Short Account of the Women's Associations of Germany under the Red Cross. Crown 8vo, 1s. 6d.

—— Some Personal Recollections of the Later Years of the Earl of Beaconsfield, K.G. Sixth Edition, 6d.

—— Employment of Women in the Public Service. 6d.

—— Some of the Advantages of Easily Accessible Reading and Recreation Rooms, and Free Libraries. With Remarks on Starting and Maintaining Them. Second Edition, crown 8vo, 1s.

—— A Sequel to Rich Men's Dwellings, and other Occasional Papers. Crown 8vo, 2s. 6d.

—— Encouraging Experiences of Reading and Recreation Rooms, Aims of Guilds, Nottingham Social Guild, Existing Institutions, &c., &c. Crown 8vo, 1s.

SCHILLER. Wallenstein. A Dramatic Poem. By FREDERICK VON SCHILLER. Translated by C. G. A. LOCKHART. Fcap. 8vo, 7s. 6d.

SCOTCH LOCH FISHING. By "Black Palmer." Crown 8vo, Interleaved with blank pages, 4s.

SCOUGAL. Prisons and their Inmates; or, Scenes from a Silent World. By FRANCIS SCOUGAL. Crown 8vo, boards, 2s.

SELLAR. Manual of the Education Acts for Scotland. By the late ALEXANDER CRAIG SELLAR, M.P. Eighth Edition. Revised and in great part rewritten by J. EDWARD GRAHAM, B.A. Oxon., Advocate. With Rules for the conduct of Elections, with Notes and Cases. With a Supplement, being the Acts of 1889 in so far as affecting the Education Acts. 8vo, 12s. 6d.

[SUPPLEMENT TO SELLAR'S MANUAL OF THE EDUCATION ACTS. 8vo, 2s.]

SETH. Scottish Philosophy. A Comparison of the Scottish and German Answers to Hume. Balfour Philosophical Lectures, University of Edinburgh. By ANDREW SETH, M.A., Professor of Logic and Metaphysics in Edinburgh University. Second Edition. Crown 8vo, 5s.

—— Hegelianism and Personality. Balfour Philosophical Lectures. Second Series. Crown 8vo, 5s.

SETH. Freedom as Ethical Postulate. By JAMES SETH, M.A., George Munro Professor of Philosophy, Dalhousie College, Halifax, Canada. 8vo, 1s.

SHADWELL. The Life of Colin Campbell, Lord Clyde. Illustrated by Extracts from his Diary and Correspondence. By Lieutenant-General SHADWELL, C.B. 2 vols. 8vo. With Portrait, Maps, and Plans. 36s.

SHAND. Half a Century; or, Changes in Men and Manners. By ALEX. INNES SHAND, Author of 'Against Time,' &c. Second Edition, 8vo, 12s. 6d.

—— Letters from the West of Ireland. Reprinted from the 'Times.' Crown 8vo. 5s.

—— Kilcarra. A Novel. 3 vols. crown 8vo, 25s. 6d.

SHARPE. Letters from and to Charles Kirkpatrick Sharpe. Edited by ALEXANDER ALLARDYCE, Author of 'Memoir of Admiral Lord Keith, K.B.,' &c With a Memoir by the Rev. W. K. R. BEDFORD. In two vols. 8vo. Illustrated with Etchings and other Engravings. £2, 12s. 6d.

SIM. Margaret Sim's Cookery. With an Introduction by L. B. WALFORD, Author of 'Mr Smith: A Part of His Life,' &c. Crown 8vo, 5s.

SKELTON. Maitland of Lethington; and the Scotland of Mary Stuart. A History. By JOHN SKELTON, C.B., LL.D., Author of 'The Essays of Shirley.' Demy 8vo. 2 vols., 28s.

—— The Handbook of Public Health. A Complete Edition of the Public Health and other Sanitary Acts relating to Scotland. Annotated, and with the Rules, Instructions, and Decisions of the Board of Supervision brought up to date with relative forms. 8vo, with Supplement, 8s. 6d.

—— Supplement to Skelton's Handbook. The Administration of the Public Health Act in Counties. 8vo, cloth, 1s. 6d.

—— The Local Government (Scotland) Act in Relation to Public Health. A Handy Guide for County and District Councillors, Medical Officers, Sanitary Inspectors, and Members of Parochial Boards. Second Edition. With a new Preface on appointment of Sanitary Officers. Crown 8vo, 2s.

SMITH. For God and Humanity. A Romance of Mount Carmel. By HASKETT SMITH, Author of 'The Divine Epiphany,' &c. 3 vols. post 8vo, 25s. 6d.

SMITH. Thorndale; or, The Conflict of Opinions. By WILLIAM SMITH, Author of 'A Discourse on Ethics,'&c. New Edition. Cr. 8vo, 10s. 6d.

—— Gravenhurst; or, Thoughts on Good and Evil. Second Edition, with Memoir of the Author. Crown 8vo, 8s.

—— The Story of William and Lucy Smith. Edited by GEORGE MERRIAM. Large post 8vo, 12s. 6d.

SMITH. Memoir of the Families of M'Combie and Thoms, originally M'Intosh and M'Thomas. Compiled from History and Tradition. By WILLIAM M'COMBIE SMITH. With Illustrations. 8vo, 7s. 6d.

SMITH. Greek Testament Lessons for Colleges, Schools, and Private Students, consisting chiefly of the Sermon on the Mount and the Parables of our Lord. With Notes and Essays. By the Rev. J. HUNTER SMITH, M.A., King Edward's School, Birmingham. Crown 8vo, 6s.

SMITH. Writings by the Way. By JOHN CAMPBELL SMITH, M.A., Sheriff-Substitute. Crown 8vo, 9s.

SMITH. The Secretary for Scotland. Being a Statement of the Powers and Duties of the new Scottish Office. With a Short Historical Introduction and numerous references to important Administrative Documents. By W. C. SMITH, LL.B., Advocate. 8vo, 6s.

SORLEY. The Ethics of Naturalism. Being the Shaw Fellowship Lectures, 1884. By W. R. SORLEY, M.A., Fellow of Trinity College, Cambridge, Professor of Logic and Philosophy in University College of South Wales. Crown 8vo, 6s.

SPEEDY. Sport in the Highlands and Lowlands of Scotland with Rod and Gun. By TOM SPEEDY. Second Edition, Revised and Enlarged. With Illustrations by Lieut.-Gen. Hope Crealocke, C.B., C.M.G., and others. 8vo, 15s.

SPROTT. The Worship and Offices of the Church of Scotland. By GEORGE W. SPROTT, D.D., Minister of North Berwick. Crown 8vo, 6s.

STAFFORD. How I Spent my Twentieth Year. Being a Record of a Tour Round the World, 1886-87. By the MARCHIONESS OF STAFFORD. With Illustrations. Third Edition, crown 8vo, 8s. 6d.

STARFORTH. Villa Residences and Farm Architecture: A Series of Designs. By JOHN STARFORTH, Architect. 102 Engravings. Second Edition, medium 4to, £2, 17s. 6d.

STATISTICAL ACCOUNT OF SCOTLAND. Complete, with Index, 15 vols. 8vo, £16, 16s.
Each County sold separately, with Title, Index, and Map, neatly bound in cloth.

STEPHENS' BOOK OF THE FARM; detailing the Labours of the Farmer, Farm-Steward, Ploughman, Shepherd, Hedger, Farm-Labourer, Field-Worker, and Cattleman. Illustrated with numerous Portraits of Animals and Engravings of Implements, and Plans of Farm Buildings. Fourth Edition. Revised, and in great part rewritten by JAMES MACDONALD, of the 'Farming World,' &c., &c. Assisted by many of the leading agricultural authorities of the day. Complete in Six Divisional Volumes, bound in cloth, each 10s. 6d., or handsomely bound, in 3 volumes, with leather back and gilt top, £3, 3s.

STEPHENS. The Book of Farm Implements and Machines. By
J. SLIGHT and R. SCOTT BURN, Engineers. Edited by HENRY STEPHENS. Large
8vo, £2. 2s.

STEVENSON. British Fungi. (Hymenomycetes.) By Rev. JOHN
STEVENSON, Author of 'Mycologia Scotia,' Hon. Sec. Cryptogamic Society of
Scotland. 2 vols. post 8vo, with Illustrations, price 12s. 6d. each.
Vol. I. AGARICUS—BOLBITIUS. Vol. II. CORTINARIUS—DACRYMYCES.

STEWART. Advice to Purchasers of Horses. By JOHN STEWART,
V.S. New Edition. 2s. 6d.

——— Stable Economy. A Treatise on the Management of
Horses in relation to Stabling, Grooming, Feeding, Watering, and Working.
Seventh Edition, fcap. 8vo, 6s. 6d.

STEWART. A Hebrew Grammar, with the Pronunciation, Syllabic Division and Tone of the Words, and Quantity of the Vowels. By Rev.
DUNCAN STEWART, D.D. Fourth Edition. 8vo, 3s. 6d.

STEWART. Boethius: An Essay. By HUGH FRASER STEWART,
M.A., Trinity College, Cambridge. Crown 8vo, 7s. 6d.

STODDART. Angling Songs. By THOMAS TOD STODDART. New
Edition, with a Memoir by ANNA M. STODDART. Crown 8vo, 7s. 6d.

STORMONTH. Etymological and Pronouncing Dictionary of the
English Language. Including a very Copious Selection of Scientific Terms.
For Use in Schools and Colleges, and as a Book of General Reference. By the
Rev. JAMES STORMONTH. The Pronunciation carefully Revised by the Rev.
P. H. PHELP, M.A. Cantab. Tenth Edition, Revised throughout. Crown
8vo, pp. 800. 7s. 6d.

——— Dictionary of the English Language, Pronouncing,
Etymological, and Explanatory. Revised by the Rev. P. H. PHELP. Library
Edition. Imperial 8vo, handsomely bound in half morocco, 31s. 6d.

——— The School Etymological Dictionary and Word-Book.
Fourth Edition. Fcap. 8vo, pp. 254. 2s.

STORY. Nero; A Historical Play. By W. W. STORY, Author of
'Roba di Roma.' Fcap. 8vo, 6s.

——— Vallombrosa. Post 8vo, 5s.

——— Poems. 2 vols. fcap., 7s. 6d.

——— Fiammetta. A Summer Idyl. Crown 8vo, 7s. 6d.

——— Conversations in a Studio. 2 vols. crown 8vo, 12s. 6d.

——— Excursions in Art and Letters. Crown 8vo, 7s. 6d.

STRICKLAND. Life of Agnes Strickland. By her SISTER.
Post 8vo, with Portrait engraved on Steel, 12s. 6d.

STURGIS. John-a-Dreams. A Tale. By JULIAN STURGIS.
New Edition, crown 8vo, 3s. 6d.

——— Little Comedies, Old and New. Crown 8vo, 7s. 6d.

SUTHERLAND. Handbook of Hardy Herbaceous and Alpine
Flowers, for general Garden Decoration. Containing Descriptions of upwards of 1000 Species of Ornamental Hardy Perennial and Alpine Plants;
along with Concise and Plain Instructions for their Propagation and Culture.
By WILLIAM SUTHERLAND, Landscape Gardener; formerly Manager of the
Herbaceous Department at Kew. Crown 8vo, 7s. 6d.

TAYLOR. The Story of My Life. By the late Colonel MEADOWS
TAYLOR, Author of 'The Confessions of a Thug,' &c. &c. Edited by his
Daughter. New and cheaper Edition, being the Fourth. Crown 8vo, 6s.

THOLUCK. Hours of Christian Devotion. Translated from the
German of A. Tholuck, D.D., Professor of Theology in the University of Halle.
By the Rev. ROBERT MENZIES, D.D. With a Preface written for this Translation by the Author. Second Edition, crown 8vo, 7s. 6d.

THOMSON. Handy Book of the Flower-Garden: being Practical
Directions for the Propagation, Culture, and Arrangement of Plants in Flower-Gardens all the year round. With Engraved Plans. By DAVID THOMSON,
Gardener to his Grace the Duke of Buccleuch, K.T., at Drumlanrig Fourth
and Cheaper Edition, crown 8vo, 5s.

THOMSON. The Handy Book of Fruit-Culture under Glass: being a series of Elaborate Practical Treatises on the Cultivation and Forcing of Pines, Vines, Peaches, Figs, Melons, Strawberries, and Cucumbers. With Engravings of Hothouses, &c. Second Ed. Cr. 8vo, 7s. 6d.

THOMSON. A Practical Treatise on the Cultivation of the Grape Vine. By WILLIAM THOMSON, Tweed Vineyards. Tenth Edition, 8vo, 5s.

THOMSON. Cookery for the Sick and Convalescent. With Directions for the Preparation of Poultices, Fomentations, &c. By BARBARA THOMSON. Fcap. 8vo, 1s. 6d.

THORNTON. Opposites. A Series of Essays on the Unpopular Sides of Popular Questions. By LEWIS THORNTON. 8vo, 12s. 6d.

TOM CRINGLE'S LOG. A New Edition, with Illustrations. Crown 8vo, cloth gilt, 5s. Cheap Edition, 2s.

TRANSACTIONS OF THE HIGHLAND AND AGRICULTURAL SOCIETY OF SCOTLAND. Published annually, price 5s.

TULLOCH. Rational Theology and Christian Philosophy in England in the Seventeenth Century. By JOHN TULLOCH, D.D., Principal of St Mary's College in the University of St Andrews; and one of her Majesty's Chaplains in Ordinary in Scotland. Second Edition. 2 vols. 8vo, 16s.

—— Modern Theories in Philosophy and Religion. 8vo, 15s.

—— Luther, and other Leaders of the Reformation. Third Edition, enlarged. Crown 8vo, 3s. 6d.

—— Memoir of Principal Tulloch, D.D., LL.D. By Mrs OLIPHANT, Author of 'Life of Edward Irving.' Third and Cheaper Edition. 8vo, with Portrait. 7s. 6d

TWEEDIE. The Arabian Horse : his Country and People. With Portraits of Typical or Famous Arabians, and numerous other Illustrations; also a Map of the Country of the Arabian Horse, and a descriptive Glossary of Arabic words and proper names. By Colonel W. TWEEDIE, C.S.I., Bengal Staff Corps, H.B M.'s late Consul-General, Baghdad. [In the press.

VEITCH. Institutes of Logic. By JOHN VEITCH, LL.D., Professor of Logic and Rhetoric in the University of Glasgow. Post 8vo, 12s. 6d

—— The Feeling for Nature in Scottish Poetry. From the Earliest Times to the Present Day. 2 vols. fcap. 8vo, in roxburghe binding. 15s.

—— Merlin and Other Poems. Fcap. 8vo. 4s. 6d.

—— Knowing and Being. Essays in Philosophy. First Series. Crown 8vo, 5s.

VIRGIL. The Æneid of Virgil. Translated in English Blank Verse by G. K. RICKARDS, M.A., and Lord RAVENSWORTH. 2 vols. fcap. 8vo, 10s.

WALFORD. Four Biographies from 'Blackwood': Jane Taylor, Hannah More, Elizabeth Fry, Mary Somerville. By L. B. WALFORD. Crown 8vo, 5s.

WARREN'S (SAMUEL) WORKS :—
Diary of a Late Physician. Cloth, 2s. 6d. ; boards, 2s.
Ten Thousand A-Year. Cloth, 3s. 6d. ; boards, 2s. 6d.
Now and Then. The Lily and the Bee. Intellectual and Moral Development of the Present Age. 4s. 6d.
Essays : Critical, Imaginative, and Juridical. 5s.

WARREN. The Five Books of the Psalms. With Marginal Notes. By Rev. SAMUEL L. WARREN, Rector of Esher, Surrey; late Fellow, Dean, and Divinity Lecturer, Wadham College, Oxford. Crown 8vo, 5s.

WEBSTER. The Angler and the Loop-Rod. By DAVID WEBSTER. Crown 8vo, with Illustrations, 7s. 6d.

WELLINGTON. Wellington Prize Essays on "the System of Field Manœuvres best adapted for enabling our Troops to meet a Continental Army." Edited by General Sir EDWARD BRUCE HAMLEY, K.C.B., K.C.M.G. 8vo, 12s. 6d.

WENLEY. Socrates and Christ: A Study in the Philosophy of Religion. By R. M. WENLEY, M.A., Lecturer on Mental and Moral Philosophy in Queen Margaret College, Glasgow; Examiner in Philosophy in the University of Glasgow. Crown 8vo, 6s.

WERNER. A Visit to Stanley's Rear-Guard at Major Barttelot's Camp on the Aruhwimi. With an Account of River-Life on the Congo. By J. R. WERNER, F.R.G.S., Engineer, late in the Service of the Etat Independant du Congo. With Maps, Portraits, and other Illustrations. 8vo. 16s.

WESTMINSTER ASSEMBLY. Minutes of the Westminster Assembly, while engaged in preparing their Directory for Church Government, Confession of Faith, and Catechisms (November 1644 to March 1649). Edited by the Rev. Professor ALEX. T. MITCHELL, of St Andrews, and the Rev. JOHN STRUTHERS, LL.D. With a Historical and Critical Introduction by Professor Mitchell. 8vo, 15s.

WHITE. The Eighteen Christian Centuries. By the Rev. JAMES WHITE. Seventh Edition, post 8vo, with Index, 6s.

———— History of France, from the Earliest Times. Sixth Thousand, post 8vo, with Index, 6s.

WHITE. Archæological Sketches in Scotland—Kintyre and Knapdale. By Colonel T. P. WHITE, R.E., of the Ordnance Survey. With numerous Illustrations. 2 vols. folio, £4, 4s. Vol. I., Kintyre, sold separately, £2, 2s.

———— The Ordnance Survey of the United Kingdom. A Popular Account. Crown 8vo, 5s.

WICKS. Golden Lives. The Story of a Woman's Courage. By FREDERICK WICKS. Cheap Edition, with 120 Illustrations. Illustrated Boards. 8vo, 2s. 6d.

WILLIAMSON. Poems of Nature and Life. By DAVID R. WILLIAMSON, Minister of Kirkmaiden. Fcap. 8vo, 3s.

WILLS AND GREENE. Drawing-room Dramas for Children. By W. G. WILLS and the Hon. Mrs GREENE. Crown 8vo, 6s.

WILSON. Works of Professor Wilson. Edited by his Son-in-Law, Professor FERRIER. 12 vols. crown 8vo, £2, 8s.

———— Christopher in his Sporting-Jacket. 2 vols., 8s.

———— Isle of Palms, City of the Plague, and other Poems. 4s.

———— Lights and Shadows of Scottish Life, and other Tales. 4s.

———— Essays, Critical and Imaginative. 4 vols., 16s.

———— The Noctes Ambrosianæ. 4 vols., 16s.

———— Homer and his Translators, and the Greek Drama. Crown 8vo, 4s.

WINGATE. Lily Neil. A Poem. By DAVID WINGATE. Crown 8vo, 4s. 6d.

WORDSWORTH. The Historical Plays of Shakspeare. With Introductions and Notes. By CHARLES WORDSWORTH, D.C.L., Bishop of S. Andrews. 3 vols. post 8vo, cloth, each price 7s. 6d., or handsomely bound in half-calf, each price 9s. 9d.

WORSLEY. Poems and Translations. By PHILIP STANHOPE WORSLEY, M.A. Edited by EDWARD WORSLEY. 2d Ed., enlarged. Fcap. 8vo, 6s.

YATE. England and Russia Face to Face in Asia. A Record of Travel with the Afghan Boundary Commission. By Captain A. C. YATE, Bombay Staff Corps. 8vo, with Maps and Illustrations, 21s.

YATE. Northern Afghanistan; or, Letters from the Afghan Boundary Commission. By Major C. E. YATE, C.S.I., C.M.G. Bombay Staff Corps, F.R.G.S. 8vo, with Maps. 18s.

YOUNG. A Story of Active Service in Foreign Lands. Compiled from letters sent home from South Africa, India, and China, 1856-1882. By Surgeon-General A. GRAHAM YOUNG, Author of 'Crimean Cracks.' Crown 8vo, Illustrated, 7s. 6d.

YULE. Fortification: for the Use of Officers in the Army, and Readers of Military History. By Col. YULE, Bengal Engineers. 8vo, with numerous Illustrations, 10s. 6d.

www.ingramcontent.com/pod-product-compliance
Lightning Source LLC
Chambersburg PA
CBHW020310240426

43673CB00039B/763